Freedom's Gardener

Freedom's Gardener

*James F. Brown, Horticulture, and the
Hudson Valley in Antebellum America*

Myra B. Young Armstead

NEW YORK UNIVERSITY PRESS
New York and London

NEW YORK UNIVERSITY PRESS
New York and London
www.nyupress.org

References to Internet websites (URLs) were accurate at the time of writing.
Neither the author nor New York University Press is responsible for URLs
that may have expired or changed since the manuscript was prepared.

Library of Congress Cataloging-in-Publication Data

Armstead, Myra Beth Young
Freedom's gardener : James F. Brown, horticulture, and
the Hudson Valley in antebellum America / Myra B. Young Armstead.
p. cm.
Includes bibliographical references and index.
ISBN 978-0-8147-0510-0 (cl : alk. paper)
ISBN 978-0-8147-0791-3 (ebook)
ISBN 978-0-8147-0792-0 (ebook)
1. Brown, James Francis, 1793–1868. 2. African Americans—Social conditions—
Hudson River Valley (N.Y. and N.J.)—19th century. 3. Free blacks—Hudson River Valley
(N.Y. and N.J)—Biography. 4. Gardeners—Hudson River Valley (N.Y. and N.J.)—
Biography. 5. Fugitive slaves—Maryland—Biography. 6. Hudson River Valley
(N.Y. and N.J.)—History—19th century. 7. Hudson River Valley (N.Y.) and N.J.)—
Biography. I. Title.
F127.H8A76   2011
635.092—dc23   [B]   2011028251

New York University Press books are printed on acid-free paper,
and their binding materials are chosen for strength and durability.
We strive to use environmentally responsible suppliers and materials
to the greatest extent possible in publishing our books.

Manufactured in the United States of America
10 9 8 7 6 5 4 3 2 1

For Matthew and Nathan

Like valleys they spread out,
like gardens beside a river.

Contents

Acknowledgments

Many eyes, minds, hands, and hearts have contributed to the completion of this book. I am very grateful for the assistance of the staffs of the Frederick County (Maryland) Historical Society, the Maryland Historical Society, the Maryland State Archives, the Edward H. Nabb Research Center for Delmarva History and Culture, the Poplar Hills Mansion Museum, the Pennsylvania Horticultural Society, the Monmouth County (New Jersey) Historical Association, the New York Botanical Garden (New York Horticultural Society Records), the New-York Historical Society, the New York Public Library, the New York State Law Library (Albany and Poughkeepsie), Pace University Law Library, the Newburgh (New York) Free Public Library, Mount Gulian Historic Site, the Dutchess County Historical Society, the Dutchess County Clerk's Office, and the Adriance Memorial Library. Individuals associated with these research centers, officially or as volunteers, who deserve special recognition include Linda Duyer, L. Paul Morris Jr., Nancy Marasco, and Stephanie Mauri. Elaine Hayes, Executive Director at Mount Gulian, was an invaluable support all along, and I also benefited greatly from the help of Susan Konvit while she was Director of Education and Public Programming there.

Bard College colleagues who served as cheerleaders, advisers, and readers include Mark Lytle, Alice Stroup, Rob Culp, Ellen Lagemann, Joel Perlmann, Christian Crouch, Greg Moynahan, Omar Encarnacion, Julia Rosenbaum, Wendy Urban-Mead, Stephen Mucher, Mercedes Ebbert, Derek Furr, Jaime Alves, and Yuval Elmelech. Janet Schulze was a priceless student research assistant, and the students in three Bard MAT Program courses I taught—*Mystic Chords of Memory* (Summer 2008, Fall 2009–upstate, Fall 2009–NYC)—graciously heard and provided feedback on the book introduction that follows. Bard Web Services Coordinator Juliet Meyers lent her expertise to the production of the maps. Evelyn Krueger's secretarial skills were crucial for the consistency in word processing the text.

Friends and family—Tarra "Tod" Dumas, Karla M. Bressant, Kyle F. Bressant, Kim Bressant-Kibwe, Monica Brown, James Server, Karen Khan, Irene Lee, Barbara Villani, Carmen Figueroa, Cathy Hexel, Paulette Oke, Greta Davey, Bethsheba Young, Roxanne Young, Vanessa Young, Cosby Young, Letise Buckner, Larin Young, Rhenetta Banks Martin, Victoria Banks, and the members of Faith Assembly of God—offered commentary and prayers. As always, Matthew and Nathan—my two sons—were my inspiration and in several, critical instances advised me well.

I thank all of these helpers, and I thank God through Christ.

Introduction

This book is a historically contextualized reconstruction of the life of James Francis Brown (1793–1868) based on the long diary he kept from 1829 to 1866. Brown was a southern-born African American manumitted former fugitive slave who spent most of his working days as a master gardener for a wealthy white family in rural upstate New York. Politically enfranchised (a voter), he enjoyed an active social and civic life with friends and family in the Hudson Valley and in New York City. While each of these biographical tidbits may be intriguing, none of them in and of itself makes his story important. It is the sum of these facts, along with Brown's deliberate chronicling of them, that lends significance to the man's life because together they can help us better understand the early national and antebellum United States.

In one sense, James's story is not unique. He wrote the story of his own life, as did countless other Americans of his day. He relocated to better his options, improved his economic standing, and was politically engaged in a new republican civic sphere. His is the story of the first post–Revolutionary era generation in U.S. history, which grappled during the early republican and antebellum years to define exactly what it had inherited from its immediate ancestors as a legacy of the American War of Independence. The historian Joyce Appleby has argued that this generation forged a new national identity distinct from that of its colonial-born forebears—that of the American citizen. Acting in the capitalist marketplace, shaped by religious revivalism and its tenets of hard work and discipline, and voicing opinions through new literary and political mechanisms, this generation promoted a vision of American democracy and its future with which contemporary Americans still reckon.[1] That narrative was about the perception of opportunity, the wisdom of risk taking, the profitability of new ideas, and the soundness of democracy.

What makes James F. Brown's story compelling, then, is that although he was born a slave in Maryland and therefore outside the intended or expected reach of that narrative, this black man nonetheless embraced it. Its message somehow reached him while he was still in bondage and propelled him to escape slavery, to challenge the exclusions it contained, and to forge a new and successful life for himself in upstate New York as a master gardener at Mount Gulian—the estate of the Verplanck family of Fishkill Landing (present-day Beacon, New York), seventy miles north of New York City in the Hudson River Valley. James lived there in a house he owned with his wife, Julia, whose freedom he purchased from her Maryland slaveowner. During the colonial period, the descendants of the Dutch settler Abraham Isaacse Verplanck became prominent businessmen and landowners in both Manhattan and upstate New York. Samuel Verplanck (1739–1820), Abraham's great-great grandson, loaned Mount Gulian to the Patriot cause during the Revolutionary War. The homestead—today listed on the National Register of Historic Places—was used as the headquarters of Baron Wilhelm Von Steuben, the Prussian military officer charged by General George Washington with training the Continental Army in drills, fighting techniques, musketry, hygiene, and general discipline. In 1783, Mount Gulian also became the birthplace of the Society of the Cincinnati, the nation's first veterans' fraternal organization. Samuel's son, Daniel Crommelin Verplanck (1762–1834), became a lawyer, a U.S. congressman, and a judge. Daniel's son, Gulian Crommelin Verplanck (1786–1870), was also a lawyer, a U.S. congressman, and a New York state senator; in addition, Gulian was a scholar, a civic activist, and once an unsuccessful candidate for mayor of New York City. Both Daniel and Gulian helped to manumit James after he escaped Maryland. Mary Anna Verplanck (1793–1856), Daniel's daughter and Gulian's sister, worked closely with James to manage the Mount Gulian estate generally, but particularly its gardens.

James Brown recorded his days as a free man working for the Verplancks in a ten-volume diary spanning the years 1829 to 1866—a remarkable act for most Americans of his day and a virtually unheard-of undertaking for an African American man. In fact, a kind of self-consciousness about his achievements—anomalous precisely in their ordinariness *because* he was black, as he knew—can be surmised by several features of the diary besides its mere existence. His determined maintenance of the journal, the relatively big size of each of its volumes, and its high-quality paper all signal that James Brown believed that his life as a former slave and free African American living in the Hudson Valley meant something. James chided himself at various points in the diary for his own lapses in steady chronicling, and he studiously recopied sections that suffered damage by water or some other means. At the start of 1830, for instance, he noted, "From the 18th of June 1829 to the first of January 1830 I have been careless and have not kept a regular journal as I ought to have done. But I have commenced again from the first of January."[2] On January 14, 1841, James Brown recorded that he "went across to Newburgh and bought a blank book for writing." This book of blank, ruled pages that measured 6.5 inches wide by 8 inches long was the sixth of the ten volumes of similar dimensions that he purchased for daily personal note taking. All of the books had hard, darkish pasteboard covers with a marble design, somewhat like today's black and white–covered composition notebooks used by schoolchildren. Indeed, Brown acquired the fifth volume in the chronology, spanning May 1837 to July 1841, from Mahlon Day, a Pearl Street retailer of "School Books, Children's Books, . . ." in Manhattan. He bought another blank book in 1841 from Rich and Loutrel, a "General Stationery Establishment" on William Street in New York City that advertised its stock of account books "made of the best linen paper."[3]

Brown's diary reflects a particular genre of antebellum writing. The blank books he purchased were of a type increasingly used both by American farmers and merchants from the late-eighteenth-century colonial period and into the early national period for keeping track of operations and transactions, and they were a variation of the almanac-diary. Printed almanacs contained calendars listing holidays; astrological and climatological information about the cycle of seasons; "tables of interest, currency conversions, and other financial instruments"; miscellaneous essays and poems; and lists of roads, coach fares, local officeholders, and the like. This combination of features invited almanac buyers to manipulate the form for practical purposes by inserting blank pages into the calendar to record daily events, according to the historian Molly McCarthy. In this way, for any given diarist, the seasonal climate predictions prompted the chronicling of weather conditions, the monetary data spurred the recording of fiscal transactions, the road information suggested travel notes, and holidays inspired the inclusion of special, personal days and events, for example births, deaths, and visits by guests.[4] In its contents, Brown's diary closely, though not exclusively, follows this pattern of journal keeping throughout its length.

Brown's use of blank books combined the older almanac-diarist's range of recorded information and the new pocket-diarist's more *individualized* information. A diary introduced to the United States in the last quarter of the eighteenth century by a Philadelphia bookseller contained several printed, ruled blank pages. Although this printed form also included some of the usual almanac information, such data were now greatly abridged so that the lined writing pages that formed the bulk of this new kind of publication permitted diary owners *themselves* to provide most of the final content. By 1825, the new pocket diaries, so-called because of their easy portability (they fit in the palm of one's hand), had become the fashionable repository for personal journaling.[5] Brown, however, chose to write about the days of his life in totally blank books, larger than these, perhaps because they were more economical for serious journalers such as he. Like the stationers from whom he purchased two of these volumes, Mahlon Day and Rich and Loutrel, many others advertised such books in the booming, competitive publishing industry of the 1830s. Blank-book or account-book making was just one niche in this field.[6]

Despite the personalized information kept in blank books, these journals rarely, if ever, revealed the secrets of their keepers' hearts in any overt fashion. Like the diary entries of farmers, ordinary housewives, and common people in the years predating the Civil War, Brown's were generally telegraphic, often consisting of only one or two lines, and offered readers no explicit revelation of the writer's interior life. One bibliographer of the diary frustratedly noted, "The entries are matter-of-fact accounts of mundane events which offer little insight into Mr. Brown's character, apart from his obsession with weather, gardening, and death." The apparent minutiae it contained were well in keeping with nineteenth-century conventions. Again, according to Molly McCarthy, nineteenth-century diaries "recorded terse, matter-of-fact comments ranging from information on the weather and daily chores to remarks on the health and well-being of friends and family."[7] Far from consisting of open and deeply self-reflective, psychologically revealing entries, nineteenth-century diary keeping was "rarely taken as opportunities for private introspective confession."[8] One can speculate on the reasons for this: Simply noting the events of one's life requires time, a precious commodity for ordinary working people; and translating one's feelings about those events on paper takes even more time. Additionally, as will be discussed in Part II regarding the cultural meanings of work, for Americans in Brown's era, activity per se and one's accomplishments more than one's musings about them was what mattered in a journal. Victorian-style diary writing providing explicit details about one's inner thoughts, often associated with young girls and women, would not become commonplace until the very late nineteenth century, more than twenty years after Brown's death.[9] For the years of Brown's diary, to the extent that American men who kept daily journals tended "to write of their public activities" and in crisp, concise fashion, Brown was well within this trend.[10] Gardening, his source of income, was his main public activity, so it, along with related weather entries, unsurprisingly accounts for a large number of his postings.

The encyclopedic nature of the diary has made it a valuable research source for writers of Verplanck family history, horticultural history, and Hudson Valley history, while simultaneously obscuring the life of its author. The Verplancks (to whom the diary passed, probably after Julia Brown's death in 1890) used it to verify events in their own family chronicle; William Edward Verplanck (1856–1928) referred to the diary in writing his 1892 Verplanck family history. Alice B.G. Lockwood, a researcher for the Garden Club of America, included an essay that referenced Brown's diary when she edited a seminal two-volume history of gardens in colonial and early republican America that was published in the 1930s. A. J. Williams-Myers used the diary in his 2003 historical overview of blacks in the Hudson Valley. But who was the man behind the pages? What did he believe in and care about? How did he act on these concerns? What was his social world like? How did he move in and/or against the currents of his times?

This biography is inspired by the conviction that the most meaningful aspects of James F. Brown's life have been hidden in plain view for too long, and that it was his intention that they be uncovered. James's life, significant in several ways, is a palimpsest perceived here against the backdrop of national developments. For sure, it substantiates and expands extant knowledge about slavery, fugitive slaves, and free blacks in the Hudson Valley and in the North. In so doing, it confirms a picture of both black agency and quintessential American self-invention. In fact, the story of the free black antebellum community in the North is very much about self-creation. As a people, African Americans were able to leverage the relative flexibility of urban milieux, fluid social relations in new settlements, the work skills they learned as slaves, black–white demographic balances, patron–client relationships, distinctive worldviews, and other factors in order to survive and to improve their lives. Such findings regarding black agency have been duplicated in numerous studies of antebellum black institutional life, antislavery and self-manumitting activity, and family life in the North in both rural and urban areas.[11] As we will see in this book, Brown was certainly a case in point reflecting both American and African-American initiative, ambition, and activity as he manipulated the flexibility of town and city life in Maryland in order to escape slavery and then to make useful connections in New York.

The obstacles to advancement that free northern blacks such as Brown faced in the new nation were numerous. Antebellum northern whites— even those opposed to slavery—generally held low expectations for blacks and treated them accordingly. Suffrage was not extended to or was severely restricted for African American men who most white Americans thought were intellectually and morally incapable of exercising citizen rights responsibly. In several parts of the Midwest, especially those where many of the white settlers were from the South, restrictions were placed on black migration to the region. Fears of black criminality led to disproportionately high African American incarceration rates. As public schools were created, African Americans found that they were excluded, relegated to racially segregated facilities, or forced to find alternatives in the private sector. And everywhere, blacks were limited in employment opportunities.[12] Important regional and city case studies confirm this pattern in New England, Philadelphia, and New York as these places experienced the generally slow, hostile passage of blacks from slavery to freedom.[13] As a free black in the North, Brown was certainly aware of the invisible color line affecting northern race relations and of his relatively rare status as a voting, propertied black man in antebellum America.

But Brown's life is ultimately about the permeability, albeit rare and tenuous, of the line between slavery and freedom even in the pre–Civil War South and how African Americans in the North at this time could and sometimes did replicate the larger struggles and successes of white Americans. In some aspects then, James F. Brown, although obscure, was exceptional: He managed to escape slavery, establish a good life as a manumitted man, and live to tell the story. But in so many other ways, despite the restrictions of race he experienced, he might easily have been a case study or an exemplary life in Appleby's work. His life is significant, then, because, as an ordinary black man, he nonetheless participated in and personally embodied the creation of a new *American* definition of citizenship at the very time that the crafting of this definition itself was a national project—one that negotiated, cautiously and contentiously, the substance of the bequest left by the country's founders.

The contours of Brown's life as recorded in the diary reveal a great deal about the meaning of freedom in antebellum America. Freedom—a much-lauded concept, the harbinger of national identity and citizenship—was a very unstable and contested notion in the years preceding the Civil War. There was, of course, the big question of who might officially claim freedom in law. The overwhelming majority of African Americans certainly could not do so by law in the southern states and had not been so entitled since the colonial period, but as the abolitionist *v.* proslavery debate was enjoined after 1830, such legal proscriptions were buffered by pseudoscientific arguments against the mental capacities of black people. As a result, in the minds of many, not only were blacks naturally relegated to the ranks of the unfree by chattel slavery, but they supposedly benefited from the paternalistic, benevolent, and necessary tutelage of the peculiar institution as well. Just as strenuously, antislavery forces argued against barriers to freedom for blacks. This controversy was settled only, and then only temporarily, by the Civil War. The trajectory of James Brown's life was itself a study in this national struggle as he moved from bondage to emancipation, from a slave master to a manumission-minded employer.

The changing structure of work in the antebellum period called into question the meaning of freedom as well, and this, too, is reflected in Brown's biography. Freedom meant the opportunity to rise, the chance to experience a level of financial success, security, and independence—a livelihood and property. Yet a growing commercial economy and the slow spread of industrialization interrupted those traditional occupational arrangements that had guaranteed the attainment of these goals for previous generations. New territorial settlements drew sons westward, away from their fathers' pursuits; and mechanization interrupted craft-based labor systems. In a rapidly transforming marketplace, could one attain and/or retain freedom through work? Did the risks of falling into economic dependency, debt, and poverty in this fluid economy outweigh the chances for upward mobility? And what steps might one take, what interventions on one's own behalf ought a laborer pursue, in order to ensure the freedom suggested in the term "free labor"? In several ways, James Brown's life may be read as his consistent endeavor to seal his freedom in economic terms.

Freedom in its fullest form also came to mean involvement in public life. James Brown, like antebellum Americans almost everywhere, participated in the evolving civic sphere that Alexis de Tocqueville so astutely observed. Nationally, new clubs and social organizations continually appeared as reflections of a menu of religious, labor-related, ethnic, and racial identities as well as the assortment of intellectual, social, aesthetic, cultural, economic, and political concerns within the American populace. On top of that, the electorate expanded by the removal of property qualifications for most adult white males who wished to exercise suffrage rights. As a rare black male property holder in antebellum New York state, James Brown swam in several of these streams of public engagement.

The pages that follow seek to tell James Brown's life, then, as a reflection of these three nationwide struggles—regarding personhood, regarding work, and regarding democratic association—in the years before the Civil War. Part

I is about the country's ongoing and growing struggle between chattel slavery and legal freedom. It plunges the reader into quite opaque historical waters—the beginning of James's life—and describes his experiences in Maryland as a slave. It attempts to explain why and when he determined to leave the South as a fugitive in search of a free existence in the North. It also surveys those experiences in his life as a slave that provided him with resources for his later life as a free man. Part II explores the national tension between "wage slavery" and freedom by surveying Brown's life as an employed laborer in the North. It mostly discusses his work as a gardener for the Verplanck family; how this work tied him to a regional and national horticultural movement with cultural, social, political, and economic dimensions; and the meaning of such work in shaping his identity as a free man. Part III examines the matter of political freedom as expressed through antebellum America's teeming associational life. This third section of the book traces Brown's political concerns and activities, both formally and informally, and interprets their larger significance.

Although it inescapably contains examples of defeat and systemic victimization, James's story is not a tragic hero's tale; it has a happy ending, at least for James, because of his successful self-reinvention. This narrative is one that consistently recognizes the atypicality of his experience as a southern-born black, the sad normality of his frustrations as a free African American, the unusualness of the safe routines he was able to enjoy as an ordinary man of color, and the commonness of the challenges he faced as an American who, along with others, etched the portrait of freedom for all national citizens prior to the Civil War by his daily choices.

PART I

Life as a Slave

Who was James F. Brown, the bondsman? And what precisely did freedom from slavery mean to him? It is a game of shadows, following the outlines of the life of James Brown during his years as a slave. He appears and disappears through the light of this or that written fragment from his time, but always in murky form. His figure is blurry, sometimes only chimerical before the viewer, and then vanishes from sight. This is not entirely surprising. After all, the details of the lives of most slaves as individuals are elusive. James and Julia Brown were the settled identities of a married couple, former slaves, whose passage to freedom included the use of family names, names bestowed by owners, names assumed as aliases in order to avoid detection, married names, and/or names selected to mark the attainment of freedom. There is a strong possibility that James F. Brown, Anthony Chase, and Anthony Fisher were one and the same man. It is also even more likely that Julia Williams, Julia Chase, and Julia Brown were the same woman. James picked up, shed, and changed names as part of his quest for full manhood in early-nineteenth-century terms, with Julia alongside as his chosen mate in life. Dotted in places, the line documenting the connection between James and his two aliases—one definite, the other likely, but tenuous—is not always continuous and it does not always appear in sharp relief. Consider the following events.

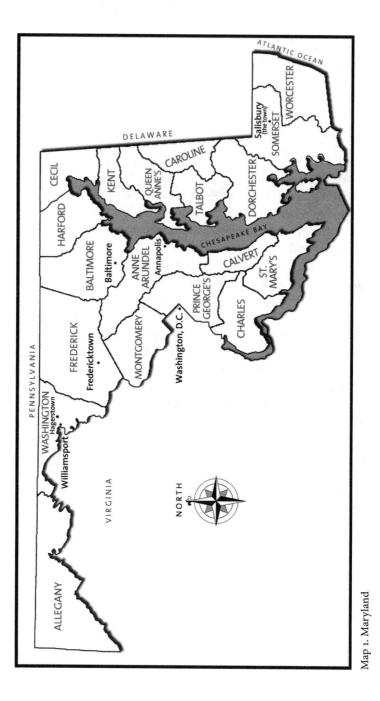

Map 1. Maryland

What Can a Man Do?

The life of James F. Brown, the slave, begins with questions about his birth date. A late-nineteenth-century newspaper profile of him put his year of birth at 1783, but James was probably born ten years later than that, as the Mount Gulian Historic Site's Web site claims. The 1850 federal census lists him as being fifty years old, thus making 1800 his year of birth. And if he was sixty-seven in 1860 as indicated by the federal census in that year, then he was born in 1793. As for a birth*day*, the diary itself consistently fixes it on October 1. So the best, cumulative conclusion is that James F. Brown was born on October 1, 1793.[1]

James was born in Maryland. The Mount Gulian Web site pinpoints Fredericktown (present-day Frederick) as the city of his birth, but there is no ironclad verification of this. Several diary entries indicate that he had correspondents there, but they are untraceable and/or mostly unnamed. In January 1829, he "received a letter from Louis Carroll of Frederick town, Md." The fact that there is no federal census evidence of such a person living in Frederick County under any spelling of that name in either 1820 or 1830 is a good indication that Louis Carroll was black, because census notation of free blacks was notoriously iffy and not individualized for slaves. Early in the holiday season of 1832, James "wrote to Fredericktown." At the start of 1833, James also "received a letter from Fredericktown Md"; early in 1846, he again recorded that he "received a letter from Frederick Town, Maryland" and this time that he "wrote a letter to Frederick Town, Maryland."[2] In addition, the diary mentions someone born there who may have been a close relative of Brown's: In the family history section of his diary, Brown recorded that "John Robert Brown was born on the [illegible] day of June 1799 and was baptized on the 23rd day of June by the Rev Shaffer of Frederick town and died the 4th day of Feb. 1824 ages 5 years, 7 months and 10 days." Indeed, a Reverend David Frederick Schaeffer simultaneously served Evangelical Lutheran Church in Fredericktown and a Bethel Church in Frederick County early in the nineteenth century. However, Reverend Schaeffer's pastorate of the two congregations began in 1808—nine years too late for him to have baptized John Robert.[3] Still, the careful record of John Robert Brown's short life in the diary section where James safeguarded some of the most important events of his life—his marriage, his manumission of Julia—and the closeness of John's year of birth to James's own hint that John Robert was perhaps James's younger brother. Yet James curiously reported an age-at-death for John Robert that suggests the latter may have been a son James fathered when he was twenty-six years old. If John Robert *was* James's younger brother by nearly six years, then James would have been thirty years old when John Robert died in 1824, so that the "5 years" James assigned to John at death might have been a simple writing error.

In fact, James may have been the eldest of several siblings who lived to adulthood. He mentions a sister, Comfort Dennis, in several places in the diary; she was born about 1795. Then there was another probable sister, Esther, married to Levin Huston of Salisbury, Maryland. Esther was born in 1797. James also had a brother William Brown, whose age cannot be ascertained from existing sources. Another possible brother was Samuel Brown, who was born in 1803.[4]

James was born of "negro parents," according to a late-nineteenth-century newspaper biographical sketch of him. This would seem to be true. There is no description of his being light-skinned or being able to pass for white. He is described as "colored" in the 1840 federal census and as a "mulatto" in the 1850 federal census, as was his sister, Comfort, in the 1880 census. But in 1860 the enumeration listed James as "black."[5] Colored, mulatto, black—these were notoriously subjective categories used inconsistently by census takers with highly individualized understandings of the spectrum of African American skin tones throughout the nineteenth century. Materials are silent about James's mother and who she was exactly. We know nothing about when she was born and died, where she lived, her owner(s), if any, or her racial or ethnic background. James's father, however, was a man named Robert Chase who died in Maryland, possibly in Baltimore, on July 22, 1838. Robert Chase was a "free Negro" who leased a small three-acre plot of land in Somerset County, Maryland, called "Little Belane" for twenty-four years after securing the rental rights to farm it in 1814. Before his death, Robert had lived for a time in Salisbury, Maryland— probably with Esther and Levin Huston at Poplar Hill Mansion, because that is where James sent his father letters and money. Levin was his brother-in-law, but just how is unclear because Esther's maiden name was Polk.[6]

As a slave, James would have received his last name from his owner. Throughout the English-speaking Atlantic world, once slavery was firmly established in a region, in most cases it was slavemasters and not the slaves themselves who came up with slave names.[7] Even when slaves retained African names, owners or overseers often assigned them an additional familiar English name as well, and this generally consisted only of a forename, for example Mary, Dinah, Harry, or George. In this way, whites asserted their authority over their human property and a racialized distinction between "negroes"—a category of being requiring no more than one name—and themselves, people known by a first name, generally one or more middle names, and a last or family name. In those cases in which African Americans went by first and last names, they were free or else were situated as slaves within a relatively fluid regional slave system, one in which the hierarchy of power dividing whites and blacks was not so rigid.[8] Certainly, this was the case in Frederick County during James's childhood and youth.

Frederick County, Maryland, was founded in 1748, less than half a century before James Brown was born. It was located in northern Maryland, a region distinct from that of southern Maryland. There were in fact two separate Marylands that took shape between 1790 and 1850. For one thing, the northern part of Maryland, which included Fredericktown and Baltimore, had a more diverse population than did the southern part. There were more European immigrants in northern Maryland than in southern Maryland. The evidence for this in Fredericktown was the existence of four German congregations in the eighteenth century when James was born there—a German Reformed church, a Lutheran church, a Moravian church, and a Church of the Brethren. In fact, Fredericktown had been settled by a group of German immigrants some time after 1745. Many Germans (Pennsylvania Dutch) moved to Fredericktown as part of their migration southward and westward through the Great Valley that included the Shenandoah Valley into the western piedmont of North Carolina during the late eighteenth century when James was born. Southern Maryland did not experience a similar immigrant influx. There, the demographic divide was chiefly between British-descended whites and African-descended blacks.[9]

The relatively higher degree of ethnic, racial, and cultural heterogeneity in northern Maryland, and particularly in Frederick County, contributed to a somewhat more liberal culture than that in the southern half of the state. For instance, there was relatively little divisive sectarianism among Christians in Frederick County during the late eighteenth century. Until the 1750s when the Moravians built their own church, people of Anglican, Reformed, Lutheran, and Moravian persuasion all worshiped together. Then during the Revolutionary War era, Anglican Church growth was stunted mainly by animosity toward Loyalists and their flight; in fact, the county's Episcopalians had no rector from 1776 to 1786. From 1785 to 1813, they met only monthly: every fourth Sunday in the neighboring county at a church in Hagerstown.[10]

The shaky standing of the Anglican church in Frederick County during James Brown's formative years meant that if he was indeed living there then, he was likely to have been taught basic literacy skills through one of the German churches while a child or adolescent. While a 1760 Maryland statute blocked Christian baptism as a path to emancipation for slaves, the opportunity to learn to read and write remained at least as one way in which Christian religion offered a better life on earth for them.[11] Lutheranism in the early republic was concerned with promoting Christian education, Protestant unity, and Christian benevolence in the service of national greatness. All of this conceivably had a positive impact on slaves within the geographical reach of Lutheran congregations. The afore-mentioned Reverend David Frederick Schaeffer, a father of the General Synod of the Lutheran Church in America, pastor in Fredericktown from 1808 to 1837, and also the minister who may have baptized one of James's likely brothers, participated in the burgeoning Sunday School movement, which taught children to read and write through Bible instruction. Reverend Schaeffer also believed in cross-denominational fellowship and African American uplift through colonization; he was an officer in the Fredericktown auxiliary of the American Colonization Society, which equated black welfare with the resettlement of freed African Americans in Liberia. James and other interested slaves would have been readily accommodated in their desire for literacy by such a man.[12]

Although slavery was legally recognized and practiced throughout Maryland prior to the Civil War, the institution was more pervasive in the southern part of the state than in the northern counties. Moreover, even as Maryland emerged during this period as an exporter of slaves to points farther south, the trend in the state as a whole was toward the freedom of blacks held in bondage for economic reasons. Northern Maryland, and the Fredericktown area more specifically, boasted a more diversified economy in relation to southern Maryland. In the northern part of the state, farmers grew mainly cereal crops, and slaves were a smaller part of the society. So as a young man, James probably was not engaged in the tobacco–slave plantation economy normally associated with the Chesapeake region. Fredericktown was an important market town for its area, Frederick County, which was on its way by 1830 to becoming a mining center for such resources as coal, iron, limestone, copper, marble, and gold.[13] In 1810, besides farms, Frederick County boasted 2 gun powder mills, 2 glass works, 3 carriage manufacturers, 4 paper mills, 5 flaxseed oil mills, 4 breweries, 7 tanneries, 102 shoe/boot/slipper manufacturers, 20 saddlers, 20 stills, 1 still manufacturer, 5 clock and watch makers, 2 furnaces, 3 forges, and 36 hatteries.[14] In contrast, southern Maryland was devoted almost exclusively to agriculture and depended heavily on tobacco cultivation as the backbone of its economy, even though tobacco was a steadily unprofitable crop because of soil overuse and erosion. Some farmers in the area engaged in wheat production, but tobacco was the mainstay in southern Maryland in the late eighteenth and early nineteenth centuries.[15]

Figures on the proportion that slaves represented in the two sections of Maryland reflect the differences in their economies. In 1790, around the time James Brown may have been born, slaves were 14.9 percent of the population in northern Maryland (including the counties of Allegany, Baltimore, Carroll, Harford, Washington, and Frederick) and had decreased to 4.8 percent by 1850. On the other hand, in southern Maryland (including the counties called Anne Arundel, Calvert, Charles, Prince George's, Montgomery, and St. Mary's), 45.6 percent or just under half of the population total consisted of slaves. In 1850, slaves made up 43.7 percent of the population of this area.[16]

Statistics on free blacks also underscore the difference between northern and southern Maryland in the antebellum years. While in southern Maryland free blacks increased over time as a percentage of the total population from 2 percent in 1790 to 10.2 percent in 1850, their increase was slightly steeper in northern Maryland, where James may have spent his youth. There, the percentage of free blacks in the whole population increased from 1.9 percent of the population to 11.2 of the total. More strikingly, in Frederick County specifically, the proportion of free blacks crept up slowly from 12.5 percent of the population around the time of James's birth to 18.7 percent by 1850.[17]

The ratio between slaves and free blacks changed dramatically, but differently, over six decades in northern Maryland as opposed to southern Maryland. In the northern part of the state, in 1790 the ratio of slaves to free blacks was 7.9 to 1, but by 1850 it had dropped to 0.4 to 1. By 1850, free blacks were more than twice as numerous in northern Maryland as the slave population there. In southern Maryland, in 1790, the ratio of slaves to free blacks was 22.7 to 1 and dropped to only 4.3 to 1 by 1850. In other words, in 1850, slaves still outnumbered free blacks in southern Maryland by more than four times. James then presumably grew up in a region where he could observe the number of black bondsmen shrinking all around him as the number of free African Americans expanded absolutely and proportionately. Focusing more narrowly on Frederick County, the ratio of slaves to free blacks declined steadily during the decades of James's youthful maturation. In 1790, it was 17.1 to 1; in 1800, 9.7 to 1; in 1810, 4.7 to 1; and by 1820, just 3.8 to 1.[18]

Imagine the effect of such population shifts on everyday life: Race relations loosened, and slaves gained a sense of widening possibility for themselves in such an atmosphere. Given the sometimes historically inverse relationship between laws and reality, the consequences of these demographics may be reflected in the fact that Fredericktown imposed a new nighttime curfew of 10 o'clock on its slave population in 1817. The law was intended "to restrain the slaves from wandering around the town at night" by providing for the arrest and jailing of violators. In other words, the strictness of the statute ironically revealed both the lax hold many owners had on their slaves and the desire of some of them and other whites to hold the line on black–white/slave–free distinctions more tightly, as the free black population rose in number, proportion, visibility, and influence.[19]

So if James Brown lived as a child slave in Fredericktown or Frederick County, who was his master or mistress? There are no slaveowning Browns among the sixteen household heads with that last name listed for those places in 1790, just before his birth. In 1800, just after James's birth, only one of the twenty-three household heads in all of Frederick County with the last name Brown was a slaveowner, and that was Stophel Brown, who had one slave. It is unlikely that this was James. Because he would have been only seven years old at the time, too young for serious farm work, at least his slave mother should have been present for him in Stophel's household, but there is none, and extant sources reveal nothing more about Stophel or his human chattel at this time.[20]

The combination of relative religious liberalism toward slaves in Frederick County with the steady transformation of the area away from its economic dependence on slave labor suggests a comparatively loose system of race relations there, the kind into which those born as slaves would have been permitted and/or given full names—first, middle, and last, as in James Francis Brown. In 1810, when he would have been about seventeen years old, there were twenty-six Browns listed as household heads in the federal census of Fredericktown, but only two owned slaves. Because this census did not provide first names, merely initials for first names, and listed only household heads by name, there were only two possible owners of a slave named James Brown—one P. Brown, who claimed two slaves, and one M. Brown, who was master of nine slaves. Nothing more can be said of P. Brown from available sources, but judging by the number of slaves within the household, this M. Brown may very well have been Matthew Brown, co-owner with his brother, William, of the Fleecy Dale Factory, a business that provided dyeing, fulling, and dressing services for wool. As a complement or supplement to the wool factory, Matthew probably also owned a sheep farm, judging by an advertisement he placed—"Ewes wanted"—in a Frederick County newspaper in 1816.[21] In all likelihood, Matthew Brown grew grains on that same farm; this assumption is based on another of his ads, which mentioned "corn for sale at [his] farm on [the] Monocacy [River] near the mouth of Bennett's Creek."[22] Between the wool factory and the farm, Matthew Brown's enterprises would easily have benefited from the use of slave laborers. If Brown bought James right after starting the Fleecy Dale Factory, it is possible that James assumed the last name of his new owner as a teenager—perhaps moving from Chase to Brown—as sometimes happened when slaves changed owners.[23]

The Brown operation was probably started during the years of hostility between the United States and England that became the War of 1812, when interrupted trade with England provided sheltered possibilities for the establishment and growth of American manufacturing because British imports were no longer readily available.[24] Regarding the wool industry specifically, production of American items especially benefited from these circumstances when "embargo, non-intercourse, and war meant opportunities for the domestic wool manufacture."[25] In 1812, Tench Coxe, as an enthusiastic supporter of American industry, surveyed the status of wool production in the United States. His report was bullish: Between 1810 and 1812, there had been growth in domestic wool production to a total of just over 20 million pounds; the quality of domestic wool had improved as a result of the introduction of Merino long-wooled sheep; the introduction and use of fly shuttles had made fulling or wool-thickening operations, like those run by Matthew Brown, possible; a market for fulled wool could be readily found in the army; and simple, drab colors like maroon, brown, and "bottle green" that were preferred in woolens were well within the capabilities of relatively unsophisticated American dyeing operations, presumably like Matthew Brown's. In these ways, the wool industry enjoyed a competitive advantage at the time against imported Scottish Shetlands, English Herefordshires, German Saxons, French Rousillons, and Spanish Merinos.[26] Indeed, the Fleecy Dale Factory may have commenced operation immediately after Tench Coxe's survey in 1810. That would be one way of reconciling the fact that that year, Coxe reported no wool factories or fulling mills in Frederick County, yet the census registered M. Brown's nine slaves.[27] Slaves working for Matthew Brown might then have been employed as skilled laborers on wool-manufacturing machines, agricultural laborers tending to grains and sheep herding, and/or as domestic servants within their masters' houses.

If James F. Brown was one of Matthew Brown's slaves, he might have been a victim of the downturn in the domestic wool industry after 1815 following the end of the War of 1812. The impact of the resumption of British woolen imports on the American market was "harmfully great after the war."[28] Indeed, Matthew Brown advertised in the fall of 1816 for the sale of a 180-acre stretch of his property called Hope Hill; another adjoining, 120-acre spread of land; his residence; and a mill.[29] It is very likely that slaves were included in his inventory reductions. In 1827, James Brown would write that he had been a servant of the Williams household for eleven years—that is, since 1816. In other words, when William E. Williams purchased James, it might have been because Matthew Brown sold him to offset business reversals.

The family from which Brown later escaped—the family of William E. Williams (1797–1822)—was looking to acquire slaves at the very time that wool operations like Matthew Brown's were looking to sell their bondsmen. The Williamses resided in Frederick County from 1814 to 1822 in Ceresville, a neighborhood a few miles northwest of Fredericktown and named for the Roman goddess of agriculture and grain. The Williams estate was a diversified farm. William E. had inherited the place from his father as the eldest living son in 1808 at the age of 21.[30] Sixteen years before that, his father had described it as "a farm of 300–500 acres, with a suitable number of hands, animals and implements; crops are wheat and other cereals, potatoes, hay and other food for stock; stock in horses, cows, sheep, pigs and poultry."[31] The spread also included "a grist mill, a saw mill, and a ferry."[32] Otho H. Williams (1749–94) had made improvements to the property before his untimely death so that it also included an orchard and garden, but following the War of Independence, he had mostly resided in Baltimore as the Collector of the Port and had left the daily operation of the Ceresville lands to managers about whom he received occasional reports from a close friend in Frederick County.[33] By 1810, however, Otho's son, William E., had returned to Maryland after a stint in the U.S. Infantry and turned his attention to farming on his father's Ceresville land. Over the next five years, William E. would have the property surveyed and appraised, contemplate adding Merino sheep to his stock, search for a mason to build him a house there, buy another 119 acres, look for a blacksmith, consider the purchase of slaves, get a sawmill operating, and advertise for a gardener. By 1814, two years after marrying Susanna (Susan) Frisby Cooke, William E. had established with his family a country seat at Ceresville. In 1816, William E. was still in an expansive mood regarding the estate; he was supplying a flour mill with new stones, debating the hire of a new miller, and making inquiries about a new overseer.[34] By

1820, William E.'s Ceresville estate required the work of 28 slaves, including four males between 26 and 45 years old. One of these might have been James Brown.[35]

As owner of a restored farm with a new, accompanying flour milling operation, William E. Williams had much use for slave laborers. A couple of years before the start of James's life with the Williamses, William E. apparently made known his interest in acquiring slaves. He received offers of slaves for purchase during the fall of 1814. One Mrs. West had "some boys . . . to dispose of" during the winter of 1814. Richard Tilghman of Queen Anne's County was trying to get rid of the "too many" he owned and wrote William E. to describe "two negro boys aged about 20 years, both stout, active, and handsome" whom he would sell for $400. The two slaves would have been about James's age at the time, an age for which William E. was apparently advertising.[36]

If James lived with the Williams family at Ceresville, he certainly would have had ample opportunity to gain experience in the kinds of work he later performed in New York as a waiter, a coachman, and a gardener. As a substantial household and a leading family in the community, the William E. Williamses entertained neighbors and visiting elites frequently. Those dining with them would have been served by slave waiters. Regional gentry—including Susan's family from Baltimore; William E.'s family from elsewhere in Maryland and Virginia; and Philadelphians like Colonel J. H. Powell, his mother, and his sister—also stopped by the Ceresville estate.[37] In 1815 William E. apparently inquired in Philadelphia about a fancy new riding gig—a carriage that might include a Dickey seat, one for servants, and painted panels—that would have been driven by a slave coachman. William E. also ordered a new wagon from York, Pennsylvania, probably for transporting farm produce back and forth to Baltimore because the builder explained that the extra iron in the tire wheels was "according to the rules of the Lancaster Turnpike for 30 barrel wagons." A slave driver would have been assigned to this transport task as well.[38] In 1815, a year after moving to Frederick County, William E. sent instructions to advertise in the Baltimore newspapers for a gardener, but no one applied for this position. Perhaps James filled this gap.[39]

By 1818, however, James Brown was living on Frederick Street in Baltimore as a taxpayer. This "Negro Boy," as he was described in the city tax list, was twenty-five years old at the time and had made an improvement to an "old frame" house on a lot on Frederick Street. This seems to reflect some sort of arrangement that had been brokered on his behalf through a Joseph Brown, an "agent" of some sort according to the tax listing, with Captain

Daniel Howland (1758–1837). Nothing more can be discerned about the agent and his business from available sources, but the captain was a gentleman of high social standing in early national Baltimore. Howland was a mariner-shipowner who had begun his career modestly as the owner of a single, small vessel, the *Erin*. His entrepreneurship had proven successful enough to lift Howland to the rank of merchant-shipowner by 1816. This meant that the captain no longer accompanied or commandeered his ship at sea but rather functioned as a sedentary Baltimore-based merchant in possession of an active sea-trading vessel. The financial security he had obtained in his climb is reflected in several real estate transactions between 1815 and 1816 (and others after 1820). In 1818, Howland had become president of the newly incorporated Savings Bank of Baltimore; dedicated to helping the poor, in its first year of operation especially this largely benevolent institution encouraged local African Americans to become savers. It is easy to imagine that James deposited his savings in this bank, and he may have received from this bank the loan to buy his Baltimore house through his association with Howland. By 1819, Howland was listed in the city directory as a "gentleman"; by 1824, he had become president of the Phoenix Fire Insurance Company of Maryland. Throughout this period, he resided on Frederick Street, as did Brown.[40]

This set of circumstances speaks volumes about the fluidity of slavery in antebellum Baltimore. It seems that at this point in his life, James had become one of the city's quasi-free slaves, those whose masters permitted them atypical, extralegal privileges as slaves. Throughout the antebellum South, especially in urban areas, a tiny minority of bondsmen conducted their own affairs—hiring themselves out, operating their own businesses, finding their own residences—with the knowledge and sometimes assistance of their masters and/or highly influential whites. These were not legally free blacks, nor were they bondsmen held under the watchful eye of strict owners who monitored their every move. Yes, there were legal, official prohibitions against such activity. Slaves were not supposed to buy real estate, own personal property, earn cash, or run businesses—but these *de facto* free blacks did.[41] James Brown was one of them.

Moreover, in Baltimore, free blacks greatly outnumbered enslaved blacks in the antebellum period. The historian Barbara Fields provides an explanation for these demographics, which were anomalous in the South:

> The slave system could never be the center of Baltimore's social existence. By the nature of the city's economic activity, the market for labor was highly seasonal and to a large degree casual. . . . The slave system did not

meet those irregular demands. The internal dynamic of a city like Baltimore excluded slavery as a dominant principle of organization. Though Baltimore in 1860 had a population of over two thousand slaves, it was not then or at any time in its history a slave city.[42]

The numbers tell the story: In Baltimore, the percentage of the total population represented by slaves decreased by nearly 7 percent between 1810 and 1820 and by another 5 percent over the next decade. Meanwhile, the proportion of free blacks rose by 82 percent in Baltimore between 1810 and 1820 and by another 43 percent between 1820 and 1830. In fact, in 1820 there were 10,326 free blacks and 4,357 slaves.[43]

Indeed, the historian Christopher Phillips has labeled Baltimore "freedom's port"—"a city through which North and South reached each other, a notorious entrepôt for fugitives between the slave states and the free states, and a safe harbor for the development of autonomy as well as community"—particularly during the early years of the nineteenth century when James was there.[44] The atmosphere in Baltimore that nursed any slave's interior musings about the prospects of acquiring freedom, then, would have been promising. Most blacks in the city were free. The city also contained so-called term slaves—slaves with delayed manumission contracts with their masters stipulating that they would be freed within a specific number of years. For economic reasons, masters were willing to extend a kind of leniency to both term slaves and quasi-free slaves by allowing them to hire themselves out for wages and then to purchase their freedom and/or the freedom of loved ones. And in the circle of African Americans there, it was easy to blend and mingle with the free black majority in 1820, to become camouflaged as such, to enjoy an independent social life, and to imbibe the heady elixir of freedom by association with former slaves.[45] Significantly, Phillips found that "slaves and freed people worked much like common whites in Baltimore. The city hired slaves as well as free Negroes and paid them the same wages that they paid white laborers."[46] He elaborated further:

> Slaves and free blacks had remarkable confidence in their futures in Baltimore, both individually and collectively. Hundreds, perhaps even thousands, of escaped slaves . . . remained in Baltimore and risked capture by masters or their masters' acquaintances who lived only a mile or two away. Thousands of freedpeople from all over the state and region left the oppression of slavery in the countryside and came to Baltimore rather than move to the free states.[47]

In sum, for many slaves, self-hiring with their owners' permission provided a means to earn wages, support their families, and enjoy some measure of autonomy. In cities and towns of the Upper South like Baltimore, Fredericktown, and Hagerstown, hired-out bondsmen worked as "coopers, carpenters, and millers, also loaded and unloaded steamboats, labored on the docks and along river fronts, became servants, domestics, cooks, coachmen, and found employment as tobacco twisters, woodchoppers, and day laborers."[48] For the owners of such quasi-free slaves, allowing their bondsmen to enter into yearly employment contracts with other whites and to collect a portion of the earnings was profitable; indeed, the most successful hired-out slaves benefited from the endorsement and patronage of well-connected, powerful whites like Howland and the Williamses who vouchsafed for the bondsmen's fidelity and/or industriousness.[49] James was apparently in this category.

It is James himself who mainly related the next, scattered details of his life as a slave. Acting as a quasi-free slave, he corresponded with his former master's widow, received mail from a white Fredericktown resident, and evidently traveled about northern Maryland on his own. On March 30, 1824, he wrote his owner, Susan F. Williams, "on business of some importance" and received an answer the following day. In typical fashion, James did not specify in his diary the contents of their correspondence with each other. Perhaps the note was about his sister, Comfort Dennis. Perhaps James had appealed unsuccessfully to his mistress to prevent his sister's sale away from Maryland because he recorded in his diary that Comfort "went to Augusta, Georgia the 19th of April." A little more than a year after this family loss, Jacob Engelbrecht, an indefatigable antebellum diarist from Fredericktown, recorded on August 9, 1825, that he had just written "a letter for the Reverend James Harper (colored man) addressed to James Brown (colored man) care of Enoch Kinsell Hagerstown Maryland."[50] Somehow living in Hagerstown then, perhaps through a hired-out arrangement, James was asked by Harper to pass on the news to one Emily Graham of the drowning suicide of her husband, Thomas. The fact that Harper was an African Methodist Episcopal (AME) minister suggests that James may have been connected with that denomination at this time. Back in Baltimore by September of the next year, during that month James was a busy man indeed: According to his diary, he married Julia Chase, manumitted her for $100, and resigned his seat at Bethel Church, probably the local AME Church.[51] The resignation may have been an indication of James's resolve to relocate again, but this time permanently.

James Brown faded from the literary trail in Maryland in 1826, but he seemingly resurfaced as Anthony Chase later that year. In order to illuminate how Brown may have morphed into Chase during the mid-1820s, we must backtrack a bit. William E. Williams removed his household from Ceresville to Baltimore some time after 1818. That summer, William E. busied himself with his farm, mill operations, and financial ventures, but by late summer he became ill and in early fall began searching for a farm manager.[52] By early 1819, Williams put his Frederick property up for sale, and by August 1822 he took up residence in Baltimore.[53] William E.'s illness—some sort of "throat and respiratory ailment"—became quite serious during the late summer of the previous year. The move and new doctors did not improve William E.'s health. He died shortly after moving to Baltimore at the very young age of thirty-five; his death may have been a consequence of the prescribed mercury cure and not the condition itself.[54]

William E.'s widow, Susan, and his younger brother, Henry Lee Williams, became executors of the elder Williams' estate while Susan and William E.'s children inherited his property, including the slaves.[55] One of these slaves, named Anthony Chase, was hired out to Henry Lee, also a resident of Baltimore, at some point in 1823. This arrangement continued for the entirety of 1824 and 1825, and six months into 1826; Susan expected $10 per month from this arrangement.[56] Sometime in 1826, apparently near death, Henry Lee promised Anthony his freedom through the following note:[57]

In consideration of the faithful services of my servant Anthony, I do hereby authorize the Executors of my last Will and Testament to purchase him from his mistress for the sole purpose of setting him free and I do further authorize my said Executors, as soon as such purchase shall be effected, to execute as the law directs a deed of manumission giving full freedom to the said Anthony.[58]

Encouraged by this promise of freedom, Anthony decided to marry in that same year, 1826, and did, but Anthony's widowed owner, Susan F. Williams, proved unwilling to cooperate in his release from bondage. Instead, after Henry's death, Susan allowed Anthony to hire himself out to Jeremiah C. Hoffman, another wealthy gentleman in Baltimore—perhaps as a domestic servant, a coachman, or even a gardener. The Hoffman home would certainly have required the use of all three. Hoffman had resided in London for many years as a commission merchant for his family's mercantile firm before returning to Baltimore in 1825 and purchasing Chatsworth House, a "large and elegant brick mansion, with coach house, stables and other offices, all first class." The house was so impressive that proximity to it served as a selling point for real estate listings for other properties in Baltimore. The extensive grounds were landscaped in a decidedly English style that would have required a gardener's attention.[59] From Susan's point of view, Anthony was less of an expense to her as a hired-out slave. A portion of his cash earnings from Hoffman would come to her. But from Anthony's point of view, the cash he gained at Hoffman's could be put toward purchasing his freedom. Susan was unbending about the possibility of Anthony's self-purchase in this way, however.

Desperate for an enlarged life and frustrated by Susan's refusals to free him, Anthony took matters into his own hands. In August 1827, roughly a year after marrying, he determined to run away and wrote to Jeremiah Hoffman to inform him of the plan:

Chatsworth House August 8 1827

Sir

I know that you will be astonished and surprised when you becom acquainted with the unexspected course that I am now about to take, a step that I never had the most distant Idea of takeing, but what can a man do who has his hands bound and his feet fettered He will certainly try to get them loosened by fair and Honorable means and if not so he will ceartainly get them loosened in any way that he may think the most adviseable. I hope Sir that you will not think that I had any fault to find of you or your family no sir I have none and I could of lived with you all the days of my life if my conditions could have been in any way bettered which I intreated with my mistress to do but it was all in vain. She would not consent to any thing that would melorate my condition in any shape of measure. So I shall go to Sea in the first vesel that may ofer an opportunity and as Soon as I can acumulate a Sum of money suficent I will Remit it to my mistress to prove to her and [the] world that I dont mean to be dishonest but wish to pay her every cent that I think my Servaces is worth. I have served her 11 years faithfully and think it hard that I offered $5.00 [of] what I was valued at 4 years ago and also to pay 4 per cent until the whole Sum was payed which I believe I could of done in 2 years and a half or 3 years at any rate but now as I have to Runaway like a criminal I will pay her when I can. Though I am truly sorry that I must leave you in the situation that I do, but I will Recommend to you as a servant Samuel Brown that I think a good and honest man and one that is acquainted well with his business but you can Refer to Mrs. Snyder who is well acquainted with him and has lived in the house with him. As my mistress is not in

Town I [have] taken the Last months wages to defray my exspences but that money and the five dollars that you lent me the day before I left you I shall ceartainly Return before I ship to Sea. I Don't supose that I shall ever be forgiven for this act but I hope to find forgiveness in that world that is to com. I don't take the step mearly because I wish to be free but because I want to do justice to myself and to others and also to procure a living for a family[,] a thing that my mistress would not let me do though I humblely Requested her to let me do so.

Before I was married I was Promised my freedom. Then after find this Peace of writeing which you will find incloesed I was then confident that I was free at Mr. Williams Death, and so I married. I must now beg for your forgiveness and at the same time pray to God for your helth and happyness as well as that of your family. I am Sir your most Obedient Servant

Anthony Chase

P.S. People will say that my wife has persuaided me to this but I do declare that she is inocent of any thing of the kind and was always opposed to any thing of the kind. AC.[60]

The letter's postscript was warranted. Anthony Chase, a slave, had indeed married Julia Williams, also a slave, in Baltimore, Maryland. The event appears twice in the historical register. First, the Reverend William Nevins—pastor of the First Presbyterian Church in Baltimore City from 1820 to 1835, and a white clergyman who was probably friendly to the city's blacks—noted the wedding in official church documents; he recorded the occurrence on September 12 between "Anthony Chase and Julia Williams (slaves)."[61] Then near the back of the last of the diary volumes, in a section quite apart from the daily chronicle—a section he called his "Memorandum Book"—James Brown reported, "James F. Brown was married to Julia Chase—The Rev Mr. Nevins on Tuesday Evening the 12 of [illegible] 1826." There are a couple of explanations for the discrepancy in names between the Presbyterian Church records and Brown's diary. Perhaps James was now going by the last name Chase after his own father's name, Robert Chase. But his choice for a new first name, Anthony, simply remains mysterious. Or else, in the diary, James F. Brown, the manumitted slave, years after the fact registered the marriage between his former self, Anthony Chase, and his slave bride, Julia, who therefore became known at the time of the ceremony as Julia Chase. Julia's change in last name reflected Western and English custom, which Maryland followed even for slave marriages. Unlike some southern states in which slave marriages had no legal standing, they had been recognized in Maryland state law since 1777.[62] But then, who was Julia Williams—the woman embodying the name recorded by the Reverend Nevins? A reasonable assumption is that Susan F. Williams owned Julia as part of William E.'s estate, and that Anthony had met and courted her within the Williams household.

Case closed, right? Not quite. It seems that the Reverend Nevins had performed another marriage between African Americans in 1826. This one was between "James Brown (slave) and Charlotte Rice (colored)," and it had taken place on March 21. The precise dates don't line up with those James recorded for his marriage in his diary, but it is remarkable that James Brown, slave, appears in Nevins's log *as James Brown*. Given that there were two different black men the Reverend Nevins married in 1826, did Anthony Chase later assume the name of this other, married James Brown once he ran away as a decoy in order to disguise his trail as Chase and still return to Baltimore later to claim a "colored" wife he left behind? Or did the Reverend Nevins simply mix up the names of the slave grooms in his church register, which he might have finalized toward the end of the year when his memory of the ceremonies might have been faded and compromised? Here the shadows of James Brown and Anthony Chase overlap in confusing ways.

What followed one week after Chase's flight was communication, first between Hoffman and William Cooke, Susan's father, and then directly between Hoffman and Susan.[63] Hoffman informed Cooke that Chase had "deserted" him after he had given Chase permission to visit New Castle, Delaware. Ostensibly, it was for that visit that Chase had borrowed five dollars from Hoffman. Hoffman rationalized his own delay in notifying Chase's owner about her slave's absence: "I would have called on Mrs. Williams to tell her about the rumors, but I myself did not believe them, and she was not in town."[64] Then, accompanying a payment to Susan Williams for a sum he felt due her, Hoffman wrote in a separate letter to her, "I apologize for not having before sent the amount I now enclose as the sum I think you consider to be the value of Chase."[65] Here, Hoffman did not pay Susan the purchase value of Anthony. Rather, he paid her for her portion of the wages Anthony had earned as Hoffman's hired servant.

Did Anthony Chase actually go to sea in order to avoid recapture while earning money to buy his manumission? Certainly this was a plausible option for any slave living in an antebellum American seaport. In fact, southern port cities like Baltimore were notorious for harboring runaways; and the most celebrated of antebellum fugitives, Frederick Douglass, slipped away from his Baltimore owner on a coastal sea vessel. Quasi-free blacks worked the docks as stevedores, caulkers, sailmakers, fishermen, carters, and roustabouts. An average of 14 percent of seamen shipping out from Providence, New York, Baltimore, and Savannah between 1803 and 1866 were African American. And in his earlier incarnation as James Brown, Anthony would have also gathered an acquaintance with local maritime rhythms through Captain Howland.[66] So Anthony Chase might have signed up for a stint as a sailor aboard a ship in order to acquire the cash for self-manumission. With so many African Americans used as crew members in the Atlantic maritime world during the nineteenth century, it was not hard for a slave to seize the opportunity to pass himself off as a free sailor in order to gain freedom.[67]

But here is another wrinkle. Susan Williams appears to have known Anthony as both Anthony Chase and Anthony Fisher. This would become clear when the itinerant black man emerged in New York state later that year.

Into the Promised Land

Somehow Anthony made his way to New York City and re-christened himself James F. Brown. Apparently, he had not become a sailor. Perhaps it was never his intent to do so. Maybe he meant only to provide a cover for himself from both Jeremiah Hoffman and Susan Williams during his escape. Or if he had become a "jack," his jaunt was very short-lived. According to Verplanck family folklore, Daniel Crommelin Verplanck hired a black waiter around this time for the family's Manhattan residence. At a dinner, a guest, presumably from the South, recognized James to be a slave associated with the Baltimore Williams household. The guest secretly informed Susan Williams of the whereabouts of the elusive Anthony.[1]

During March 1828, Susan F. Williams of Baltimore began communicating with Daniel C. Verplanck for compensation for her missing servant. It appears from the date of this correspondence, just eight months after Anthony Chase's letter indicating his intention to run away, that Anthony Chase/James Brown had gone not to sea but rather directly to New York City. Somewhere between Baltimore and New York, Anthony Chase had adopted the name Anthony Fisher, as seen in Verplanck's dispatch to Williams: "Madam, I have been informed that you are desirous of emancipating your slave Anthony Fisher who has lived with me as a servant by the name of James F. Brown."[2] The note continued by setting terms for Brown's manumission. Susan replied with a conciliatory letter in which she referred to the servant in question as only "Anthony":

Sir:

Your letter of 22 Mr. [March] proposing to guarantee the pay of 300 $ in annual instalments by Anthony has been received, and in consequence I have give to Mr. Needles his manumission bond—you state that you would prefer to pay this amount deducting the interest, this proposition meets my approbation as I had rather have it finally settled at once.

You can make the deduction and forward me a check for the balance, when I will return you, your obligation.[3]

Susan F. Williams and Daniel C. Verplanck both agreed that Anthony Fisher and James Brown were the same person, but one may well ask whether Anthony *Fisher*, first and mentioned only by Daniel Verplanck in his letters to Susan, was Anthony Chase. Three sets of circumstantial evidence strongly support this conclusion. First, both men had a common owner, Susan F. Williams, and in separate correspondence she implicitly confirmed "Anthony Fisher" and explicitly confirmed "Anthony" as one and the same slave who had gotten away from her. Next, James, in his diary, identified himself as the man whom the Reverend Nevins had married to Julia—the bride of Anthony Chase, according to Nevins's records. Finally, there is the corroborating timing and flow of events. 1826: Anthony Chase was promised freedom by a master-through-hire presumed to be dying. 1826: Anthony Chase married in hopes of soon starting life as a free man. 1826: Anthony Chase's master-through-hire died; futilely, Chase sought to work out manumission terms with his new owner, Susan Williams, who hired him out instead to Jeremiah Hoffman. 1827: Anthony Chase borrowed money from Hoffman and somehow took money from his absent owner in order to run away. 1828: Susan F. Williams agreed to manumit James F. Brown, whom she referred to simply as "Anthony"—not Anthony Fisher.

Still, the apparent overlap of James's life in Maryland as James Brown and as Anthony Chase or Anthony Fisher is baffling in one respect: How could his dual identities have escaped the notice of Susan F. Williams, his longtime mistress, and Henry Lee Williams, his hired master? The fact that they did underscores the degree of independence of quasi-free slaves like James. In surviving correspondence, the one name these two both called James was Anthony. How and why did James pull this off within Maryland? It is possible that when James first entered the Williamses' household at the age of twenty-three, he decided that having two names might work to his advantage. "Anthony" would be used in his dealings with the Williams family while "James" would be for his other, more "independent" or secret life, wherever and whatever that might entail. Ultimately, the answer to this question remains a mystery.

As to the specific terms of James's manumission, it seems that it was James himself who ultimately paid for his own emancipation, but this arrangement would not have been possible without the assistance of Daniel C. Verplanck, who offered a kind of down payment or bond for the deal. The exchange of written commitments from a man of his stature and wealth was the kind of satisfaction or financial surety that Susan needed in order to agree to relinquish claim to James. On March 23, 1828, Daniel wrote to Susan from his Mount Gulian estate:

> Mrs. Susan Williams,
>
> I have been informed that you are willing to emancipate your slave Anthony Fisher on receiving security for the payment of the sum of three hundred dollars in annual instalments of a hundred dollars. I have no objections to becoming security for the above sum but prefer making payment being allowed the Discount payment 1st May next.—Should you think proper to accept the terms of offer in addition to the sum paid you by Anthony you will be so good as to inform me of it by letter directed to me at Fishkill Landing. I am Madam very respectfully
>
> Your humble servant
>
> Daniel C. Verplanck[4]

In another version of the letter penned by Daniel on the same day, he made clear that he was asking Susan to accept an initial "security" payment of $264 toward Anthony's manumission. This was a "discounted" amount for one of two possible reasons. Perhaps Anthony/James apparently had already paid Susan $36, which when combined with Daniel's security would make up the first installment of $100 annual installments toward a total manumission price of $300.[5] This price was in line with market conditions and the reality of James's situation. In the neighboring Chesapeake state of Virginia, for example, young black male slaves could buy themselves for $350 at this time. Because James was already at a distance and Susan was anxious to have matters with him "settled at once," she agreed to a lower price.[6] Alternatively, the discounted price for James may have indicated that he was, in fact, a term slave because such slaves generally fetched a lower price than life slaves (slaves held for life) of "similar age, health, and labor skills." By the former calculation, James should have paid completely for his time by the end of 1830. Indeed, he recorded in late November of that year that he "received a letter from Miss Williams of Baltimore" and that, in reply, he "wrote a letter to Mrs. Williams of Baltimore . . . by the honorable G.C. [Gulian Crommelin] Verplanck," Daniel's son.[7] One imagines that this was about his final payment of three installments, beginning in 1828, for his freedom. Unfortunately, no manumission deed in any Maryland public archive or in the Williams family papers exists for a James F. Brown, Anthony Chase, Anthony Fisher, Julia Williams, Julia Chase, or Julia Brown for the years 1826 to 1828, when they escaped and ultimately found freedom. Perhaps it is for this reason that James noted in his diary after the fall of 1841: "This memorandum book was written by an old colored man Contains a record of his marriage and of purchasing his wifes time for one hundred dollars This page is about recording the deed." When one considers that self-hired or hired-out slaves in the antebellum South usually netted between $25 and $150 yearly from their labors, James's ability to pay for Julia and to execute a self-purchase is significant.[8] Perhaps in Julia's case, his savings were augmented by the sale of his Frederick Street property.

James's "recording of the deed" was a chivalrous act toward his wife, performed quite self-consciously as a black *man*. Just as he had freed Julia before freeing himself, he saw the necessity of verifying her manumission by his own writing, something he did not do even for himself. Similarly, when James-as-Anthony penned his letter indicating his intent to run away, he explained his planned course as a necessary, manly act. He further couched his decision in moral terms. Anticipating disbelief, disappointment, a sense of betrayal, and perhaps outrage from his owner and Jeremiah Hoffman, James sought to present his case in sympathetic terms. He wanted it known that his escape was an act of conscience incumbent upon any man, that the principle of manliness compelled him to flee. But what in fact was manliness to him? And what was the connection between manhood, morality, and freedom?

Men living in the United States and coming of age in the early nineteenth century inherited definitions of manhood forged in the colonial and Revolutionary War eras, as well as emerging notions of masculinity. In the colonial era, to enter manhood meant that one headed a household and as a husband wielded authority over a wife by virtue of God-ordained superiority of mind and body over women. To be a man also required the suppression of one's own will for the sake of duty or social obligation. The Revolutionary War injected a political dimension into this notion of duty, as manliness came to be associated with resistance to despotic rule.[9] Then, as the nation entered the nineteenth century, new definitions of manhood melded themselves onto the older ones in the early Republic. To be a man required drive, ambition, and individual self-actualization. A man sought to improve his lot in life, to better himself by competing in the marketplace in order to gain economic and social standing.[10]

But there were two versions of the new century's invigorated manhood. In one version, manhood expressed itself through physical adventure and conquest or wars of territorial expansion. This was a boisterous masculinity—all-out, no-holds-barred machismo. In antebellum America, this was the manhood of Daniel Boone in coonskin cap, of Lewis and Clark hiking through the Louisiana territory, of Andrew Jackson in his Indian wars, and of every male pioneer who cleared a forest or set his wagon for points west to push back the frontier. Such "martial manhood" also displayed itself in boxing matches, militia membership, alcohol consumption, minstrelsy, and marching bands. An alternative version of antebellum masculinity measured itself by the degree of discipline and self-control its claimants displayed. This type of manhood, "restrained manhood," funneled itself into leadership roles in social causes like temperance, abolitionism, and penal reform; into activities like commerce, law, preaching, and politics; and into interests like evangelism, horticulture, family life, and debating clubs.[11] The two masculinities coexisted, and any individual man might display both martial and restrained forms of manhood, but in the early nineteenth century the restrained model of manhood held the upper hand as men mainly "grounded their own sense of manliness in virtue, honor, and public service."[12]

Of course, slavery threw a monkey wrench into these notions of manhood for African American men. The prism of race transformed black male aggressiveness into brutishness because submission to white authority was a fundamental tenet of white society. Black ambition, in white eyes, became "uppity" behavior, because society could not imagine black aspirations to be anything more than an extension of the white owner's will. Duty to family became an impossibility because of the reality and threat of separation from kin by white masters who had the legal right to move black bodies across the southern landscape at will. In effect, nineteenth-century manhood was outside the realm of possibility for African American enslaved men—at least officially. Virtue and honor, however, might be imputed to African American men by more enlightened owners, but these were usually reserved for those black slaves deemed the most loyal and faithful servants. And typically, such slaves would be called good Negro *boys*, not men.[13] Thus, James Brown, taxpayer in 1818, was noted by the clerk recording his data as a "Negro Boy."

Yet as Anthony Chase, James Brown–the–slave argued that his decision to run away was a manly act. On the one hand, it seemed that he wished to be viewed as a faithful, "obedient servant" and even signed his letter to Hoffman with that closing. But was he serious? How could he have construed his deliberate act of self-emancipation to be that of an obedient servant? Or was he simply using contemporary literary convention for ending letters in a gentlemanly fashion? Both were true. James wanted it known that he was trustworthy, that he had "served [the Williams family] 11 years faithfully." But is also clear that Anthony had absorbed and was operating from mainstream notions of genteel manhood, not just the narrow, hegemonic prescriptions of perpetual black male boyhood.

Like his white male contemporaries, James understood manly duty to include protecting and providing for his family in the best way possible. That is why he paid for Julia's manumission, and why he sought to liberate himself from the uncertainties of chattel slavery. As James explained, he "want[ed] to do justice to [him]self and to others and also to procure a living for a family." James also possessed the kind of manly ambition expected of white men of his era. He wanted to "melorate [his] condition," to better himself. "[H]is hands bound and his feet fettered," James argued, "[h]e [would] certainly try to get them loosened by fair and Honorable means and if not so he [would] ceartainly get them loosened in any way that he m[ight] think the most adviseable." Such a course would only be reasonable for any man, he insisted. And it would be the right thing to do. It was important to James to emphasize the fundamental rectitude of his actions. Correctly anticipating the swirling emotions that his escape would trigger among the whites who trusted him—"sorrow," "disquiet," confusion about his "desertion," shock at such a reversal of "fidelity"—James crafted, however futilely, a response designed to counter and/or neutralize this reaction. Any infractions involved, he argued, were only temporary, superficial, and amendable; they were not the measure of him as a man. For this reason, he took pains to explain that it was frustration about the roadblocks put in his path, a desperate reach for full manhood, and not criminality, that drove him to steal from his mistress. A higher ethic was at stake—manly duty to family. This was not theft; it was a loan taken for an honorable end.[14]

How did James come to absorb mainstream notions of manhood—that is, manhood in terms that crossed racial boundaries? After all, he was living in a highly racialized milieu, one in which a slave like him was constitutionally counted as only three-fifths of a man. Constructions of manhood in mainstream antebellum American society were hardly inclusive. They pointedly excluded African American men and, in fact, depended upon the political, social, economic, and cultural subjugation of black men. In the South, particularly, white men advanced and fulfilled their ambitions because black men as a group were prohibited from doing the same.[15] As the historian Walter Johnson explained:

Among the white men who owned [land], many were living lives of constant motion, moving west, gaining a stake, building it into a legacy, dreaming of growing old in a place far removed in space and class from the place of their origin. As they grew up and moved on, these white men marked their progress by buying slaves.[16]

Again, in Johnson's words, white "men [were] made out of slaves."[17]

The answer lies in several aspects of the slave system in Baltimore and northern Maryland. First, permitted to hire out and live out, many slaves experienced lives of semi-independence in which they gained practice in the habit of pursuing opportunities before them. In fact, when slaves hired out, the yearly work contracts linked them as slaves to the same kind of material goals as the whites involved, both owner and hirer. In this limited way, bondsmen like James followed their ambitions. Second, although sources do not specify James's work while a slave, it was almost certainly of the domestic labor sort because this category included "cooks, dining room servants, nurses, laundresses, coachmen, houseboys, gardeners, shoemakers, carpenters, blacksmiths and mechanics"—all of whom interacted closely with white masters.[18] These slaves were the most likely to gain literacy, and it was they, as opposed to field hands, who "entered into the traditions and spirit of the family to which they belonged, defended its name and its honor, accepted . . . its ideas of country, morality and religion, and thus became to a considerable degree inheritors of the civilization of the white race."[19] The sensitivity to the charge of infidelity and the effort James expended in his letter to counter any such charge attest to his identification with and awareness of the values of slaveowners because masters were vocal about choosing and keeping domestic servants based on their demonstration of a preferred list of character traits—"'goodness,' 'truth,' 'diligence,' 'patience,' dependability,' 'devotion,' 'probity and loyalty.'" [20] Then too, an especially appealing model existed for James as an aspiring young black man in a port city, and that was the life of a sailor. Racially egalitarian pay rates and social treatment as well as the means to support a family and even advance made seafaring an attractive vocation for black men. So, surveying his options in a port city like Baltimore, it only made sense for James to speculate about going to sea, for as one contemporary noticed, "In the presence of the sailor the Negro feels as a man."[21] In the antebellum years, there was also the influence of African Bethel Church, Baltimore's AME Church, of which James might have been was a member. The AME Church, established formally in 1816, was the first independent African American church denomination in the United States. Its very existence was a testimony to "black self-assertion," a rebuttal to the charge that "the colored man 'always was, still is, and ever must be a mere cipher.'"[22] Surveying the history of the church, AME Bishop Daniel Payne wrote in 1891:

> The separation of our church from the [white-controlled] M. E. [Methodist Episcopal] Church, which was brought about by the agency of our venerated fathers, the Rev. Richardson Allen of Philadelphia and Rev. Daniel Coker of Baltimore, has been beneficial to the man of color by giving him an independence of character which he could neither hope for nor attain unto, if he had remained an ecclesiastical vassal of his white brethren. This is evident from the training which the force of circumstances has given. These circumstances have been such as to produce independent thought; this has resulted in independent action; this independent action has resulted in the extension of our ecclesiastical organization over nearly all of the States and also into Canada; this ecclesiastical organization has given us an independent hierarchy, and this hierarchy independence has made us feel and recognize our individuality and our heaven-created manhood.[23]

In other words, the AME Church nurtured a sense of African American masculinity. Moreover, with leaders like Baltimore's Reverend Daniel Coker, a manumitted slave who was once a fugitive slave, the church's antislavery stance encouraged self-manumission on the part of its slave membership, whether by payment or by flight, as a positive good. In sum, because of his quasi-free status, because he was likely a domestic servant, because of the maritime model he encountered, and through his probable associations with the black church, James viewed himself as a man—just as his white masters viewed themselves. And manhood required freedom.

Despite the fact that he was held in legal bondage, James Brown also inherited the legacy of the philosophical arguments developed by the white male founders of the nation and white male Revolutionary War–era patriots against tyranny, against the abuses of power, and in defense of liberty. Political debates of that day had led many of them to bump hard against the contradiction between freedom and slavery, and to see the need for an adjustment in political realities. James was born during early federal-era Maryland, just ten years after the war's end. Because he was a slave, he was not officially recognized at this time, or during his youth and early manhood as a citizen of the newly wrought United States of America. Yet he and other slaves were unintended beneficiaries of the spirit of freedom that had inspired the young nation's conflict with its mother country in the first place. This was especially true because the metaphor frequently used by protesters against English colonial rule to describe what they saw as their unjust treatment by the Crown was that of "slavery." John Dickinson, for example, had written, "In freedom we're born and in freedom we'll live; Not as *slaves* but as *freemen* our money we'll give." John Adams had prodded fellow colonials against the Stamp Act and similar English laws with the query "Is it not High Time for the People of this Country explicitly to declare, whether they be Freemen or Slaves?" In the nation as a whole, therefore, the logic of the Revolution inspired a spate of manumissions. For the North, where there was no large-scale dependency on plantation crops requiring permanent, year-round supplies of cheap labor for profit, this would take the form of state constitutions that eliminated slavery or provided for gradual manumissions. In the South, where reliance on slave labor for wealth was deeper, far more widespread, and endemic, there was some noticeable movement toward private manumissions.[24] Certainly the latter was the case in Maryland as a whole, and especially in the northern part of the state.[25] This was so much the case that during James's formative years, he was encouraged by the rhetoric and the reality surrounding him to imagine an enlarged life as a free man as part of his birthright.

Without ever explicitly invoking the terms "slavery" or "freedom," James's letter to his master implicitly referenced the rhetoric of rights initially unleashed in the Revolutionary era. In a kind of informal legal brief, he established the tension between his natural rights as an American man and his "fettered" position. Using lawyerly discourse to establish the untenability of his situation, James, as both plaintiff and defendant, empowered himself by pressing his claim and legitimizing his decision. This was a device frequently employed by his abolitionist contemporaries, black and white, who fought to expose the contradiction between slavery and freedom in the United States, who proclaimed the inconceivability of legalized human bondage as a survival of the Revolution. Among African American abolitionist writers, however, this kind of literary strategy—whether in sermons, letters, appeals, or slave narratives—was generally employed by those who had been born free or by those who had become free.[26] What is extraordinary about James F. Brown is that he employed this rhetorical scheme while still in the clutches of the peculiar institution. For all its diffidence in tone, James's missive was a bold document. And despite his disclaimers, James was a bold man.

Finally then, James Brown took his cues from both mainstream and African American prescriptions concerning manhood and liberty. The time of year was right; there would be several more weeks of warm weather. He was still relatively young—thirty-four years old—and strong. And he wouldn't have to travel far to find free soil.[27]

The mention of a Mr. Needles in Susan F. Williams's letter to Daniel Verplanck provides a clue as to how James may have escaped and why he ended up in New York. Friendly whites, especially Quakers, may have helped him. The Needles family—John; his brother, Edward; and his sister, Elizabeth—were among these. John was a stalwart supporter of a fellow Quaker, Benjamin Lundy, after Lundy relocated his antislavery paper, *The Genius of Universal Emancipation*, from Tennessee to Baltimore in 1824. Both Needles and Lundy were active abolitionists on the national scene through the American Convention of Abolition Societies and another organization they set up in 1826, the National Anti-Slavery Tract Society. As a cabinetmaker, John Needles even used to wrap the furniture he sent customers down South in antislavery tracts.[28] Through Quakers like Needles and Lundy, James could have learned that the law in New York had changed; slavery had been illegal there since 1827. One can speculate that Needles and his associates may have put James in touch with other Quakers in nearby Delaware in order to plot his getaway. Concealing this purpose and using his quasi-free status, then, James may have gotten permission from Jeremiah Hoffman to visit Delaware in the summer of 1827. That may be where James learned about the Newlins—Quakers and Delaware residents with ties to New York state. This line of conjecture makes sense because, as an absentee landlord, Cyrus Newlin once owned acreage and a flour mill in Dutchess County, where James would later live and work. When Cyrus's son, Robert, was a newlywed seeking an independent living back in 1811, he had moved his young family to Fishkill Plains, New York, less than three miles from Mount Gulian, to manage both the farm and gristmill that his father had started. Cyrus Newlin was dead by the time James may have consulted Cyrus's other children in Delaware about antislavery associates in New York. But in August 1827, when James visited Delaware, they could have told him of their brother, Robert, whose operation was not too far from Manhattan, where James surely could find work. They could even have asked some of their New York acquaintances or Quaker associates in the Hudson Valley if they needed help. Many of them were eager to assist free blacks and especially runaway slaves.[29] James may have been led to the Verplancks through this chain of contacts.

So in order to fulfill his moral obligations as a responsible family man, in order to participate in the national patrimony of male self-advancement, in order to receive his political inheritance of male citizenship, perhaps going by sea as he had indicated he would, perhaps guided instead from Baltimore to Delaware to New York by sympathetic whites, James escaped chattel slavery completely. He "loosed" himself "by fair and Honorable means." He ran. Heading north to New York, he discarded the ruse of plural selves to assume one identity—James F. Brown, free man.

PART II

Free Man and Free Laborer

After 1829, James F. Brown was legally free and came to enjoy, along with Julia, a measure of economic security. During his life as a free man, he could claim several positive experiences in the workplace—membership in an occupational fraternity of sorts, upward mobility in a competitive labor market, affirmation of his moral rectitude, and escape from wage slavery. He accomplished these things as a successful gardener for the Verplancks at the family's Mount Gulian estate.

Map 2. Hudson Valley

3

A Horticultural Community

When Daniel Crommelin Verplanck—lawyer, banker, U.S. congressman, and Dutchess County judge—relocated his family from its Manhattan residence to Mount Gulian at Fishkill Landing in 1804 and started a garden at this estate in the same year, he joined a trend among other men of his background, education, and station in the Hudson Valley, in New York state, and in the country at large—a trend that eventually shaped the identity of James F. Brown. Only three years earlier, for instance, Alexander Hamilton had acquired a farm in northern Manhattan, then quite undeveloped, and laid out a garden there in 1802. Daniel moved to Mount Gulian the same year that David Hepburn published *The American Gardener*—an indication of the popularity of gardening within the nation's upper class. This trend only partly reflected Thomas Jefferson's agrarian vision of a virtuous American Republic—the idea that farming, rather than commerce and industry, ought to be the economic foundation for the new country. In addition, gardening was one aspect of the "New Husbandry" that had emerged in England in the previous century and crossed the Atlantic to Britain's colonies to germinate among America's educated, high-ranking, landed gentry as one aspect of the Enlightenment.[1]

In England, the Scientific Revolution had transformed approaches to the natural world at every level in that country in the beginning of the late seventeenth century, and this change affected biology along with its subfield of agriculture. Soil cultivation became an arena for methodological observation and experimentation in order to achieve the most effective farming methods. In the seventeenth century especially, following the writings of Jethro Tull, Charles Townshend, Arthur Young, and Sir John Sinclair, the English gentry broke away from centuries-old agricultural techniques that depleted the soil and caused declining output, substituting new methods, the so-called Norfolk system of horse-hoeing (improved tillage), rotating such crops as "wheat, turnips, barley, clover, and grass," and following this land use with cattle grazing. The result of such changes was vastly increased agricultural productivity, and an outpouring of English manuals on scientific farming.[2]

In North America, Benjamin Franklin, George Washington, and Thomas Jefferson sought to import such improvements. They noted that most American farmers in the late eighteenth century were mired in antiquated farming techniques. Wanting to make the country's agricultural output internationally competitive, these leaders complained about the need for domestic crop rotation, better farm implements, stronger livestock, and enriched soil. At the same time, they encouraged scientific agriculture through research and education.[3]

Daniel, as James's first Verplanck employer and an "enlightened" 1788 graduate of Columbia College (today's Columbia University), was in this circle.[4] Probably either he or his father, Samuel (1739–1820), had even produced a farm book around 1790 based on his Mount Gulian experiences that he entitled *A Treatise on Agriculture and Practical Husbandry*. The book's introduction explained the author's intent and placed him squarely within the New Husbandry school:

> My design in writting and Compiling this Treatise on agriculture and practical Husbandry was to instruct the Country Gentleman & land owner how he may enrich himself and his land, or by a little skilful management, keep his land in a constant state of fertility . . . The advatages [sic] arising from the new Husbandry are so great that it would be doing an Injury to the publick not to endeavor to make it practise in the United States of America, . . . [M]en of every Rank & ability should lend a helping hand to forward and Improve this art of agriculture this Science was the favourite employment of the greatest Roman Senator . . . now agriculture is left to the feeble Efforts of the poor and Illiterate Peasants & we have nothing for their Examples but their gross ignorence [sic] and unattention & what is still more lamented is, that the common Farmer perhaps is the least inquisitive of any man after Improvement out of his beaten tract, is frequently the most obstinate attached to the Practise of his Predecessors, let them [be] ever so absurd . . . it might not Consist with predence [sic] for him to risque his little Competence upon the Success of Experiments. No Imployment of life is more respectable nor more beneficial than husbandry. [I]t hath been honored & promoted by learn'd men in divers ages.[5]

Daniel's interest in scientific and practical agricultural experimentation, of which horticulture was a subdivision, was an active one: He relocated his residence to the upstate family farm with his second wife, Ann Walton Verplanck, and four of his five children. He planted all the nearby streams at Mount Gulian with watercress with seed brought from Washington—an innovation because watercress cultivation for the market was only in its infancy during the early nineteenth century in the plant's native England. And notably, with the help of the eldest of those children accompanying him in the move to Mount Gulian, eleven-year-old Mary Anna, he laid out a shrubbery and flower garden on the estate.[6]

By the time James F. Brown became a Verplanck family servant in 1828, the range of cultivating work at the estate was substantial. There were European and New World grain and vegetable crops, familiar to residents of British America and now the new American republic since the seventeenth century—corn, squash, potatoes, peas, beets, carrots, tomatoes, cabbages, string beans, peas, brussels sprouts, celery, cauliflower, broccoli, cucumber, and onions. But because the Verplancks participated in a rising national horticultural movement, the variety of produce exceeded these common types. There were also vegetables of global origin from Africa, the Middle East, and Asia, not entirely unknown in the United States but only recently gaining in popularity—salsify, okra, spinach, rhubarb, Swiss chard, asparagus, and eggplant. These last plants, along with the strawberries, raspberries, melons, pear trees, and numerous types of flowers, reflected the Verplancks' involvement with contemporary thought and trends regarding fruit and vegetable cultivation.[7]

When James took over as master gardener in 1836, it was Mary Anna's gardening interests that he most closely followed. By that time, her father was dead. Mary Anna's only older sibling, her half-brother Gulian Crommelin Verplanck, centered his life as a lawyer, civic activist, scholar, and politician mainly in New York City and Albany. Her mother, Ann, was an invalid. So she, as a forty-three-year-old childless, unmarried woman, was free to devote her efforts to the pastime she loved. Moreover, her father had depended upon her "for the management of the household and the entertainment of the guests," and Mary's central role as Mount Gulian mistress only intensified after his death in 1834. James would have noticed that it was a role she relished. In fact, according to Verplanck family history, "She [Mary Anna] it was who laid out the garden, in which she took great pleasure and pride all her life."[8]

So from the very start, James took his cues from Mary Anna. As an educated woman and her father's favorite, Mary Anna was aware of the intellectual and scientific currents that informed early-nineteenth-century agricultural practices. Following Mary Anna and Daniel's lead, then, with the intention of securing his position, James participated in the scientific agricultural movement in practical ways by introducing new plantings—no doubt sometimes at their or other family members' suggestion, but also by his own initiative. For example, in the spring of 1838, he recorded in his diary that he had gone "over to Mr Downings garden and bought some fruit trees for Miss Mary and myself to set out in the garden." Again in the fall of that year, he "went over to Mr. Downings and bought sundry plants for Miss Mary Verplanck—also some fruit trees." He planted melon seeds and a "Rohn potato" in the spring of 1839, after Mary Anna's younger brother and farming enthusiast, Dr. William W. Verplanck, returned with them.[9] But Brown also anticipated his employers' pleasure in botanical experimentation on his own when he "sowed some wild flower seeds brought from the west by Mr. Isaac Knevels," "took some passion flowers over to Mr. Knevels hot house for safe keeping," or "planted some potato skins by way of exsperiment."[10]

Mary Anna was also familiar with the aesthetic trends that shaped contemporary gardening, and this was reflected in the design of the flower garden on which she collaborated with Daniel, and later instructed Brown. Mary Anna's core garden layout, described by one of her twentieth-century relatives, Virginia E. Verplanck, can be categorized as decidedly picturesque:

> Taking a few steps into the garden from the shrub-shaded entrance along the gravel walk, seven feet wide, which is one of the main arteries of the garden, on the right the principal formal garden is disclosed. It extends fifty feet by fifty feet; the smaller box beds are forty feet by fifteen. The plan of this main box garden begins with a circular bed in the center, from which run out four little graveled paths twenty-one inches wide which divide the formal garden into four large sections, which in turn are subdivided into three beds each, making thirteen beds, all encircled by the narrow gravel walks.[11]

To say that an 1804 garden was picturesque is to denote more than its visual appeal. Rather, such a garden was a reflection of an aesthetic sensibility and approach to the natural world arising in the eighteenth century, particularly in the model English garden idealized by the writers and poets William Gilpin, Uvedale Price, Edmund Burke, Richard Knight, and Alexander Pope. This aesthetic rendered outdoor settings pleasing, manageable, and approachable for humans.[12] It represented a controlled irregularity that stood in stark contrast to the structured and highly designed geometry of classic seventeenth-century French gardening. In these qualities, the Picturesque can be understood as the middle sensibility to nature positioned between two other eighteenth-century artistic motifs—the Sublime, focused on those natural scenes and occurrences evoking awe, reverence, and trepidation, and the Beautiful, based on a classical Greek sense of proportions.[13] As an upper-class educated woman, Mary Anna would have been fully aware of these aesthetic trends because they were disseminated, discussed, and experienced by Americans in her circle through poetry, fiction, painting, and even travel. The Hudson Valley especially in the early national period was a favorite site among the nation's elite for encounters with the Sublime, the Beautiful, and the Picturesque.[14]

Much of James's work, then, was about maintaining a sophisticated visual appeal of the garden, as his employer desired, with attention to floral health and the balance of colors. Mary Anna had planted "box, shrubs, peonies, fraxinella, lemon lilies, roses, and tulips" in the original garden of 1804. So James maintained and replenished these plantings throughout his gardening years, as when he "[laid] down rose bushes from Downings" and "planted bulbs from Holland" in the late fall of 1836, "brought trees and shrubbery" from Downings' nursery in the late fall of 1837 and "[set] boxwood edging around the flower beds" in the spring of 1849. James made sure the garden pond remained visually appealing by keeping it clean, maintaining its dam, and adding goldfish to its waters. He kept the garden fence in good repair by replacing pickets as needed.[15] Mary Anna's garden was a riot of color given the variety of flowers it contained, but the lemon lilies, the Austrian Gold Leaf roses, the Harrison roses, some of the Crown Imperials, and certain tulips revealed her penchant for yellow. James was mindful of this detail. Before returning to Mount Gulian from a trip to Manhattan, he "bought a yellow carnation . . . for Miss M Verplanck." And again before returning to Fishkill from New York City five years later, he "bought a yellow [China] rose" for her.[16]

The successful performance of his work in all its phases not only aligned James with the Verplancks' gardening interests, but it also attested to his participation with them in the burgeoning national horticultural community. This community was defined by the formal establishment of horticultural societies, regular society meetings, society publications, and society exhibitions. James Brown was linked to practically all of them.

First, although Brown may not have been an official founder or member of any agricultural, botanical, or horticultural society because of racial proscriptions, through his employers and associations he was much aware of their existence and closely followed their activities. The New-York Horticultural Society, founded in 1818, was the first horticultural society per se organized in the United States. Its early existence lasted until roughly 1837.

(After a decades-long hiatus, it was reorganized in 1900 as the Horticultural Society of New York.) In the more immediate vicinity of Mount Gulian, the Horticultural Society of Newburgh began in 1828.[17] Then there was also the Horticultural Society (or Association) of the Valley of the Hudson, founded in 1839 by Andrew Jackson Downing. Reflecting his great ambition, Downing intended this second regional group to be an association that embraced "the whole of the river counties of the Hudson" especially in order to reach "numerous prosperous communities with commercial nurseries and the estates of wealthy individuals.[18] Clearly, this included Mount Gulian, right across the river.

Brown was at least informally included in these new organizations by his work-related associations with its members, chief of whom was Andrew Jackson (A. J.) Downing. The existence of an informal fraternity over gardening between Brown and A. J. is revealed throughout Brown's diary. Brown "went over to Downings and exchanged a green house plant with him," for instance, in the spring of 1830. In July 1836, Brown noted that Mr. Downing "of the Botanical Gardens at Newburgh payed us a visit," and in the August 1836 diary entry listed above, Brown brought Downing some apple buds; later, Brown noted in the following 1840 diary entry: "Went up to Fishkill Village on some business for A J Downing." From Downing Brown bought quince trees for Mary Anna Verplanck and fruit trees for himself. He consulted with Downing about nursery equipment like a garden engine, and in the spring of 1843, he "went over to Mr. Downings and bought 3 plum trees."[19]

In addition to Downing, Brown communicated with other important local horticulturalists. John W. Knevels, Mary Anna's brother-in-law through marriage to her sister Elizabeth, was one. Knevels developed an extraordinary garden on his Newburgh property. Downing described it as a botanical paradise in these effusive terms in 1836:

> The truly superb collection, now in possession of this gentleman, is the largest amateur collection in the State of New York, and, considered in regard to its richness in tropical plants and the individual beauty of many of its specimens, we do not hesitate to pronounce it unsurpassed in the Union. All the fine exotics formerly belonging to J. B. Smith, Esq., of Philadelphia . . . were purchased by Mr. Knevels, and form the mass of the collection now at Newburgh; but it has also been enriched by a great number of the choicest and rare specimens, in addition, from the different nurseries in this and other States. Some idea may be formed of the ardor and enthusiasm of Mr. Knevels as an amateur, when we mention that the

whole of these plants have been selected and transported here under his own direction during the short space of the past five months. The large structures which now contain them, have also been built since the first of September, and recollecting this, we were certainly much surprised and delighted to find the plants now (Feb. 1st) in such a vigorous and healthy state.

We believe that Mr. Knevels is rather a botanical, than a floral amateur; and we are gratified to observe it, because, though a less common, it is, in our opinion, a more refined, as it is a more scientific taste. Where there will be one individual who will possess sufficient knowledge to appreciate and cultivate the palms, and their rarer tribes of vegetation, there will be fifty who can admire and enjoy a beautiful bed of tulips, or a handsome collection of camellias.[20]

In fact, Brown regularly turned to Knevels for cuttings of strawberry plants and rare specimens like bishop orange, to borrow plants like geraniums and azaleas, and to store some of his more delicate holdings like cactus and lemon trees in the Knevelses' greenhouse.[21]

Edward Armstrong was another important member of the horticultural circle with whom Brown associated. "A gentleman of refinement and wealth" who lived just north of Newburgh, Armstrong was a key, formative, and influential acquaintance of and informal mentor for A. J. Downing as he aggressively climbed the Hudson Valley social ladder. Armstrong was also a very active member of the Horticultural Society of Newburgh. Armstrong, in fact, was a speaker at the fifth-anniversary ceremonies of that organization.[22]

Henry Winthrop Sargent was also a member of Brown's horticultural network. His sprawling estate at Matteawan, New York (with Fishkill Landing, part of present-day Beacon)—called Wodenethe—was impressive for its horticultural delights, "a paradise of exotics."[23] In raptures over the place, a *New York Evening Post* writer gushed:

Weeping birches, weeping beeches, weeping ashes, weeping arches, weeping elms and weeping willows are specialties there, and so are purple-leaved trees and shrub, and the silver and golden tinted evergreens from Japan, while oaks, elms, chestnuts, maples and other standbys appear in choicest varieties. The magnificent palms constitute a show by themselves. There is scarcely a mountain, a shore or a plain in Europe that has not contributed to Wodenethe.[24]

Brown visited Sargent's home in late summer of 1842 simply to examine the garden. After hearing that Sargent had erected "a fine grapery and new green house" in the fall of 1845, James again visited the place in December of that year. Brown set out a bed of strawberries he had acquired from Sargent in October 1847 and requested geranium cuttings from him in July 1851. Theirs was a comfortable and easy arrangement, allowing Brown to collect cuttings from the Matteawan home throughout the 1850s.[25]

The connection among Brown, the Verplancks, Downing, the Knevels, Armstrong, and Sargent—cemented by a common passion for horticulture—is seen in many diary entries of the next decade. In a single day in early February 1830, Brown drove with John Knevels to Fishkill Village; next, to Newburgh to see one of the Downings; and then continued on to visit Armstrong. In June 1830, for instance, Mary Anna and Louisa Verplanck "went up to Mr. Armstrong's in the barge and returned in the evening." Brown himself "went to Mr. Armstrongs with Mr and Mrs Christie [Fishkill neighbors]" in July. Verplanck family members dined with Armstrong twice that same summer—once in July and again in August. In the fall of the same year, Brown recorded that "Mr. D [perhaps Downing or Daniel, Mary Anna's father] dined with Mr. Armstrong." In the fall of 1836, he noted that "Mr and Mrs P went up to Mr. Armstrong's." On July 7, 1840, Brown "budded some cherry stocks with some very fine buds from Mr Armstrong" that Mary Anna had picked up during a visit, and two years later, he "grafted some fine cherries for Mr Armstrong."[26] Inspired by Wodenethe, Andrew Jackson Downing even included descriptions of its interior furnishings in *Architecture of Country Houses* (1850); following Downing's death, Sargent reciprocally contributed a supplement to a revised sixth edition of Downing's *Treatise on the Theory and Practice of Landscape Gardening* in 1859.[27] Brown's membership in the horticultural community of the region via his employment by the Verplancks is reflected in these and similar interactions.

Layering the circle of gentlemen gardeners were other local servant-gardeners like himself with whom James also communicated. One of these was Sargent's gardener and general laborer at Wodenethe, an Englishman named William Bennett. In the fall of 1847, Brown "went to see Mr. Bennet and got some rose cuttings." In the spring two years later, he "went to Sargents to see Mr. Bennet (gardener) and got some achamoneas [achimenes?] roots." In the winter of 1852, Brown again "went to Mr Sargents and got some green house plants and some cuttings from Mr Bennetts garden." Later, during the summer of the same year, he acquired even more cuttings from Bennett.[28] Another gardener-colleague of Brown's was B. Manning, the

Irish-born gardener for Robert Bayard, nearby neighbor of the Verplancks. In the early spring of 1849, Brown sowed eggplant that had been "presented" to him by "Mr. Mannin[g]." In November 1852, James "potted some wall-flowers from Mr Byards gardener." James also corresponded with Manning during January 1855.[29] It is also clear from the diary that Brown sometimes chatted with the gardeners—Michael Ross, Irish, and William Lucas, English—on the Downing estate across the Hudson.[30] Brown picked up plants from Mrs. Deacon in Wappingers Falls; her husband was a servant-gardener as well.[31] This informal web of Hudson Valley horticulturalists apparently cut across ethnic, class, gender, and, by the participation of James F. Brown, racial lines—all in the interest of better and more varied flowers, fruit, plants, shrubs, trees, and vegetables. At the same time, it is noteworthy that Downing nearly always referred to the white gentleman gardeners and to the white servant-gardeners mentioned in his diary as "Mr.," "Miss," or "Mrs.," while nearly always omitting the honorific for the mostly African American garden-laborers under his supervision to identify them by their first and/or last names directly. This distinction suggests that contemporary racial codes still prevailed both in his mind and in fact at some level within this horticultural community.

Brown united with horticulturalists not only through visits and floral exchanges but also through acquaintance with a common literature. The years 1820 to 1855 witnessed a national explosion in agricultural and/or horticultural literature with the appearance of representative magazines such as *The American Farmer* in 1819, the *New England Farmer and Horticultural Journal* in 1822, the *Genesee Farmer and Gardener's Manual* in 1831, the *Horticulturalist* in 1846, *The American Fruit Culturalist* in 1849, and the *Country Gentleman* in 1853. There were all sorts of books on the topic, like Robert Buist's *The Family Kitchen Gardener*, which included in its end pages advertisements for other popular horticultural publications. In addition, newspapers regularly carried agricultural and gardening columns with details on fruit, flower, vegetable, and grain growing.[32]

The New-York Farmer and Horticultural Repository, the monthly magazine of the New-York Horticultural Society (NYHS) began publication in 1828—one year before James Brown began his diary. Through this monthly magazine, general, practical horticultural knowledge was shared in articles on soil management, recent agricultural patents, recipes, improvements in farm equipment, and particular crops and species.[33] The *Repository* featured contributions from regional horticulture and information and contributions from the Caribbean and Europe as well.[34] Thus, the NYHS and its monthly magazine, like other similar associations and publications throughout the nation during the antebellum era, fostered a local, regional, national, and international community of garden cultivators among its subscribers and their associates. This community was defined by its exchange of expertise and practice.[35]

Judging by the source of many of his plantings, James Brown probably read the *Repository* regularly. It may have been available in the Verplanck home or in the Downing nursery. Barring those possibilities, however, Brown was a library subscriber, and at least one of the local libraries—the Newburgh Library Association, started by Andrew Jackson Downing in 1836—was open to the public twice weekly in the afternoons and evenings. Significantly, it carried foreign and American periodicals, and with Downing as its president, it is difficult to imagine the absence of the *Repository* from the new library's shelves.[36]

More evidence of Brown's familiarity with the *Repository* is found in the sources for some of his nursery purchases—Parmentier's, Prince's, Thornburn's, Hogg's, and Bridgeman's nurseries. In June 1830, Brown visited "Parmentier's garden" in Brooklyn and "Prince's garden" in Flushing.[37] André (Andrew) Parmentier was the owner of the Horticultural Botanic Garden in Brooklyn, served on the NYHS council, and exhibited his produce at NYHS fairs. He enjoyed a national reputation.[38] Parmentier advertised regularly in the *Repository* during 1828.[39] Similarly, William Prince ran a nursery on Long Island—the Linnaean Botanic Garden and Nursery, which had been in existence since the late eighteenth century. Prince had been able to capitalize early on the English-inspired "rage for gardening and landscaping" that had spurred New York gentlemen to decorate their country estates with "vast lawns and flowerbeds, orchards, greenhouses, conservatories, fish ponds, and fanciful grottos."[40] In fact, his was the "first commercial garden in America."[41] He had been "famous throughout the colonies" for scouring the entire North American continent for flora. Prince wrote several horticultural treatises and continued to enjoy national patronage and attention into the early nineteenth century. Major botanical finds from the Lewis and Clark expedition had been brought to Prince's nursery. Like Parmentier, Prince contributed articles to the *Repository* and advertised prominently on its back cover.[42] Brown planted apple trees he received from Prince's in 1836.[43]

Another leading commercial gardener Brown patronized was G. Thornburn and Son of Manhattan's Liberty Street, who, like the other New York City nurseries he preferred, marketed garden seeds in the *Repository*. A recurring advertisement announced the sale of garden seeds to readers: "The subscribers have on hand an extensive assortment of Garden and Field seeds, the growth of the present year. . . Among them are many varieties of early and late peas."[44] James was lured by the pitch because an 1837 diary entry records, "A dish of peas from a new sort called Eagles new dwarf marrow pea. Just imported by Thornbourn [sic]." For the next twenty years, Thornborn was James's most frequent seed supplier.[45]

Brown also bought garden stock from the Rose Hill Nursery, run by Thomas Hogg. Hogg advertised "a very general assortment of indigenous and exotic Plants" in the *Repository*.[46] In April 1838, Brown "planted out some grape vines bought of Mr. Hogg."[47]

Brown was influenced in his purchases by Thomas Bridgeman's horticultural expertise as well. Bridgeman, a New York City–based seedsman, published *The Fruit Cultivator's Manual* in 1847 and *The American Gardener's Assistant* in 1850.[48] Brown probably read both, or at least he was aware of Bridgeman's ensuing reputation because in 1852, he ordered house plants from Bridgeman, evidently for the first time.[49]

A final way in which Brown participated in a local, regional, and national horticultural community was by involvement in exhibitions and society meetings. James attended these events along with Mary Anna in the years before the Civil War. It was rare for women to place entries in horticultural shows in the antebellum era, and, as a black man, James was an exceptional participant in them as well. So it is difficult to say on what basis—whether as a hired man or as an equal—Brown accompanied Mary Anna in such instances, especially given that the diary is silent on this point. On the occasion of its tenth anniversary in 1828, the NYHS put on a gala exhibition of fruits and flowers at Niblo's Garden on Broadway in lower Manhattan, which was a prototype for similar shows of the period. Founded in the same year, at a time when New York City's population remained for the most part settled south of City Hall, Niblo's opened its doors in what was still considered a rural landscape. The establishment was at first a resort, "a garden where coffee and refreshments were served" to guests. The grounds had originally been a part of the Bayard farm but then were sold to the Van Renssalaer family before William Niblo purchased it. The drive there from Wall Street, where the Verplancks owned a home until 1822, passed by many "suburban farms."[50] Niblo's, already surrounded by beautiful countryside, was itself transformed into a verdant paradise for the 1828 NYHS festival. The main banquet hall was decorated with "a variety of shrubbery, green boughs, and vases of plants and flowers, indigenous and exotic"; down the center of the room ran a long dessert table of fruits, part display, part buffet, containing grapes, apples, strawberries, peaches, plums, pears, and melons. Hudson Valley contributors to this celebration included T. Ash of the Beekman clan (apples) and a Professor Gimbrede who sent grapes from his West Point vineyard.[51]

According to the Brown diary, James and Mary Anna participated in similar exhibitions. For perhaps the first time, in June 1830, he presented lettuce and strawberries at a Newburgh exhibition. Again, nearly three weeks later, Brown "went over the river with some beans for exhibition." In September 1830, James recorded that he attended a horticultural exhibit in Newburgh, organized in all likelihood by the Horticultural Society of Newburgh; perhaps the event was held at the Downing nursery.[52] In the same year, Mary Anna presented some of her botanical prizes on a wider stage. First, in July, she and a Mr. D. L. Walton (probably a cousin on her mother's side) went to New York City, presented lima beans in the NYHS exhibit, and were awarded a cash premium for them. One month later, she and her brother Gulian came up from New York City in order to present celery and melons at a Newburgh exhibit.[53] While Downing's Horticultural Association for the Valley of the Hudson held its spring show in Albany and autumn show in Manhattan at Niblo's in 1839, Brown brought only fruits and vegetables to the downstate exhibition.[54] In his diary, James noted fruit and flower exhibits, which he may or may not have attended, in the fall of 1848. During January 1849, he presented "apples and winter pears" at "the farmers and gardeners Association," the location of which he did not specify. Later, in April of the same year, he showed radishes and other vegetables before the same group.[55]

The horticultural community, in Brown's experience, functioned as a kind of informal, *de facto* craft guild. Membership in the guild was officially limited to membership in horticultural societies and/or to those who participated in horticultural events. Botanical expertise or exclusive possession of horticultural skills that were highly individualized, as well as finely honed ability at tasks that were unreplicated by machines, defined this guild's membership. The guild's publications supplied both rudimentary information to relative novices and advanced knowledge to experienced practitioners. Within this "guild"—master to apprentice, master to master, master to avocationist, avocationist to master, and avocationist to avocationist—craft skills were shared along multiple lines. James Brown began as an "apprentice" in the horticultural guild during the late 1820s while in his early years of employment with the Verplancks and pushed himself to "journeyman" status in the early 1830s by visiting, reading, learning, producing, and "showing" with other guild members like Andrew Jackson Downing—colleagues, if not peers. Upon achieving master gardener status in 1836, he ran his own "shop"—the Verplanck garden—overseeing and tutoring several apprentices and staying ever attuned to new horticultural developments by using guild contacts. In contrast, the several black apprentices he supervised remained laborers all of their lives. Even within the context of an overwhelmingly agricultural society in the antebellum United States, admission to this rarefied club for a black man required more than readiness. It required the support of white patrons, whether amateur gardening enthusiasts, gentlemen farmers, or garden professionals. In James Brown's case, his place within the antebellum horticultural community was enabled by the special endorsement he enjoyed as the Verplancks' employee. But to this he added his own will and his own preparation.

4

A Gardening Career

A free black man in the North, James Brown advanced up the pro-
verbial occupational ladder as he worked his way from the bottom to the top
with increasingly skilled labor. Starting off as a waiter for the Verplancks,
he next became the family's coachman. But less than ten years after fleeing
slavery, he achieved the status of master gardener at Mount Gulian and a
comfortable existence.

Shortly after his arrival in New York, he began work as a waiter for
the Verplancks in their Manhattan residence, probably from 1826 through
the end of 1828. A published Verplanck family history reported, "At first
he was a waiter for a short time"—the period immediately following his
escape.[1] Although the same family history asserts that James "was gardener
from 1829 to 1864,"[2] he did not jump immediately from the waiter's position to that of full-time gardener. Rather, there was an intermediary phase
in which he was a jack-of-all-trades and general household manservant.
So by the start of 1829, when he commenced his diary and was living with
the Verplancks at Mount Gulian, James worked chiefly as family coachman
but also performed gardening and general household duties. This multi-
tasking was reflected even in single-day entries. For example, on January
5, 1829, he "[h]ad the horses (Old Tom and Bute) shoed then went to the
Long Dock for salt"; on April 16, 1829, he "[t]ook a ride to Mrs Schencks
and got some plants from Paige for Miss Mary Verplanck"; and on April
24, 1829, he "[w]ent to Newburgh and bought things to make blacking."
James reported that "[a]ll hands [were] very bu[s]y cleaning house, painting, glazing etc." In early May 1829, and one day about three weeks later,
he "[w]ent to Fishkill Village with Gulian Verplanck Junr to school and
then went to Newburgh and painted the boats."[3]

James continued into 1830 and 1831 in this position, which involved miscellaneous duties—washing windows "in the large room," "painting the
kitchen," buying a bedstead for Mrs. Verplanck, rowing Verplanck family
members across the river to Newburgh, "clearing out the old dining room,"

buying "a set of new brass mounted coach harness[es]," driving Verplanck family members to church and social events—but his preoccupation with gardening grew simultaneously.[4] For one thing, if one is to judge from his diary, he seemed to spend more time at garden work than anything else. In 1830, for example, nearly half (nineteen of forty-one) of the entries describing chores were related to gardening or horticulture.

The next year was an anomaly, or at least so it seems. James kept up the diary only through March 4, 1831, after which time he went down to New York "to live with Peter A Jay" (1776–1843)—lawyer, abolitionist, reformer, philanthropist, president of the New York Manumission Society (NYMS), and son of Federalist founding father John Jay, himself a charter member of the NYMS.[5] This was just one year after James had secured his legal freedom from his former mistress, Susan F. Williams of Baltimore. Using the diary as an indicator, we know that James was with Jay for an entire twelve-month period because his diary entries from Mount Gulian ceased and did not resume until March 1832. If James was in fact away from the Verplanck estate at Fishkill Landing during this interlude, for what reason did he take up residence with Peter Jay, and who initiated this arrangement? There is no mention in Peter Jay's extant official correspondence or the personal papers of James during this period, nor is there any listing of him in the Manumission Society minutes or registers for this time. But an association between the Jays and Brown makes some sense because Peter held strongly to the antislavery views of his father and had, in fact, been influential in 1821 in blocking the complete exclusion of African American men from the electoral franchise in New York state. During this time, Peter Jay's main residence was at the corner of Broadway and Walker Street in Manhattan, so if James had been employed temporarily as a domestic servant for the Jays, he would have been living in New York City—the headquarters of the Manumission Society.[6]

The Manumission Society, first formed in 1785, charged itself not only with encouraging private manumissions, enforcing gradual abolition, and interceding on behalf of kidnapped fugitive slaves and free blacks but also undertaking the moral guardianship of the growing free black population in New York, of which James was now numbered. Regardless of James's specific duties within the Peter Jay household, moral tutelage would have been extended to him under Jay's supervision, and such tutelage would have promoted diligence, sobriety, and punctuality as virtues. Jay's commitment to encouraging such habits was also marked by his service as one of the founding managers of the Bank for Savings of the City of New York, which was incorporated in 1819. Savings banks were aimed at instilling the values of industry and thrift in the laboring poor.[7] James would have been familiar with such institutions based on his connection in Baltimore with Captain Daniel Howland. In linking himself somehow to Peter Jay, then, James exhibited a pattern of association with influential elites who were sympathetic both to those they deemed the needy, yet deserving poor and to African Americans. Besides the Manumission Society and the Bank for Savings, such whites also supported similar organizations aimed at assisting the free black population like the African Free School, begun in 1787, and the Society for the Encouragement of Faithful Domestic Servants (SEFDS), founded in 1825. Gulian Verplanck and James Verplanck (1805–81), sons of James's Fishkill employer, were early subscribers to the SEFDS, which dedicated itself to curbing job transience, the use of unscrupulous "intelligence offices" (employment agencies), and "loose" behavior among domestics by distributing cash prizes and Bibles for longevity of service. In its own words, the SEFDS existed "to teach [domestic servants that] the way to become *respectable* is by *respecting themselves*, and by acting well the parts which Providence has assigned to them."[8] So perhaps Peter Jay and Gulian Verplanck had agreed between themselves and with James that an informal "internship" sponsored by the SEFDS would enhance James's work prospects. Ambitious African Americans like James Brown tolerated these paternalistic overtones in order to benefit from the practical aid such institutions and their operators could provide in the quest for job security and upward mobility.

Certainly, the diary's chronology suggests such motives behind James's apparent "leave of absence." Whatever really transpired in Manhattan under Peter Jay's patronage or employment, James was back in Fishkill Landing at Mount Gulian one year later with a singular, relentless, work-related focus on gardening. James resumed the diary in March 1832. In that month and in every daily entry for April through October, the sole activity he noted is gardening work—nothing else for nine straight months. Here is a representative sample from the spring of that year:

March 7. This day hauled Earth in the garding [*sic*] To level some part of the ground that was very uneven.

March 17. The greater part of this day has Been raining and in afternoon came on a very severe snow storm which continued all night. On Friday the 16th Removed the old hot-bed and transplanted some cherry trees that stood by it. Michael also finished a stone wall on one side of the brook in the garden.

Monday 19th. Very cold and three or four inches of snow in the ground, so There can be no work done in the garden as yet. On Wednesday the 14th of March Set out 6 Peach Trees of asorted kinds, from Mr. Downings, and have tried an Experiment to present with them to prevent the frutes from droping off, by Laying some flat stones at the bottom of the roots and also tried the Experiment with an Apricot.

This day the 6th [of April] Planted six rows of Early June Peas, and dressed the asparagus beds sowed Radishes, Salad, etc.

7th [of April] sowed celery and some yellow Turnip Radishes (a new sort)

The 11th Sowed onion, parsley, Beets, carrots, spinage. Bought some manure from B. Thorne and hauled it home.

12th dug all the seed beds and planted Early String Beans.

13th. Pulled Radishes This day, and transplanted some Salad.

Evidently, on his return to Mount Gulian, James increasingly perceived gardening as his top priority because it became the main, single topic in the diary for the next several years. In 1833, the number of entries of nongardening work outstripped those related to gardening by a ratio of 2.5 to 1; that ratio declined to 2 to 1 for 1834.[9] But the following year, of the merely two work-related entries James made of only seven total diary entries, both were about gardening: He "planted out peach trees, cherry trees, pear trees" and received "200 apples trees [that] came up in the tow boat Washington from Princes Nursery."[10] One gets the sense that in 1835, he was simply working too hard at gardening to chronicle what he was doing. James was now fixing his eyes on the prize of becoming a master gardener.

The next year, James reached his goal. At the start of spring planting, nine years after beginning the diary at Mount Gulian, James recorded on March 12, 1836, "Resigned my place as coachman today." In fact, through 1840, when he would experience a singular horticultural triumph with Andrew Jackson Downing, he mentioned chauffeuring only four times. On one occasion, he rowed the "[Verplanck] young ladies" across the river in order to make a gardening purchase. At all the other times—when he rowed some Verplanck servants across the Hudson to catch the steamboat at Newburgh, when he took Mrs. Verplanck to the steamboat, and when he drove the Verplancks to church—he probably filled a temporary gap that was due to the absence of a coachman. Indeed, it seems that a John Butler succeeded James as coachman. Then Butler was replaced: In the winter of 1838, James "bought a pair of coach reins" for Mrs. Daniel Crommelin Verplanck and helped her bring on a new coachman from New York City, one Anthony Bradford.[11] James's coachman work had formally ended and he had become master gardener.

Again, his diary revealed his new main preoccupation. In 1836, his gardening entries outnumbered his nongardening labors exactly 2 to 1; in 1837, 2.6 to 1; in 1838, 2.1 to 1, in 1839, 2.3 to 1, and in 1840, 1.6 to 1.

During the 1830s, Brown and his fellow horticulturalist across the river, A. J. Downing (1815–52), displayed tremendous ambition as gardeners. A. J. strove for a national reputation as an expert nurseryman during this decade as James labored to claim a similar spot on the Verplanck estate. When he was 15 or 16, A. J. joined his older brother's business, and the impact that the extremely driven young man had on the family operation was immediate and striking. Within a year, the outfit's name changed from the prosaic Downing Nursery to the illustrious Botanical Gardens and Nursery, and its greatly amplified stock of more than 150 kinds of apple tree and 200-plus pear trees alone began drawing customers from a wide geographical perimeter. By 1836, it gained the notice of Freeman Hunt, writer and soon-to-be publisher of the New York City–based *Merchants' Magazine and Commercial Review*. Hunt visited the brothers' nursery and reported, "[M]any strangers are drawn hither . . . to draw from the rich resources of fruit and ornamental trees collected here." Hunt further praised the pair for their "profound [botanical] knowledge, both theoretical and practical," and for their ongoing communication with European botanists and gardeners.[12] Upon the death of their widowed mother in 1838, Charles and A. J. divided the property— a part to Charles, a part to A. J., and a part jointly owned. On his portion, A. J. erected a stately Gothic residence in 1839—one that "proclaimed the owner was a person of substance," according to his biographer David Schuyler. The surrounding grounds and their design were prototypes for the kind of Romantic architecture and naturalistic, informal English landscaping for which he would become nationally celebrated over the next dozen years. During that period, landscape design replaced horticulture as Downing's chief preoccupation after he published his widely read *Treatise on the Theory and Practice of Landscape Gardening* in 1841.[13]

But just before moving on to landscaping, Andrew Jackson Downing evidently collaborated with James Francis Brown during the fall of 1840 in a brilliant horticultural success. Downing decided to present at that time at the Pennsylvania Horticultural Society's annual exhibition. After nearly ten years of developing his gardening expertise, the twenty-five-year-old young man seemed determined to make a major advance in his burgeoning national reputation as a premier horticulturalist. And if ever there was a city from which to launch his ambitions, it was Philadelphia. Floriculture and horticulture there were perhaps the most advanced in the country; in fact, the first European-styled garden in colonial America was planted there in 1728 by John Bartram.[14] So Downing sent a cornucopia of his best fruit to the Philadelphia event, in all likelihood entrusting Brown to accompany the shipment and assist with its display. The diary does not contain explicit reference to such a Downing–Brown partnership because Brown recorded his trip to the Philadelphia show in typically concise terms: "Went to NY on my way to Philadelphia to the Pennsylvania Horticultural Exhibition."[15] But Brown's association with Downing was established among local Hudson Valley horticulturalists.

Brown was experienced at this kind of assignment and probably enjoyed it. Just the previous fall, he had taken vegetables and fruit down to the New York Horticultural Exhibition, and the new coat and pair of pants he purchased the weekend before traveling to Philadelphia probably reflected the excitement and seriousness with which he approached the task.[16] The Philadelphia show was a three-day botanical extravaganza. Attendance was probably excellent because it had been well advertised. The *Magazine of Horticulture, Botany, and All Useful Discoveries and Improvements in Rural Affairs* had anticipated a "splendid" showing, especially given the "liberal premiums" being offered for top specimens.[17]

The Downing display was a huge success. The Committee of Superintendence for the Twelfth Exhibition of the Pennsylvania Horticultural Society reported that for sheer variety, the New York contribution "had never been surpassed": [18]

> But that which attracted the attention of all visitors was a display of *one hundred varieties* [emphasis added] of fruits from A. J. Downing & Co., of Newburgh, New York, consisting of thirty-six specimens of Pears; fifty-one of Apples; ten of Plums; and three of Grapes, all of which were arranged with the greatest care and attention, and are well deserving an honorary premium of Ten Dollars.[19]

The positive reception that both Downing and, by likely association, Brown enjoyed from the Hudson Valley fruit display in Philadelphia in 1840 was a confirmation of a particular dimension of both men's status as free men—their ability to acquire economic security for themselves as free laborers, even if at different levels. There was, of course, a distinction between the kind of recognition the two men received. Downing was celebrated nationally and publicly while Brown was known only locally and privately. No matter. The professional reputations of both were now solidified. And this was especially remarkable for Brown, because he had been born a slave.

For the rest of James's career, while he regularly performed assorted non-gardening service tasks for the Verplanck household as needed—driving, cleaning, house maintenance, waiting tables—and assisted with fixing public roads each spring, the diary suggests that he did so from a head man's position.[20] As master gardener and head man, James was never exempted from menial, unskilled manual labor about the Verplanck house, grounds, farm, and garden—such jobs as filling the ice house, polishing silver, hauling gravel and manure, harvesting wheat, or burying dead pigs.[21] Rather, along with these duties, his major responsibility was horticultural work performed on Verplanck property or on behalf of the Verplancks within Dutchess County, across the river in Newburgh and Ulster County, down the river in New York City, and occasionally farther afield.

James didn't work alone on the Verplanck grounds. As head man and master gardener, he also managed other garden and farm laborers. The Verplancks hired additional nursery and farm staff—black and white—and assigned them to specific tasks in consultation with Brown.[22] At the same time, Brown could and did conduct hirings on his own, as when he hired a Fishkill cartman/teamster, John Bloomer, "to haul greens to dress the Episcopal Church at Matteawan" during the Christmas season of 1841. Garden, farm, grounds, and household assistants are frequently mentioned in Brown's diary. He noted when they began work, what kinds of tasks they were assigned, when they completed their jobs, when they were ill or absent, when they married, the welfare of their children or relatives, and how they conducted themselves as laborers. Throughout the diary after the mid-1830s, James wrote of the working and personal lives of the Verplanck hired help: "E. Chancelor [was] going to N Y" in May 1836, "John Annin [was] on a drinking frolic" in July 1837, "John Annin began to haul the winter wood on [a] Tuesday" in November 1841, "John Annin went off to the county [alms?] house at Poughkeepsie—Was a great search for him, thinking he might have fallen in some place and perished to death," "Coleman & Warner agreed with Edward Bush to work in the garden for Miss Mary Verplanck at 50 cents per day," "Ephraim Chancellor has got better and gone to work" in January 1849, he (James) "went to Newburgh to get C A Reynolds spectacles mended" one early spring day, and "Christian a Reynolds had the 5th child born last night" in January 1851.[23] Brown's helpers consisted of regulars from year to year—the African American Reynolds family (father William and brothers Frederick and Christian), John Annin (white), Ephraim Chancelor (black), Lott Jones (black), and Robert Williams (black). Then there were those who seemed to work more sporadically or for only a few growing seasons—Edward Bush (black), Cornelius Jacocks (black), Stanford Rose (black), Leara Slavin (white), "Jimma," James Cearman, Henry Henry, and others.[24]

Work for James and his colleagues was seasonal, offering the steadiest employment from spring through early fall, and then only intermittent work in the remaining months. In the late fall after harvest and during the winter months, James and his co-workers fell back on alternative household duties. In November 1838, for instance, James himself "began putting up the curtains . . . in the drawing room" while another laborer "quit work in the garden and commenced chopping wood for Mrs Verplanck"; similarly, in December 1845, Ephraim Chancelor was kept busy by "salt[ing] the pork."[25]

Often, the slow winter months—November through late February or early March—prompted the estate's outdoors staff to take time off or to seek employment elsewhere, so as head man, Brown also kept close track of the movements of his co-workers at such times: how and when they shuttled back and forth between home and Mount Gulian, or New York City (probably for supplemental employment).[26] For example, that "Ephraim Chancelor [was] gone to Montgomery to pay a visit to his Mother" on November 21, 1840, and then returned three days later warranted entries in James's diary. So did the fact that "John Annin came up to work by the day" on December 22, 1840. It was similarly important for James to record that "William Reynolds and C A Reynolds went down to N Y" on December 7, 1841, and came back after four days. At other times during early winter, James busied himself by hauling dung to the garden, filling the ice house, selecting seeds for spring planting, paying bills owed area retailers by the Verplancks, or else literally listening for the chirping of birds because they were a sign of warm weather, the coming of spring, and a return to his preferred work: gardening.[27]

As master gardener and head man, James was regularly charged with making important purchases for the Verplanck garden and house, especially those concerning their upkeep, and with settling of related accounts with area merchants and employees. For example, one fall day in 1841, he crossed the river "to Newburgh and bought some cranberries and paid for [a] sash and [some] glass," the last item probably for a greenhouse or house window repair.[28] The confidence of the Verplancks in James's judgment revealed itself in the diverse and significant tasks and purchases he was dispatched to perform. He bought both low-priced items such as a tool shed lock and high-priced items such as a furnace for the garden greenhouse. He selected good seed. He bought and maintained tools—hoes, sharpened shears, pruning knives, and shovels. He made purchases of superior quality such as apple trees from Prince's Nursery, a patent saw set, or an Ames spade. James paid contracted workers as when he "Paid a bill to Sam Bogardus for Miss Mary VP of $19.47 for carpenters work." Brown not only obtained items specifically requested by Mary Anna—for example, dahlias or nectarines—but he also made independent decisions concerning the garden's basic and ongoing needs, such as fertilizer or a garden engine at good prices. Evidence of the family's belief in Brown's horticultural and business sense can be observed in his participation in nursery auctions such as the one in November 1839 from which he acquired some "bulbous roots." At another in Manhattan in 1848, Brown "bought some hyacinth and crocus roots." With no pre-set price for goods at these auctions, the family was beholden to Brown's own determination of what constituted an advantageous purchase.[29]

The Verplancks also trusted James to market their garden produce. He sold "some new potatoes for . . . fourteen shillings per bushel" in early summer 1839, for instance. In September of 1840, 1847, and 1849, Brown either sent or took grapes down to market in New York City. He "sold 2 bushels of cherries at $2 per bushel" in June 1848. In September 1850, he took "sickle pears" to market in Manhattan, and a couple of years later, he sent mostly the virgilius variety of that fruit.[30] In assigning such tasks to James, the Verplancks demonstrated their certainty that James would travel responsibly with valuable products and then return with money from his sales.

As head gardener for the Verplancks at Mount Gulian, James Brown found himself in rare company with a decidedly tiny minority of other, free African American men in the antebellum period performing farm or service work, but in a supervisory capacity. These included stewards, butlers, headwaiters, and head porters in hotels. Such workers were distinctive, not only because of the managerial aspect of their jobs but also because of the specialized expertise their employment required. They oversaw mixed-race staffs in such posts that usually resulted from the patronage of wealthy whites. They regularly interacted with white elites, as occasioned by their positions. In addition, they were able to hold on to their jobs after 1830 when competition from white, largely Irish immigrants displaced them as household servants. Laborers such as Brown straddled occupational categories somewhere between domestic servants—the majority of all African American wage earners (66 to 75 percent) who were unpropertied and poor—and skilled workers, a minority of blacks (under 25 percent) who helped constitute an early black middle class. Although they performed service work, the high level of responsibility associated with their jobs set them apart and resulted in greater financial reward than was available for other domestics—black and white.[31]

Joseph Smith—a southern-born African American and apparently a free man, who came north from South Carolina in 1850—provides an example of the small circle of antebellum black workers in the Hudson Valley to which Brown belonged. During the summer of 1854, as a young man of twenty, Smith moved to Hudson, New York—about fifty miles upriver from Mount Gulian—in order to take a new job. This was a kind of promotion from his previous position as an assistant for a traveling exhibition company. In his own words, he moved "to conduct a private house." This would be The Hermitage—home of Charles Coffey Alger (1809–75), "the iron king"—founder of the Hudson Iron Corporation, established in either 1848 or 1851.[32] An extensive operation for its time, annually producing some 22,000 tons of pig iron and returning a 40 percent yearly profit, this was the third most profitable iron manufacturing business in the nation at some point in the mid–nineteenth century. C. C. Alger eventually owned two Hudson Valley residences—both run by Smith. In addition to The Hermitage, he acquired the former estate of Andrew Jackson Downing some time after his untimely demise in 1852. Alger used the Newburgh home as his family residence and The Hermitage as a secondary home, close to the ironworks and a place for entertaining guests. Alger's social circle at The Hermitage drew notables from the nation's leading commercial and intellectual elites, such as the Verplancks' guests at Mount Gulian. As a manservant in the Alger household, like Brown in the Verplanck household, Smith would come to occupy a managerial position. His success in service and Brown's longevity as the Verplanck gardener attest to the way in which both men adhered to the advice Smith's father had given him at the age of eighteen as he embarked upon his career: "Make a confidante and friend of your employer. . . . I beseech you, do nothing to forfeit the confidence he has in you. Study his interests constantly."[33]

Aligning his interests with those of his employer was the ticket to Brown's job security and mobility. Wherever early industrialization of this period interrupted traditional work relationships with the introduction of machines and their exacting regimen, laborers responded in one of three ways. Some resisted through new-found workers' organization and political parties. Some clung to long-established habits or more lax work codes. Others embraced the new methods and expectations of their employers wholeheartedly. In villages, cities, mills, and firms throughout the nation, it was this last group that experienced the most upward mobility relative to the others.[34] So it only made sense for Brown to stand guard at the Mount Gulian garden one entire day in June 1848; he was protecting the space against intrusion by the railroad commissioners for the Hudson River Railroad. The men were visiting the estate in order to conduct land appraisals for the property their company planned to purchase to build a line on the western edge of Verplanck land along the Hudson. Brown was aware of the family's opposition to the railway. He therefore made it his business to stand sentinel against these invaders.[35]

As reward for dedicated, expert service and as a measure of his career advancement, James enjoyed a comfortable lifestyle. With his income, Brown was able to afford a house mortgage, house and school taxes, and house and furniture insurance. According to the diary, he rented a place for three years from John P. DeWindt to the south of Mount Gulian in 1833, one year after he returned from his residency with Peter Jay. By 1836 when he shifted chiefly to gardening, he bought the modest house and paid the one-shilling school tax on it that year. A mere three years afterward, Brown retired all of his mortgage debt to DeWindt, the holder of the mortgage loan. Brown owned that house, valued at $1,200 in 1850, for just over twenty years. In the summer of 1857, he rented the "big room" in his residence to one Dianah Sailes, probably a domestic worker. At some point within the next three years, Brown decided to give up home ownership. He sold the house to Julia Gile, a white neighbor, in January 1859; he is not listed as a landowner in the 1860 federal census. In August 1860, in fact, he rented from a "Mrs. J. Neal" a house that he occupied on September 1 at $3.50 per month. Was this Jane Neal of Fishkill? Illiterate and apparently a widow in 1850, Mrs. Neal lived with seven children, five of whom were under sixteen years old. Owning $600 worth of real estate that year, Mrs. Neal probably could have used the steady extra income from renting part of her property to James ten years later when all of her children would have been grown and she, at fifty-eight years of age, was possibly alone. At the end of 1861, James was still renting from Mrs. Neal. Finally, in the middle of the Civil War, James moved into Mrs. Verplanck's wash house, which he rented as a residence, presumably until his death in 1869. Perhaps after shouldering the responsibility of homeownership from 1836 through at least 1857, James sought relief from the physical maintenance of a house, particularly as he and Julia aged without children to assist them or to whom to deed it.[36]

James F. Brown's steady advances as a laborer permitted him to become a homeowner and to move beyond subsistence in order to enjoy a lifestyle of modest comfort. It had been auspicious indeed in January 1833 when James bought his first-ever pair of buckskin mittens and leased a house one month later. His later income as a master gardener enabled him to rent Pew Number

3 at the Episcopal Church in Matteawan, the church attended by the Ver-plancks, and to outfit the pew with a fashionable cushion. It allowed him on one Good Friday to purchase expensive velvet cloth for $6.00 a yard for pants, probably to be styled at the following Easter morning service. It pur-chased him a tailor-made "pair of cloth pants and vest" which in all likeli-hood he sported at a fireman's ball in Newburgh two days later. James's sal-ary provided him not only with everyday shoes, but with boots and slippers too. It allowed him to pay a dressmaker in Newburgh for clothing, presum-ably for Julia, and to provide his wife with fashionable hats as well. It bought him credit with area merchants. Of course, Julia's labors as a paid domestic helped the family coffer as well. Considering that she earned $6.50 per week cooking for the DeWindts in 1838 when female domestics in the Brandywine River Valley (a region that attracted workers from Baltimore) averaged only $8.50 per month in the same year, and when free, black agricultural workers in Maryland in 1847 earned $10 per month, Julia must have often thanked her husband for ignoring her cautious advice against his escape from that state some years earlier.[37]

James's material success may also be measured by the kinds of leisure opportunities he enjoyed. Topping this list was the range of spectator amuse-ments, those that engaged the audience's passive gaze upon any number of popular nineteenth-century "curiosities" and entertainments—a display of "a man without arms," exhibits of live Indian warriors or exhibits on magne-tism, a boat race, a trotting match, fireworks. Despite contemporary criti-cisms of the circus by many Protestant clergymen, James also crossed the river in the spring and/or fall to take in the offerings under "the big top" in Newburgh rather steadily from 1833 to 1854. He attended local lectures on Indians and antislavery talks. Participating vicariously in new inventions and technological advances, he traveled all the way to Buffalo for the splashy, opening ceremony marking the completion of the New York and Erie Rail-road in 1851 and attended the celebration of the first successful transatlan-tic telegraph cable connection in the summer of 1858. James enjoyed pub-lic balls in Newburgh and Fishkill Landing. He regularly visited Baltimore friends in Manhattan and once returned to Baltimore to renew contact with acquaintances there over a period of nearly two weeks. Taking advantage of Julia's occasional summer job—probably as a hotel maid or cook—in Sara-toga Springs, he even visited the spa resort in 1841 and was struck by the fashionable crowds and all the hotels there at full capacity. Such excursions and activities generally required transportation fares, admissions fees, dona-tions, sometimes extra outlays for lodging, and of course surplus time. Poor, laboring workers or "wage slaves" had no such advantages as they struggled merely to keep body and soul together. Only the nation's gentry and its emerging middle class were privileged with these benefits, as James's recreational pursuits demonstrated.[38]

James's career advancement is also revealed within the field of gardening itself. John Loudon, the British (Scottish) botanical expert whose *Encyclopedia of Gardening* was widely read by the wealthy American horticultural set for whom gardening was an avocation, provided a typology of worker-gardeners for the early nineteenth century. Brown straddled several slots in this categorization scheme. Loudon divided garden laborers into two types: (1) "tradesmen gardeners," of which there were twelve sorts or ranks and (2) "operating or serving gardeners," of which there were ten sorts or ranks (see Table 1). Loudon drew his categories from English and western European practices and systems in which job distinctions were relatively rigid. Still, his model supplies a useful basic framework for understanding the gardening profession in the United States, where more fluid conditions were in place. Using this occupational chart, it is clear that Downing fell into the first category and by 1840, the year of his showing at the Pennsylvania Horticultural Society's annual exhibition, had attained the highest rank of tradesman gardener as a "nursery gardener/nurseryman," while Brown had reached what was virtually the highest rank of a serving gardener within the United States on a private estate as a "master gardener."[39] According to Loudon, a master gardener was "a journeyman . . . appointed to the management of a garden, even if he has no labourer, apprentice, or journeyman under him" and one who had "been a year in such situation." But by this typology, James simultaneously occupied the job rank just above that of a master gardener as well—that of "head gardener"—"a master who has apprentices or journeymen employed under him" if one counts the several garden workers under him as informal apprentices. In fewer than thirteen years, James had progressed from the lowest or entry-level post among serving gardeners, that of the "garden labourer"—"occasionally employed to perform the common labours of gardening, as trenching, digging, hoeing, weeding, etc [without] any professional instruction, farther than what they may have obtained by voluntary or casual observation." This upward movement within the field of servant gardening distinguished Brown from Downing through 1840 (see Table 1). Both men deepened their erudition and consequently enjoyed a deepening respect from others for their work. While Downing became famous as a gardener, he remained on the same rung within the range of tradesmen gardeners; in contrast, the obscure Brown climbed several rungs within the range of serving gardeners.[40]

TABLE 1

A Typology of Early Nineteenth Century Gardeners in Ascending Order

Operators (Serving Gardeners)	Tradesmen-Gardeners
Gardener laborer-digs, hoes, weeds*	Jobbing-gardener-lays out, repairs garden grounds
Apprentice-under master or tradesman	Contracting-gardener-jobber on larger scale
Journeyman-has experience in private gardens, botanic gardens, and public nurseries	Seed-grower-farmer contracted to seed-merchant
Foreman-most senior journeyman in large garden; has authority over other journeymen in master's absence	Seed-merchant/seedsman-seed wholesaler
Master-gardener-garden manager*	Herb-gardener-grows herbs for medicinal purposes or for perfumery for sale
Head-gardener-master-gardener over apprentices*	Physic-gardener/herbalist—grows herbs and wild plants for medicine or perfumery for sale
Nursery-foreman-master-gardener or head-gardener working as clerk in nusery; also keeps account of workers' time in a nursery	Collectors-collects berries, nuts, cones, and tree seeds for sale to seedsman
Traveling gardener-gardener or collector sent on scientific exhibitions to acquire plant specimens and to note the soil and climatic conditions for same	Orchardist-grows fruit on orchard grounds or in hot-houses for sale
Satanic curator-superintendent of a public botanical garden	Market-gardener-grows fruits and vegetables for shops in own garden or in towns
Royal gardener/court-gardener/gov't gardener-gardener for a monarch or for head of state; White House gardener	Florist-grows flowers for market Botanic gardener-grows large collection of indigenous and exotic plants for sale
	Nursery-gardener/nurseryman-grows and stocks from seed every variety of vegetable, plant, and tree for sale and shipment to distant places; also a seed-merchant**

Source: J.C. Loudon, Allen Robert Branston, and Jane Webb Loudon, *An Encyclopedia of Gardening* (London: Longman, Green, Longman, and Roberts, 1835), pp. 1223-1224. Loudon supplied a third gardening category or column, that of "Garden Counsellors, Artists, or Professors," with six tiers. Under this heading, A. J. Downing would have occupied the top two—that of landscape-gardener and of gardening author after the 1841 publication of his book on "domestic architecture." Also see Richard Drayton, *Nature's Government: Science, Imperial Britain and the 'Improvement' of the World* (New Haven: Yale University Press, 2000), pp. 139-146 for a discussion of the high and low ends of botany and horticulture as occupations in Britain.
* Positions held by James F. Brown. At the top of his career, his work combined that of a master-gardener and a head-gardener.
** A. J. Downing's position in the gardening world through 1840.

After establishing a local reputation and a place for himself as a master gardener by 1840, Brown was able to relax somewhat and enjoy the security based on this momentum for the next twenty-four years of his life until his "retirement" in 1864. Now that he was relatively confident about the surety of his employment, gardening took up dwindling space in James's diary. During the decade of the 1840s, he made about twenty-one entries per year related to gardening, garden workers, gardening associates, or gardening clients. In the 1850s, the number of similar entries dropped to about eleven per year, and in the 1860s, there was an average of one garden-related entry per year. These numbers corresponded with the diary's overall focus—heaviest in the 1830s and 1840s and tapering off in the 1850s with James's declining health, the deaths of several gardening friends, and his growing interest in local and national politics.

Brown's physical vitality waned slowly but steadily after 1840. During the winter of 1839, while lifting a log, he badly sprained his back. This kept him from work for a few days and later seems to have occasioned a doctor's visit for bleeding. In February 1841, James cut his hand while trimming grape vines. Certainly such accidents were occupational hazards for a gardener, but one imagines that over the years, such mishaps began to take their toll and slow him down in his work. Three years later, he "had a very severe fall . . . and was much hurt by it" and also found himself "too lame in the hands to work" the next day. In early 1842, he suffered with erysipelas, a streptococcus infection of the skin that often affects the body's extremities. As a gardener, James was at risk of fungal infections, which in turn put him at risk for this painful, unsightly skin ailment. He required a "strengthening plaster" for his lame back during early 1847. In July 1849 he again was "taken with a lame back & not able to work." During May 1853, James badly sprained his ankle and described himself as "very lame" as a result. Even after nearby Dr. Schenck had "applied some leeches to it," the ankle required surgery. In the fall of 1858, James sprained his shoulder. In July 1859, he was "taken early [one] morning with the ague & fever—Very bad." One year later, he suffered from "a very sore eye so as not to be hardly able to work."[41]

Over these same years when he passed from forty-seven to sixty-six years old, Brown's gardening circle slowly diminished. Ephraim Chancelor died during the cholera epidemic of 1849. In July 1852, A. J. Downing drowned while trying to save passengers who had jumped from the steamer *Henry Clay* into the Hudson River near Yonkers, New York, after an engine explosion. Mary Anna Verplanck died four years later, in December 1856.[42] At the start of the gardening season in 1860, garden staffer Robert Williams passed away. In April 1861, James Haight, the main farmer at Mount Gulian, moved away and was replaced, and in the fall of 1863, another garden helper, Frederick Reynolds, died.[43] Blows such as these undoubtedly took an emotional toll on James; when Christmas arrived just three weeks after Mary Anna's passing, he remarked that the holiday was "very dull—No Christmas dinner today as has been for 30 years."[44] Mary Anna had been known for the gaiety of the holiday festivities she planned and hosted, and clearly Brown missed her. During these years of work-related setbacks, Brown turned increasingly to matters other than wage work, as will be seen, probably precisely because his career climb was already successful.

James F. Brown's work life formed the model arc. As a free man, he made an ascent from unskilled to skilled work that took approximately nine years. The arc continued to slant upward for another four years until it peaked in 1840 by the time of the Twelfth Pennsylvania Horticultural Exhibition. At its acme, James's career maintained its high level for another two decades until age and other interests intervened.

5

Cultural Meanings of Gardening

Gardening in early and antebellum America was more than an application of science to fruit, vegetable, and flower cultivation, and it was more than a career opportunity for some. It was also a way to affirm male hegemony, one's social class, civic virtue, commitment to a dominant American political economy, and one's respectability. While gardening in the United States during this era also reflected the spreading hegemony of Western civilization, the forms it sometimes took among the nation's black population often reflected African farming and aesthetic norms. Where did Brown stand in relation to these possibilities?

In the antebellum period, especially prior to the 1840s, horticultural societies were decidedly white male preserves wherein members established or confirmed their middle- and upper-middle-class status, so the implications of James's involvement are notable. Even white women's participation was exceptional or limited; they were not actual, official society members, although occasionally they entered displays at exhibitions. A few women published gardening books by the end of the eighteenth century, and, notably, Jane Loudon's *The Lady's Country Companion: How to Enjoy a Country Life Rationally* appeared in 1845, but gardening until the postbellum, late Victorian period was divided into separate, gendered spheres, and extant antebellum horticultural literature makes it clear that the male sphere was dominant and prescriptive.[1]

For the men, a preoccupation with the growing of fruits, trees, shrubs, vegetables, and flowers stood as an antidote to their engagement with crude, materialistic commercial pursuits—especially because most of them were wealthy merchants with relatively newly made fortunes. For example, in its decennial year, the NYHS had as its president Hudson Valley resident Dr. David Hosack (1769–1835) of Hyde Park, the son of a Scottish immigrant—a "woolen and linen draper" and real estate speculator. Jacob Lorillard (1774–1838), one of the vice presidents, earned his money during his lifetime as a leathermaker-turned-banker, tobacco merchant, and real estate developer.

John R. Murray Sr. (1774–1851), another NYHS vice president, was the son of a first-generation miller–turned–shipping merchant, marine insurance broker, and retailer of imported goods.[2]

This link between successful males and gardening was evident in the Hudson Valley. For example, the leaders of the village of Newburgh in the 1830s were New England–born merchants who had only recently consolidated their wealth following a downturn in the previous decade. The town's new-found prosperity transformed it into a village of dirt streets filled with "the near constant rumble of carts" and "herds of animals heading to market." At the same time, soaring profits allowed for the appearance of new mansions, new institutions (churches and banks), and new associations such as the local horticultural society. As commerce fueled city growth and economic recovery in the 1830s, patrons of the horticultural arts appeared there and throughout the Hudson Valley.[3] To be a horticulturalist, then, was one way to be a responsible man—one who assumed a particular role regarding the positive moral character of a city, county, and/or region.[4]

Social commentators, ministers, and the merchants themselves were often uncomfortable with the greed that accompanied the nation's expanding antebellum economy. Critical of the corrupting influence of unchecked, self-interested, individualistic pursuits, they frequently expressed their disapproval of the widespread preoccupation with business while simultaneously extolling the virtues of horticultural pursuits. Consider, for instance, the following critique that appeared in an edition of the periodical *American Quarterly Review* in the 1830s:

> Let him who is engaged in the racking cares of commerce, say in what frame of mind *his* eyes close in sleep, and what are the anxieties of his waking hours. Let the manufacturer tell of his feverish dreams by night and his dyspeptic symptoms by day . . . follow these men—look at their daily walks and occupations—and then turn to the horticulturists.[5]

This author is typical of many of the period in setting business and horticulture against each other as polar opposites. A "true gentleman" would succeed in business but temper his impulses with immersion in horticulture.

As a subfield of agriculture, horticulture was also a means for men, in their custodial role, to pursue the country's economic welfare. Practitioners believed not only that experimentation with new plant, flower, and fruit forms would result in higher and improved botanical and fruit yields for them personally, but that these in turn would strengthen the nation's overall productivity. Thus, the Hudson Valley's Thomas Storm, first president of the NYHS, explained that the founders of that organization "thought they perceived their capability of contributing to the public weal."[6] An indication that "public weal" was fundamentally an economic concept was the group's decision to extend honorary membership in the NYHS to Governor DeWitt Clinton, described by the board as "that patron of internal improvement who was then [in 1822] at the head of the state government."[7] In other words, horticulture, like Clinton's Erie Canal, was a kind of internal improvement that would solidify the state's prosperity. In the words of another NYHS president, "[T]he Society obtained very extensive and useful information respecting the actual state of horticulture in this country. Many facts were brought to light, proving the natural tendency of many of our vegetables to deteriorate. Not only the means of preventing this deterioration, but of promoting their improvement, were pointed out and understood."[8]

What, then, did it mean to and for James F. Brown, an African American man, to be a part of this horticulturalist circle? Certainly, his position was rare; horticulture was, after all, an expensive pastime for most of its chiefly white, rich, male practitioners. Its pursuit demanded three things of gardeners: time; money to put toward exotic and/or fashionable plantings and upkeep of well-trimmed, healthy gardens; and knowledge of the requirements, benefits, and sources of various flora. As a gardener by occupation, James naturally had time for this pursuit. As a gardener-employee, he obtained the money for his pursuits from the Verplancks. And he apparently kept himself well informed of the latest practices and developments in the field through his professional connections and his literacy, which enabled him to read horticultural publications. By default, then, James promoted the goals of leading horticulturalists; according to contemporary conceptions, his work by definition assisted in improving the moral climate, and his displays helped make the "gradual improvement in our [American] markets clearly manifest," as a New York agricultural periodical explained garden shows.[9]

But gardening, as work, and his chronicling of it took on an additional significance for James F. Brown, African American master gardener, because they provided a structure for him to prove his self-moderation and steadiness of character. The ten diary volumes that Brown produced over the course of his years with the Verplancks, like others of his period, left a "life record" that, according to the historian Molly McCarthy, "involved the keeping of some sort of account—of time, money, and the self."[10] Keeping a journal underscored new conceptions of time that accompanied modernization. As the nation moved steadily away from an agricultural, preindustrial economy, the mechanization of early industrialization and commercial growth entailed new forms of work that required a regimented notion of time. Whereas purely agricultural societies viewed time in cyclical or seasonal terms determined by nature, modern economies mechanized time into units determined by the clock. At the start of the nineteenth century, when most Americans participated in an agricultural economy, daily rhythms were determined by the seasons, by the weather, and/or by holidays—planting time and harvesting time, or sun up and sun down. One hundred years later, however, mechanized industrialization meant that labor could be scheduled constantly and, in contrast to the old farming rhythms, rather arbitrarily. Hence, a hallmark of factory work was that it could be performed year-round, and around the clock—as the notion of work shifts took hold. Neither weather, nor nightfall, nor traditional festivals necessarily interrupted daily rhythms. The new forms of work, in other words, required a new discipline of time and timekeeping because the efficient use of time was now regarded as an avenue to success. Diary keeping increased in popularity as a type of self-discipline—a way of literally marking one's time. It was a way, as James understood, for an individual to give account of his or her time—to prove his or her productivity. So James gave an account in the ten blank account books that served as his journal.

During the early nineteenth century, the new approaches to time first reached the nation's cities but quickly permeated the countryside, affecting rural areas like the Hudson Valley, where James lived and worked. The historians E. P. Thompson, David Landes, Michael O'Malley, Lewis Mumford, and others have written persuasively about the switch from a task orientation to work governed by the seasons (e.g., spring planting, fall harvest) toward a time orientation for work dictated by the clock. This change in work forms characterized the shift from preindustrialized to industrialized economies. These same historians have further discussed how novel thought patterns accompanied this transformation so that individuals began to govern their activities by watches and public clocks (e.g., those on factory towers) and consequently to develop sharply regimented internalized clocks, seven days a week, and twenty-four hours a day.[11]

The new industrial conceptualization of time was marked by the way Americans, including Brown, began to carry individual timepieces for governing and scheduling daily activities. At first, the price of watches was prohibitive, making them exclusive to the business and wealthy classes. However, as with any new, mass-produced technology, prices eventually fell so that by the 1820s and 1830s, the ownership of watches was democratized. In the Hudson Valley during these years, increasingly workers and middling sorts of people like James Brown—not just the elite—owned watches, used them, and traced their day's activities by them. In fact, even people like James Brown, whose gardening work might be categorized as "preindustrial," had come to depend on their timepieces by this era. For example, on March 23, 1830, the sole activity Brown noted for the day was the following: "Went over to Newburgh for my watch." The possession of a good timepiece was worth an even longer trip, if need be, for Brown; thus, on July 22, 1833, he recorded the following for future readers: "Went to NY on the s[team] boat 'Albany' and got my watch." By the 1830s and 1840s, Brown, like other Hudson Valley residents, noted all kinds of events by clock time,[12] as can be seen in the following diary entries, which reflected not only an awareness of clock time but also the increasing precision of that sensibility with the passing of years:

October 14, 1830. Today Mr. Rogers powder mill exploded in the morning about ten o'clock.

August 26, 1837. At night returned—Landed at the Long Dock at half past nine o'clock.

June 2, 1843. Mrs D C Verplanck died this day at 15 minutes past 5 o'clock.

To ensure the accuracy of his timekeeping, Brown saw to the proper mechanical functioning of his timepieces throughout his gardening career. In 1838, he "crossed the river to Newburgh for [his] watch that was cleaned by Lander." Again, in the winter of 1846, Lander cleaned Brown's watch; the fact that the job cost him 75 cents, close to two days' wages for an ordinary laborer at the time, is an indication of how much he valued his timepiece. In December 1850, he picked up his clock from Newburgh, where it had been repaired. In the spring of 1853, he traveled across the Hudson to Newburgh for a watch cleaning. Only toward the very end of his gardening career did he record actually losing his watch—a definite consequence of the dulling with age of his otherwise sharp attentiveness to time.[13] Brown was perhaps unconscious of the subtle way in which the following entry linked new notions of time with new business methods: "Went to Newburgh for my watch and settled acct. with Jimison."[14] The implied message here was that Brown had absorbed the import of Benjamin Franklin's dictum "Time is money"—a saying that had taken on a new insistence by 1800.[15]

For James to keep time in this way was to stay regular and to maintain a well-ordered personal and business life—a life of predictable, systematic, productive habits. Diary keeping was one such habit. It was a routine that conferred discipline on its authors, and the writing itself often provided a written account of how authors excercised methodical behaviors. In the expanding commercial and early industrial antebellum economy, such habits as discipline, predictability, and regularity were increasingly prized and touted as part of the new prescription for an industrial ethic. In his magisterial survey of English diaries, the British politician and writer Arthur Ponsonby noted:

> Children are often encouraged to keep a diary or enjoined to keep one for disciplinary reasons. . . . The habit having been acquired, either in youth or later, a diarist may continue without having any clear notion with regard to the eventual fate of his diary. In fact, habit and nothing else may account for the writing of a good many diaries. Habit also will make a methodical man keep memoranda of his doings, notes and accounts for future reference. . . . Daily single line notes have been entered by business men over long periods."[16]

Similarly, in his advice manual entitled *Advice to Young Men, and (Incidentally) to Young Women, in the Middle and Higher Ranks of Life,* William Cobbett—an English farmer and pamphleteer—wrote in 1830:

> Put down something against every day of the year, if it be merely a description of the weather. You will not have done this for one year without finding the benefit of it. It disburdens the mind of many things to be recollected; it is amusing and useful, and ought by no means to be neglected. How often does it happen that we cannot make a statement of facts, sometimes very interesting to ourselves and our friends, for the want of a record of the places where we were, and of things that occurred on such and such a day! . . . It demands not more than a minute in the twenty-four hours; and that minute is most agreeably and advantageously employed. *It tends greatly to produce regularity in the conducting of affairs* [emphasis added]; it is a thing demanding a small portion of attention once in every day.[17]

In the antebellum era, the mere act of keeping a diary, regardless of its contents, was viewed as morally beneficial in and of itself on both sides of the Atlantic.

Hence, the Brown diary itself and the mundaneness of its contents were quite purposeful. The very basis of frustration for one bibliographer of the diary who noted that "[t]he entries are matter-of-fact accounts of mundane events which offer little insight into Mr. Brown's character, apart from his obsession with weather, gardening, and death"[18] was precisely the point from Brown's perspective. By disciplining himself to write a line or two about his day, each day Brown displayed his good habits. In nineteenth-century terms, by committing himself to his diary, he declared his reliability in personal affairs and his steadiness as a gardener. An example of this can be seen in his notation of John Annin's "drinking frolic." Brown's decision to relate his assistant's unsteady behavior implicitly emphasized his own steadiness by way of contrast. And that steadiness could overrule sickness, as on a July day when he recorded, "Not well today but kept at work all day."[19]

Because he was a gardener, Brown reflected a combination of the old preindusrial notions of time, work, and discipline and the modern, emergent, commercial, and early industrial notions in his approach to journaling. His systematic recording of the weather certainly demonstrated the older, almanac-diary form in its embrace of seasonal meteorological time. It only made sense, after all, for a gardener—like a farmer—to note rainfall, humidity, frost, snow, ice, thaws, and heat. But recording the weather for Brown was a kind of commercialized business notation as well—an account entry of sorts. Some weather was a credit. Other weather was a debit. As in Cobbett's advice, a focus on the weather was also a convenient way to guarantee at least one daily diary entry. Weather entries—frequent and abundant in Brown's diary—thus ensured the diary keeper's practice of the new era's much-touted habits of consistency. Indeed, weather "happened" every day. Similarly, James's feverish, singular entries on gardening alone from April through October 1832 can be read as an indication of an invigorated determination to become a master gardener following his previous year's sojourn with Peter Jay. The entries reflected his conscientiousness, his diligence, and hence his worthiness for the job in terms of a very moralistic antebellum work ethic.

Personal responsibility in business affairs, another part of this ethic, was reflected in Brown's diary. James kept a register of his own careful self-monitoring regarding credit and debt from year to year. In early 1839, he proudly recorded, "Paid Mr DeWindt all the money I owe him on my house, 6 hundred dollars," received the mortgage, and "paid some debts for boots & shoes for self & wife."[20] Two years later, perhaps shortly after "[s]ettling with Miss Mary for one years work," he deliberately entered into the log of his life,

"Went to Newburgh and paid all bills owed by me."[21] Brown noted when he paid bills in August 1843, December 1850, and September 1851.[22] Just as carefully, James kept track of his debts—the house mortgage; a $300 personal loan from Benjamin H. Mace, a Newburgh lawyer, taken out in 1847; and a $30 note owed to Powell Bank in Newburgh in 1853. James recorded the loans and his repayment of them as evidence of his lifelong credit-worthiness.[23] In this regard, the diary again stood as a testament to Brown's character. The journal offers proof that the state of his personal finances mattered to him, that he cared about maintaining a reputation as a sound man of business. For the years of Brown's diary, to the extent that American men who kept daily journals tended mainly "to write of their public activities" and in telegraphic, matter-of-fact fashion, Brown was well within this trend.[24]

Besides personal account keeping, there were entries concerning other public business activities as well, as in this one when he noted the start of the Panic of 1857: "A K Chandler selling off dry goods at auction—Great panic in the money matters—Banks suspended all over the state."[25] By such entries, Brown self-consciously and deliberately left a report on his work, his fiscal reputation, and his attentiveness to important developments in the world of commerce. As he steadily filled the pages of blank books, night after night, his entries provided evidence that he was personally and professionally trustworthy and solidly accountable. In antebellum America, these were especially virtuous traits within the prevailing work ethic.

Although this ethic was articulated by mainstream sources, it was repeated as well by African American leaders of Brown's day. *Freedom's Journal*, the nation's first black newspaper, published the following advice to the free black community of New York regarding the selection of schoolteachers in 1827: "See to it then, that your school instructors are well educated moral men; apt to teach and of regular habits."[26] In an 1848 issue of *The North Star*, Frederick Douglass printed a paraphrased version of a letter to the editor he had received from a black advocate of the use of savings banks by African Americans:

> The author of the letter is a mulatto now residing in this city, who has at times assisted as a compositor in our office, and from his unassuming manner, and regular habits, has commanded the esteem of all his co-laborers. We do not, however, insert the letter merely to exhibit the ability of [a] colored man to get up a letter worthy of publication, but we do it more for the very excellent advice it gives to the colored population, in both their public and domestic economy, and as worthy of consideration

by the working portion of the white population, who determine to rise in the world by industry and frugality.[27]

In a similar vein, *The National Era*, an antislavery periodical read by free blacks, published a short piece entitled "Don't Be Afraid of Hard Work" in 1851.[28] So in keeping his diary, Brown deliberately disciplined himself to maintain predictable, regular work habits and thereby reassured himself and future readers of his chronicle of his moral worthiness as a laborer.

There were also political implications to Brown's mastery of horticulture. Exchanges of information and botanical specimens within the horticultural community did not take place within a political vacuum. Horticultural expertise connoted a power over the natural world, even as Western domination of the geographical world through imperial and colonial ventures proceeded apace in the nineteenth century. In other words, it was only because vast portions of Africa, Asia, the Middle East, the Caribbean, and South America had become increasingly dependent upon commercial ties with European and North American enterprises and/or because these same areas were under direct political control of European powers that acquiring non-European plants was even possible for Western gardeners. In England, for instance, acquisitions of orchids, rhododendrons, cactuses, water lilies, and camellias for Kew Gardens reflected "each advancing edge of British power."[29] Of course, some trading of information existed across national borders among relative political equals, as in the northern Atlantic world between horticulturalists in European countries and the United States. But countless items in the botanical paradises that were constructed by botanists, gentleman farmers, and their assistants like Brown—either on private estates or in public gardens—were parts of a bounty plucked by explorers, tourists, and merchants from increasingly subjugated lands, especially in the southern hemisphere.[30]

The Swedish botanist Carl Linnaeus's *The System of Nature* (1735), through its attempted classification of all plants on the planet Earth, paralleled this economic and political domination by enshrining the practice of "botanical imperialism." In this context, the work symbolized a kind of mastery-by-naming that stimulated similar taxonomic projects by his readers in the Western world throughout the rest of the eighteenth century and beyond. Classification of the natural world amounted to an imposition of a Eurocentric and racialized order on all living things, especially as Linnaeus preferred Latin over indigenous names in the new, official linguistic system he and his peers created. Linnaeus's pupils and disciples penetrated South America, Africa, Indonesia, the Pacific Islands, and North America in their work.[31]

In the Hudson Valley, Jane Colden (1724–66) followed the lead of Linnaeus and her father, also a botanist. Living just west of Newburgh, the daughter of Scottish immigrant, physician, and New York politician Cadwallader Colden and a correspondent of John Bartram's, Jane completed a manuscript of descriptions and drawings of New York state plants by 1759.[32] With its focus on vegetation, her work, very rare for a woman of her day and therefore an accomplishment in purely feminist terms, can nonetheless be seen as part of the project of white American subjugation of Native American territory. Such botanical undertakings enabled nineteenth-century Hudson Valley horticulturalists—generally wealthy, influential men—to express their standing in society through their gardens. The formula was straightforward: Vast horticultural knowledge and extensive garden displays garnered from various corners of the globe resulted in enhanced social visibility and social status. Both of these were forms of power. By utilizing this formula in his own life and having the right connections, A. J. Downing had risen from poverty and obscurity to become an influential national cultural arbiter by the time of his death.[33]

There is an irony, then, in Brown's involvement as an African American in this horticultural world when most of his peers were either enslaved or economically marginalized as free laborers. The order on the world's ecosystems imposed by the progress of a European natural history, a practice in which Americans participated, was conjoined with a larger contemporary political project in the Atlantic world—the racial subjugation of those of African descent. In this context, one must ask what it meant that his employer, Mary Anna Verplanck, presented James with a gift of *Lander's Travels* in the spring of 1833.[34] The primary author, Richard Lander (1804–34), was a British explorer of western Africa between 1825 and his death there. Based on his two expeditions, he published a two-volume work called *Lander's Travels in Africa*. The gift of this travelogue to James was certainly and most simply an expression of Mary Anna's appreciation of a trusted, faithful servant. But the gift was more than that. Relatively new and widely advertised in the United States, *Lander's Travels* was part of a contemporary British series called The Family Library (published between 1829 and 1834 by John Murray Publishers, London), intended for "the more respectable market for self-improvement" among the working class.[35] Consisting of travelogues of voyages to faraway places (e.g., India, the West Indies), biographies of "eminent men" (e.g., Alexander the Great, George Washington, Napoleon, Ali Pasha), political satires (e.g., Washington Irving's *Salmagundi*), histories of places (e.g., the Bastille) and political states large and small (e.g., "British India," New York), anthologies of fairy tales, a compendium of insects from around the world, descriptions of the operations of bandits and imposters, and more, the series was both entertaining and didactic.[36] Motivated by a new set of mostly middle-class publishers, books like *Lander's Travels* provided their readers with "useful" information by conveying the reformist, charitable, and, above all, bourgeois sensibilities of people in the English-speaking world. The gift, then, was an exceptional admission ticket—an invitation conveying entry to James Brown and others like himself who otherwise stood outside the ranks of the respectable middle class.

In New York, *Lander's Travels* and other volumes in the Murray Family Library were published by the J. J. Harper firm. Harper editors candidly admitted their emulation of the English model in developing a series with an "American character" typified by an emphasis on "instruction and amusement," "merit and cheapness," and accessibility to a general public. The two publishers shared several titles, including *Lander's Travels* (which appeared in 1832 as Volume XXXV in the Harper series called Harper's Family Library). Pleased with the popularity of the series, the New York editors explained in a prefatory advertising section in *Lander's Travels* that "In several instances gentlemen of wealth and of excellent judgment have been so much pleased with the character of the Library, that they have purchased numbers of complete sets as appropriate and valuable gifts to the families of their less opulent relatives; and others have been unsolicited, active in their endeavors to extend its circulation among their friends and acquaintances."[37] In this instance, then, Mary Anna Verplanck offered the two-volume work to James F. Brown because she thought it would be both "appropriate and valuable" to him. It also invited him to participate vicariously in the respectable middle class by virtue of her familiarity with him as a trusted servant-gardener.

Lander's book ultimately confirmed British imperial endeavors. Toward the end of his two volumes, Lander's efforts in the Niger River Delta—an expedition commissioned by the British government that did not result in a botanical encyclopedia of the region's flora—are summarized as "the extension of geographical science," "the laying the foundation of the civilization of the countries through which he might pass," a means "by which the general interests of the human race might be promoted, our [English] commercial relations extended, and ultimately, the blessings of Christianity diffused over the dark and unenlightened children of Africa."[38] To twenty-first-century readers, Lander's energies seem chauvinistic, condescending, racist, and jingoistic. But in antebellum terms, men of commerce—middle-class merchants and those of their class—considered such efforts enlightened. For them, the great evil of the day was slavery and the slave trade. On this, Lander's record was impeccable because he died in western Africa as a martyr of sorts in the cause of Atlantic world abolitionism. So Mary Anna's gift to James might have also reflected their mutual disdain for slavery and the slave trade, and her assumption that he held and/or was capable of holding her Western and class-based view of human progress.

While this last speculation may seem a bit far-fetched, the fact is that James shared mainstream American conceptions of gardening produce and aesthetics at least. The literature that examines African American gardening practices as distinct from prevailing American customs tends to overlook Brown's occupations—landscape gardening and market gardening—and there is no evidence that Brown engaged in any form of horticulture particular to blacks. The sources on black gardeners and gardens focus on the South, gardens kept by slaves for their masters, gardens that slaves and antebellum free blacks kept for themselves, and/or the gardens later kept by African Americans after Emancipation, rather than the gardens kept for employers by free blacks in the North such as Brown.[39] Some of these sources take up the question of West African retentions among black gardeners of the South—that is, the extent to which they transferred Old World agricultural crops, gardening, and landscaping practices to the British mainland colonies. Perhaps the most developed arguments on this subject have been put forward concerning foodstuffs, especially rice cultivation, but there have also been similar studies of yams, okra, taro root, plantains, greens, cowpeas, and peanuts. Some researchers see direct carryovers from Africa to the Americas.[40] Others like Richard Westmacott argue that despite prior familiarity among African captives with southern food crops—for example, rice—they "may not have been familiar with the methods of cultivation in a specialized cash economy" so that many specialized agricultural skills learned in Africa "probably disappeared."[41] The data the diary supplies about Brown's involvement in grain cultivation are about only corn or wheat, neither of which is a traditional African crop.[42] While there is mention of okra, there is no evidence that its cultivation at Mount Gulian reflected any uniquely African-based skills used in the process. In addition, Brown's "recipes for cures"—included at the back of one of the diary volumes—does not mention any indigenous African ingredients in the mix for any of his herbal medicines.[43]

Brown refers very sketchily in the diary to a garden he maintained for himself, but again, it appears to have been kept within mainstream American practices. The research on the gardens and yards that blacks cultivated for themselves in slavery and freedom see both African retentions and a New

World, African American vernacular art—particularly in landscaping, ornamentation, and yard-sweeping practices. Westmacott, too, argues for a distinctly African American vernacular approach to yards and gardens in those that blacks kept for themselves, as opposed to those for their masters and employers, but he documents this by targeting twentieth-century case studies, not the antebellum gardens tended by James.[44]

Perhaps best placed between the two views of black gardeners—that they either completely adopted Anglo-European forms or that they adapted African forms to their new environment and created their own new ones—is the view of Barbara Mooney. She posits that in the nineteenth century, particularly in the antebellum context, freed blacks (i.e., manumitted or emancipated blacks) such as James associated southern landscape practices with slavery and northern landscape practices with freedom. As a consequence, freed blacks with property of their own preferred the neat, modest gardening practices—including flowers—of the northern middle class.[45] This observation probably pertained to the garden James kept for himself on his own land. True, the pertinent diary references are very few and vague, and they include notes on ground preparation or food-crop planting as in "planted my own garden this day," "plowed up my garden," "planted my potato patch," or "planted potatoes, beens, beetz, etc. in my own garden."[46] But there are also references to the type of decorative gardening involving ornamental plants, flowers, and fruits—which James performed for the Verplancks—being done in his own yard:

> Planted out some fruit trees in my garden.[47]
> Setting out trees of different sorts brought from Mr Downings garden also some in my own garden.[48]
> Went to N Y and returned in the evening - brought up a rose bush . . . for myself.[49]

None of these entries indicates that Brown displayed in his personal garden plantings or a gardening style that departed from Western, mainstream American horticultural conventions, taking into account that these were partly shaped by Amerindian and African influences within the Americas.

In several ways, then, James F. Brown demonstrated his participation in prevailing horticultural practices and their cultural meanings in early-nineteenth-century America. A male-dominated field, horticulture confirmed his manhood through its chief practitioners and the membership of its societies. In theory, it allowed him to contribute to moral uplift and the strength of the national economy through associations with successful businessmen. For James, such associations and the botanical erudition they required also reflected his possession of the kind of social and cultural capital that conferred social status within the African American community, as we will see. Gardening for the Verplancks and his studious recording of it also reflected his deep embrace of middle-class sensibilities.

Figure 1. Ceresville Mill (originally the Williams Mill). Courtesy of Harry Richardson, New Market, Md.

Federal Hall and the Verplanck Mansion (the site of the present Custom House and Assay Office).

Figure 2. Federal Hall and the Verplanck Mansion on Wall Street in New York City. Picture Collection, The New York Public Library, Astor, Lenox, and Tilden Foundations.

Figure 3. Mount Gulian with 1804 addition. Courtesy of Mount Gulian Historic Site.

Figure 4. View from Fishkill looking to West Point. Spencer Collection, The New York Public Library, Astor, Lenox, and Tilden Foundations.

Figure 5. Restored nineteenth-century garden at Mount Gulian. Photo by Charles T. Lyle; courtesy of Mount Gulian Historic Site.

Figure 6. Restored nineteenth-century garden at Mount Gulian. Photo by Charles T. Lyle; courtesy of Mount Gulian Historic Site.

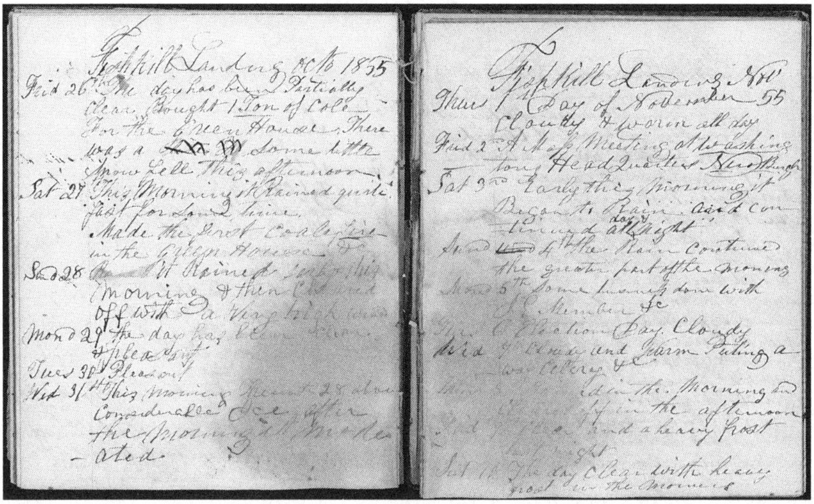

Figure 7. Detail from James F. Brown's diary from Fishkill Landing, N.Y. From the James F. Brown Papers, Vol. 7, October 27–November 10, 1855; Negative #84021d. Collection of The New-York Historical Society.

Figure 8. James F. Brown's gravestone, St. Luke's Church, Beacon, N.Y. Photo by Charles T. Lyle; courtesy of Mount Gulian Historic Site.

Escaping Wage Slavery

After his manumission, James's work engaged him successfully in another battlefront for freedom in antebellum America—the struggle against so-called wage slavery. Gardening gave him admittance into a craft guild: the horticultural world. It allowed him to experience upward mobility. And it conferred upon James a degree of middle-class respectability that most laborers desired. In the seven decades preceding the Civil War, all three benefits were being proclaimed as dimensions of an American birthright. Despite the steady advance of industrialization and its resulting impoverishment of increasing numbers of workers, Brown's life confirmed an emerging prescription for the ideal laborer—the self-made man. That James F. Brown knew such success as an African American man, particularly one who had been born a slave, makes this achievement especially significant.

Brown escaped wage slavery in ways that could be appreciated by members of both the new working class and the new middle class of his day—groups that often found themselves at odds with each other as commerce and industrialization spread. Critics of the new economic order from the laboring class railed against the disappearance of traditional paths of upward mobility as craft shops gave way to factories. In this new system, apprentices no longer progressed to become journeymen who, in turn, advanced to become masters within a particular craft. The preexisting rules of reciprocity and mutual obligations whereby an apprentice's perceived needs—food, shelter, moral shepherding—were provided by the master as he learned a trade and climbed to journeyman level in his master's shop fractured. The mechanization and de-skilling that accompanied mass manufacturing reduced entry-level workers to permanent status as poorly paid unskilled workers and set journeymen adrift. Both groups—the vast majority of the growing ranks of non-agricultural laborers—were left to fend for themselves regarding jobs, housing, and basic material needs with unsteady, meager wages as their only compensation. Experiencing and anticipating lives of intermittent, uncertain employment and inescapable poverty, the new industrial workers protested that they were being reduced to wage slavery and that they were, in fact, now wage slaves. Reformers complained further that in this form of slavery, not only were workers materially impoverished, their lives were being monotonized—dehumanized by having to perform dull, repetitive tasks unthinkingly. Wage slavery was the antithesis of freedom.[1]

Such arguments drew justification from the rhetoric of the Revolution in the early national period. Since Alan Dawley's study of nineteenth-century shoemakers in industrializing Lynn, Massachusetts, labor historians have demonstrated in numerous case studies how traditional artisans drew on the political ideology of the War of Independence to protest that the new economic order denied them "the equal rights" for which they or their fathers had fought.[2] For artisans and mechanics, the legacy of independence was freedom from dependency, their right as freeborn or free Americans to pursue "a competency"—an independent living. In the historian Alan Taylor's words,

> "Independence" meant owing enough property—a farm or a shop—to employ a family without having to work for someone else as a hired hand or a servant. A "competency" meant a sufficiency, but not abundance, of worldly goods: enough to eat, adequate if simple clothing, a roof over their heads, some consumer goods, and an ability to transmit this standard of living to many children.[3]

The fact that the colonists perceived British taxation policies in the last several decades of the eighteenth century as a threat to their notion of economic right—this particular type of independence—was what in part had fueled their break with England. Early-nineteenth-century craft laborers resisted new industrial work forms for once again jeopardizing this type of freedom.

In the two large cities where James F. Brown had worked, craft workers appealed to Revolutionary War rhetoric in their struggle against the factory system. In a study of early Baltimore, Seth Rockman focused on the broad swath of free working people (rather than artisans)—unskilled manual laborers who never achieved economic independence. They strove for a living wage but often resorted to other ways of staying alive—temporary stays in the almshouse, apprenticing their children, stealing, scavenging, pawning goods—rather than apply direct resistance to industrialization in hopes of improving their condition. At the same time, Rockman noted that skilled laborers in that city such as artisans who opposed the debasement of their crafts and life chances by mechanization did so based on the belief that "workers and employers met as equals in the marketplace."[4] Such assumptions flowed from the fact that artisans and merchants had united in Baltimore during the Revolutionary Era, according to the historian Charles Steffen, to fight English control through such organizations as the Mechanical Club, the Mechanical Volunteers (a militia), and the Baltimore Whig Club.[5] As Baltimore's economy expanded in the first three decades of the nineteenth century, employers needing cheap labor proved willing to employ blacks, free and enslaved, in a full range of industries—"brickyards, ropewalks, ironworks, shipyards, chemical plants, and tobacco manufactures."[6] White male artisans saw them as competition, a menace to their already threatened patrimony of economic independence.[7] But the willingness of business owners to use African American laborers implicitly invited these very workers to hope for the kind of upward mobility promised by the Revolution, as we have seen in James's escape letter.

Similarly, skilled workers in Manhattan when Brown arrived there in the late 1820s were appealing to Revolutionary War rhetoric through Democratic-Republican politics to resist economic marginalization. The historian Sean Wilentz has shown that there, "Artisan independence conjured up . . . a moral order in which all craftsmen would eventually become self-governing, independent, competent masters. . . . [C]raftsmen would insist on their equal rights and exercise their citizenship with a view to preserving the rule of virtue as well as to protecting their collective interests against an eminently corruptible mercantile and financial elite."[8] Such an outlook drew direct inspiration from colonial-era remonstrances again the British Crown and would have only reinforced James's own understanding of his position.[9]

Where did gardening, specifically, fall within this conflict between industrial capitalists and traditional craft workers? The voluminous literature on horticulture and scientific agriculture as a movement from the late seventeenth to the early twentieth century overlooks the labor history per se of gardeners and gardening as a profession, "trade," or "living" in the nineteenth century. The overwhelming concern in the historiography is for gentlemen farmers, businessmen with country estates, and those few gentlewomen interested in gardening as an art form or hobby.[10] Alternatively, the literature addresses yeoman and middle-class farmers as the target of scientific gardening campaigns to improve crop yields. Those who worked the land for others as paid gardeners are therefore ignored in this work.[11]

But early-nineteenth-century newspaper accounts of street parades yield clues that gardening, at least as practiced by master gardeners, was understood by other artisans to be a craft. From the medieval period through the late nineteenth century, workers in the North Atlantic engaged in public performance and civic processions as members of craft guilds, whether through religious plays, pageants, mumming (merrymaking in disguise), naumachia (enactments of naval battles), or parades. When such events were linked to election days, fair openings, the swearing-in of officials, May Day, church feast days, and patriotic celebrations, skilled laborers indicated their approval of established political authorities and the economic order and their proud identities as either subjects or national citizens.[12] In Federal-era New York City, for example, blacksmiths, sailors, and ship joiners marched in a celebration of the Constitution's ratification under an approving banner: "This federal ship will our commerce revive/And merchants and shipwrights and joiners shall thrive." Similarly, in 1825, tailors joined in celebrating the completion of the Erie Canal under a flag that featured a Native American receiving a cloak, while the chairmakers' banner prominently displayed an American eagle. Fourth of July festivities in the years between 1788 and 1825 also typically included contingents of skilled workers marching under patriotic flags. In such street politics, craft workers asserted a connection between the new American republic and support for a traditional craft system.[13] Alternatively, as "mummers" or in their own spontaneous parades—for example, English machine-breakers between 1811 and 1816—workers expressed disapproval of their sinking economic condition's being brought about by mechanization.[14]

A Washington's birthday parade in Philadelphia in 1832 suggests that gardeners, at least master gardeners such as James F. Brown, considered themselves craft workers in the preindustrial sense. On that occasion, 50 gardeners marched beneath "a splendid banner, and a magnificent bouquet of flowers and fruits" behind 250 butchers, 140 saddlers, 450 hatters, 150 bakers, 140 glass workers, 340 carpenters, 340 masons, 200 blacksmiths, 850 tailors, 390 shoemakers, several hundred printers, and hundred of others from "the trades."[15] Here, gardeners linked themselves to other artisans in celebration of the American republic's most popular founding father, thus declaring their identification with the economic promise of the Revolution.

Salaries within the field of gardening validate this impression of an artisan's identity for master gardeners such as James, while suggesting apprentice and unskilled laborer identities for beginners or paid, occasional, casual workers within the profession—Brown near the start of his career with the Verplancks and certainly those who worked under him after he quit his coachman's job to become head man for the family. Gardeners' wages varied according to their level of expertise. Common laborers were paid a daily average of $1.08 from 1828 to 1881, and $0.88 in 1836, when Brown moved from mainly coachman to gardening duties, but as agricultural workers, laboring gardeners were probably paid less than this. American agricultural workers around 1830 averaged $0.40 per day ($146 per year). The Verplancks seem to have approximated this wage, allowing for yearly increases, when they contracted with a newly hired garden laborer at the start of the growing season in 1842 for pay of $0.50 per day in 1842 ($182.50 per year). Ten years later, they paid another garden laborer $12 per month or $0.40 per day ($144 per year). Nationally, agricultural laborers earned between $100 and $200 a year in the early nineteenth century. In antebellum Dutchess County more specifically, yearly wages for farm laborers were between $100 and $400, according to William P. McDermott, a local historian, with the average day laborer on a farm earning between $150 and $160 per year. At the other extreme of the national gardening pay scale were high-ranking government gardeners. The principal gardener for the president of the United States at the White House, for example, earned a salary of $1,200 per year in 1840—more than eight times as much as his fellow-laborer on the first tier of the gardening ranking ladder.[16]

James's salary lay between these two poles if one considers him an artisan in the company of some of those in the 1832 Philadelphia parade of tradesmen. Likening Brown's salary to that of a carpenter, he earned $490 in 1836, $540 yearly in 1840 and 1850, and $630 in 1860. If one equates Brown's salary with that of a mason, he earned $540 in 1836, $630 in 1840, $540 in 1850, and $720 in 1860. Or, using McDermott's agricultural wage scale for Dutchess County, Brown possibly collected $400 per year—nearly three times the typical farm worker's earnings.[17]

Thus, James F. Brown avoided wage slavery entirely. True, his labors were not strictly artisanal in the usual sense, as were those of tailors, carpenters, coopers, and blacksmiths; his work was essentially agricultural and therefore outside the immediate and initial reach of industrial forces. However, the amount of horticultural expertise required to become a master gardener permitted the application of gradations within gardening work so that it made sense to talk of apprentice, journeyman, and master gardeners, as did Loudon and others of the day (see Table 1 in chapter 4). By moving up this occupational ladder, James experienced economic freedom—a kind of liberty that contemporary unskilled urban laborers understood as a distant possibility for them as American citizens, a kind of liberty that their skilled countrymen idealized as an American birthright, but for which so many in both sets of workers only longed.

But how typical was James F. Brown as a gardener? And how common were African American gardeners during the period of his lifetime? A survey of nineteenth-century newspapers and periodicals suggests that Scottish and German gardeners, rather than African American gardeners, were prized in the North during the 1830s when James was striving hard to become an expert in this field. In the South, certainly slaves were used as gardeners.[18] In addition, free black gardeners and other skilled clandestine runaways in that region seem to have competed advantageously with poor native whites for work in the eighteenth century, at least as measured by job advertisements. For example, *The Southern Patriot* announced: "Also wanted. To hire or purchase, a Gardener, who possesses the above qualities ['white or colored, . . . sound, sober, honest, and no runaway.']."[19] Another Baltimore ad read, "Wanted. - A good Gardener, to take charge of a garden, situated about two miles from Baltimore. No one need apply unless he can bring unexceptionable recommendations, both as to character and competency."[20] The lack of specificity regarding the race of applicants might have as easily implied a desire for whites as an openness to blacks in this last ad and others like it. But there was probably a comparatively short supply of wage-earning nurserymen in the South, or at least in Baltimore, indicating a race-neutral approach to hiring in the field. In other areas of work in Baltimore, for example, employers sometimes placed racially opaque notices for jobs—ones that did not specify race—when their demand for workers was high.[21]

In the antebellum North, black and abolitionist publications encouraged African American gardeners. The *Colored American,* a black newspaper, urged its readers to take up gardening in New York state in 1838: "There is a field of enterprise thrown open, upon which they may enter with pleasure and profit. There is no calling more healthy or more beautiful than Gardening, and its productiveness correspondent has clearly shown." One year later, the same paper advertised "an unexpired lease of a small house & 3 acres of good and well cultivated ground" as an attractive "situation for a market gardener," and again, in the summer of 1838, the *Colored American* ran an article encouraging scientific and market gardening among its subscribers. In 1841, this periodical also "call[ed] the attention of [black] people living in the cities of New York and Brooklyn, and vicinities, to the advertisement of building lots . . . that afford[ed] a fine situation for a gardener, being contingent to [the] New York market . . . where vegetable produce finds a ready sale, and always at a handsome profit." The antislavery paper *The National Era* included a piece in an 1851 issue listing "valuable books" to readers who were "agriculturalists, horticulturalists, and florists." After visiting the annual horticultural exhibition in Pittsburgh, Lewis Woodson—African American activist, AME Church minister, leader, and barbershop owner in that city—wrote to *Frederick Douglass' Paper* in 1853 and urged its readers to consider gardening "as an easy, practical, and certain means of bettering their condition, and increasing their happiness and respectability." Similarly, the Boston-based black abolitionist William Cooper Nell, who ran the employment bureau for free black and fugitive slaves for *The Liberator*, the nation's leading abolitionist publication, advertised for black gardeners, as in the following notice: "A colored man, who can come well recommended as a gardener, can hear of a [grand] situation in the State of New York . . ." The same paper was receptive to solicitations for work from black gardeners, as illustrated in this announcement: "situation wanted.—A very worthy and trusty man desires a situation as a gardener."[22]

Still, in the northern states, where European immigration was concentrated in the colonial period through the nineteenth century, Scots and Germans seemed to be in a more advantageous position compared with that of blacks regarding gardeners' positions. This was partly because of the Scots' and Germans' experiences with market gardening—growing vegetables and fruits for retail through green-grocers or in their own market stalls. But this was also because Scots and Germans held a reputation for steady, industrious work habits. Significantly, too, the botanist John Loudon was Scottish and advised in his prescriptive *Encyclopedia of Gardening*, "In horticulture, when the difficulties that German gardeners have to contend with are taken into consideration, the German gardener is at least upon a par with those of Britain and he may confidently be pronounced superior to them in forced productions and in the preservation of vegetables and fruits throughout the winter."[23]

Mainstream antebellum American literature reflected what seemed to be a stereotype of the preferred German or Scottish gardener. Numerous examples of various types of these can be found in period newspapers and magazines. For example, in a curious piece called "The Sultan and the Pine Apples," readers learned that it was a German gardener who was persuaded to take an eminent post at Constantinople with the *seraglio* there. Similarly, a Massachusetts traveler to Washington's Mount Vernon in 1845 who noted a "colored gardener" there explained that this worker had been trained by a German, as if to validate the African American's skills. An abolitionist newspaper, in order to punctuate its argument against the recapture of fugitive slaves, ended an article with a literary reference to "the Scotch gardener"—apparently a well-known type. *Godey's Lady's Book* ran a short story called "The Gardener's Daughter" in which a main character was "the Scotch gardener, Allen Palmer, in his search for a home in the New World." Mr. Palmer and his family emigrated to the United States, and "little by little they purchased, and dressed, and tilled the barren land around, turning the weedy stream to usefulness, and profiting by a knowledge of soils and favorable exposures, which then were but little attended to, or indeed understood in the busy New World." Allen Palmer, in short, was the quintessential industrious Scottish market gardener. Likewise, a romance published in *The National Era* featured a " truehearted old gardener"—a man with "genuine Scotch pride."[24]

German and Scottish gardeners understandably, then, sought to capitalize on the advantage that their nationality might bring to them in job searches by including explicit statements of their national origin in their advertisements for positions.[25] Just two examples from the *New York Herald* read as follows:

> A German gardener (married, without children) wants a situation; he is a good horticulturalist and vegetable gardener; and has several years experience in this country.[26]
>
> Gardener—Wanted, by a Scotchman, a situation as a gardener, a single man; has lived in places where horticulture has been carried on in the greatest extent; and has a perfect knowledge of his business; has had several years practice in this country, and has lived with some highly respectable families. Good references given.[27]

Similarly, a Scottish immigrant placed the following ad in a Philadelphia newspaper: "a gardener and farmer wants employment in a settled place; a person who has been bred a Farmer and Gardener in East Lothian, Scotland; he understands common Gardening, and can take care of a Greenhouse and the work of a Farm."[28] In becoming a master gardener for the Verplancks, then, James Brown as an African American may have won out over some of the most usual and sought-after competition in the North.

James F. Brown's successful gardening career validated northern apologists for "free labor"—the term used by the commercial class and industrial elite to defend the new economic order against its working-class detractors and against southern critics who argued that chattel slavery was a humanitarian system whereas wage slavery was not.[29] Wendell Phillips, a leading white abolitionist, argued:

I believe the terms "wages slavery" and "white slavery" would be utterly unintelligible to an audience of laboring people, as applied to themselves. There are two prominent points which distinguish the laborers in this country from the slaves. First, the laborers, as a class, are neither wronged nor oppressed: and secondly, if they were, they possess ample power to defend themselves, by the exercise of their own *acknowledged* rights. Does legislation bear hard upon them?—their votes can alter it. Does capital wrong them?—economy will make them capitalists.[30]

Brown's work history lent credence to Phillips's dictum "[E]conomy will make them capitalists." James followed the interests of his employers, he sharpened his botanical expertise through associations with other horticulturalists, he worked hard and steadily, and he managed his own fiscal affairs well enough to become a homeowner—a little capitalist.

Evaluating Brown's avoidance of wage slavery depends on the scope of analysis. Labor historians studying change in the United States in the antebellum years have moved past a romanticized, monolithic notion of a single group of workers represented by the noble artisan valiantly critiquing the widening grasp of industrial capitalism. Instead, they see that the expanding national economy necessarily and structurally perpetuated the poverty of many relatively passive unskilled workers, diminished life chances for some outspoken craft apprentices and journeymen, yet created tremendous opportunities for compliant, enterprising, and fortunate others. This last result was especially noticeable in comparison with other industrializing nations in the North Atlantic. James F. Brown was in this category—a group of wage earners who pursued their own self-interest by joining themselves to wealthy commercial and industrial leaders rather than opposing them. He was able to advance himself in horticulture—a growing pastime, aesthetic arena, and agricultural subfield that could yield increasing profits for many whom it employed. He advanced because he was a disciplined risk taker, a serious-minded adventurer who cleverly and providentially hitched his abilities to well-placed supporters. As a result, he was twice free—free from chattel slavery and free from wage slavery.

PART III

Free Man and Citizen

Double freedom opened the door for James F. Brown to political citizenship as an African American in the antebellum United States. Free from chattel slavery and free from wage slavery as a property owner, he could vote and pursue volunteer activities that contributed to the shaping of local, state, and national public policy. The choices he made as a political actor reflected his own experiences as they intersected with two main influences—the politics of his male employers to whose ideas he was particularly exposed as a close household servant, and the political traditions of the African American community with which he retained mostly informal yet vibrant ties in its struggle against slavery and for equal rights.

To a significant degree, James expressed his political citizenship via participation in the emerging national civic sphere of antebellum America. Alexis de Tocqueville famously noted after visiting the United States in the 1830s that "Americans of all ages, all conditions, and all dispositions constantly form associations." Here, he referred to the American penchant for forming clubs and societies reflecting their various causes, concerns, and interests in an effort to have such organizations affect public policy and/or public behavior. The ability to form such associations as well as political parties, unimpeded by a central government or without an aristocratic class, was a form of democratic freedom.[1] Voluntary associations of the period can be subdivided into two types—formal political parties and informal organizations for social betterment. By participating in both, James F. Brown helped define American democratic freedom.

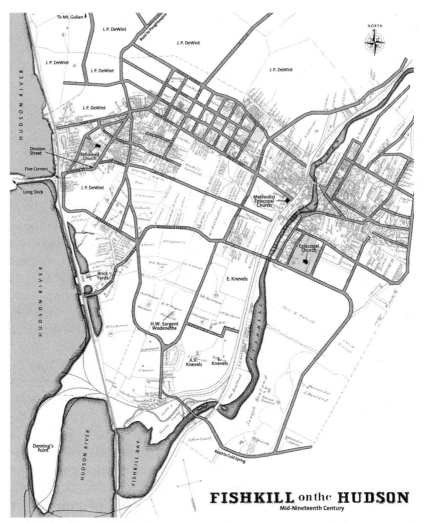

Map 3. Fishkill Landing during Brown's lifetime. Base map copyright by www.historic-mapworks.com.

A Whiggish Sensibility

One incubator for James Brown's politics was the Whiggery shared by William E. Williams, his slavemaster in Maryland, and the Verplancks, his New York employers. Despite differences where they eventually fell along the slavery divide, the Williamses and the Verplancks had a political disposition in common—Whiggery. There were two dimensions to Whiggery. First, it was a general, abstract philosophy of government and authority pioneered in eighteenth-century England but adapted by colonial Americans to criticize British taxation policies. Second, it was a specific party and political platform developed in the antebellum United States. The key aspects of a Whiggish political disposition in understanding James Brown, the political actor and voting citizen, were the restraint and moderation at its center, which determined his actions regarding the question of slavery.

Brown was probably first exposed to Whiggish ideas while a slave in the William E. Williams household in Maryland. William E. was a Federalist. In Maryland and in other states, the Federalist Party, according to one historian, "refused to recruit its leaders from beyond the narrow oligarchic circle of Maryland's aristocratic families, nor would it adopt the devices of mass political organization so successfully used by the Republican opposition" during the early republican era. As a party of the status quo, Maryland Federalists increasingly represented the interests of counties and rural areas against the ascendancy of Baltimore and other urbanized areas.[2] For the time that Brown lived within the Williams household, then, he would have been surrounded by Federalist conversations, particularly as a domestic servant, even as he probably represented Williams family interests in increasingly (Democratic-)Republican strongholds like Baltimore and other Maryland cities as a hired-out or quasi-free slave.

But it is a survey of the Verplanck family's Whiggery that is most useful for understanding James's politics. Samuel Verplanck (1739–1820), the owner of Mount Gulian during the Revolutionary War, seems to have approached the conflict with England with the sort of Whiggish pragmatic circumspection that would influence and define his own, his son's, his grandson's, and his great-great-grandson's approach to the question of slavery. During the Revolutionary War years, the nation's founders who united to oppose the absolute power of the British Crown ironically were influenced by the political philosophy of British Whigs who sought simultaneously to assert the preeminence of Parliament over the Crown. Both American dissenters and British Whigs insisted that governmental authority resided in the people, and that duly elected legislatures were the representatives of the people.[3] For some American protesters, this meant only one thing: Revolution against British rule was necessary. But other colonial leaders who insisted that the political and economic policies of the Crown toward the North American colonies amounted to "taxation without representation" balked when they confronted the fact that their political arguments led them logically to revolution.[4] In other words, many hesitated when they realized that rebellion was the next step that followed their own protests. At the end of the day, revolution flew in the face of notions of hierarchy, ascribed roles, and social order that many American colonial elites shared with English elites.[5] Moreover, civility and politeness in the public and social sphere were widely circulated ideas among eighteenth-century English Whigs, and America's founders adopted these same notions.[6] So while a revolution might be justified, it would always be messy—a chaotic, acrimonious upheaval against the prevailing order—and order was something to be preserved, although not by zealous Patriots nor by Tories. However, there was a third group—a set of cautious but dissenting colonials for whom the preferred route was diplomacy, compromise, and negotiation with Britain toward a peaceful resolution of differences. Only when statesmanship failed did this group fully support an armed struggle for independence.[7] Samuel fell within this category, and the halting manner in which he embraced rebellion against the Crown was similar to the tentative yet determined way in which Brown would later explain his flight from his Maryland owner.

Verplanck was a member of the Committee of Safety of One Hundred, or Committee of One Hundred for short, which organized in New York City in early May 1775 and through which Manhattan residents were pledged to obey the decisions of the Continental Congress. By the end of May, the committee had four companies of volunteers, had received orders from the Continental Congress for the construction of a fort at King's Bridge in the Bronx and at the Highlands (today's Washington Heights in Manhattan) against British attack, and had begun arming and training a militia. The Committee of One Hundred was not for independence per se but was instead opposed to

Britain's taxation laws, which they considered unjust. The committee wrote to Governor Cadwallader Colden in May 1775 that "though they [patriotic colonists] are arming with the greatest diligence and industry; it is not with design to oppose, but to strengthen government in the due exercise of constitutional authority."[8] Judith Crommelin Verplanck, Samuel's wife, remained in British-occupied Manhattan throughout the war in the couple's Wall Street home, where she entertained British officials and army officers, including General William Howe. Such placating measures seem to confirm William Cullen Bryant's view that "although [Samuel Verplanck] took no share in political measures, his inclinations were on the side of the mother country."[9]

However, such an interpretation is undermined by the fact that Samuel helped equip the Continental Army materially when there was a shortage of lead for bullets. The Provincial Congress of New York decided in early 1776 that lead should be taken from the windows of the inhabitants of the city of New York and delivered to the Provincial commissary to be melted down for ammunition. Samuel Verplanck along with another individual listed as a "Mrs. Verplanck" made contributions to this effort, according to public records.[10]

After war broke out fully within New York, Samuel Verplanck removed himself alone upstate to the farm and mill of his deceased cousin, Philip, where he served as a guardian for Philip's children and as administrator and steward of Philip's property farther south on the Hudson at Verplanck's Point—an important trading post occupied first by the English and then by the Americans during the war. While living in Fishkill Plains, Samuel permitted the Continental Army to use Mount Gulian as the headquarters of Baron Von Steuben until the war's end in 1783. In that same year, the Society of the Cincinnati, the country's first patriotic veteran's organization, was founded at Mount Gulian.[11]

Samuel and many of his peers approached the manumission of slaves with the same cautiously progressive outlook with which they contemplated revolution. Rather than outlaw slavery directly, they moved slowly but steadily in that direction out of fear of the social and economic dislocations that sudden abolition might cause. Such caution flowed from the kind of eighteenth-century, Whig-influenced politics to which they subscribed. In the 1790s, this thinking emerged in the new United States within a new political party, the Federalists, of which Samuel Verplanck was a member. Spurred by Quakers and by their own discomfort with the contradictions between slavery in New York and the revolutionary ideals they espoused, many saw the need to move toward a policy of general manumission. So two years after the war's end, thirty-two prominent citizens met in Manhattan to organize the New York Manumission Society. But many of these people were slaveholders themselves. As an indication of the complications attached to statewide manumission, the society's president, John Jay, owned five slaves himself, and about half of the society's founders were slaveowners. Eventually, men with similar sentiments were able to secure the passage of state legislation for the gradual abolition of slaves in New York state born after July 4, 1799.[12] The date is laden with symbolic meaning and irony. For New York state slaves affected by the law, independence was a middling place, poised between slavery and freedom, with most working as indentured servants. The law typified the moderate, accommodating, and compromising liberal political sentiments that Federalists drew from their Whiggish sources. This would explain two things: that William B. Verplanck (1770–1804), a state assemblyman representing Dutchess County and Samuel's cousin, introduced a bill (unsuccessfully) to compensate New York slaveowners for even gradual abolition, and that Judith, Samuel's wife, still had five slaves living with her at the family home in New York City in 1800, when James Brown was a seven-year-old slave in Maryland.[13]

As Federalist politics took shape between 1787 and 1800, Daniel Crommelin Verplanck (1762–1834) and those of his generation were coming of age and beginning their public careers, while men like Daniel's father, Samuel, were nearing the end of theirs. Daniel encountered Whig-informed federalism not only through his father but also through his first father-in-law, William Samuel Johnson (1727–1819), while attending Columbia College (today's Columbia University), of which Johnson was president.[14] However, when Daniel first assumed political office in 1803 as a representative from Dutchess County to the U.S. Congress, it was as a Republican, as Democratic-Republicans (or Jeffersonians) were then called—not as a Federalist. He was twice reelected to this post and served there through 1809. During Daniel's time in office, the Democratic-Republican majority voted to ban the importation of slaves, thus terminating the legality of the transatlantic slave trade. An indication of Daniel's repudiation of slavery at this time is the fact that in the 1810 U.S. Census, he is listed as owning no slaves. After serving three terms, Daniel returned to his law practice after 1809 and served as a judge in the Court of Common Pleas in Dutchess County from 1828 to 1830. These were the years when James F. Brown entered the Verplanck household in Dutchess County. By that time, the politics of the Verplanck family at or connected to Mount Gulian had evolved to the point that they were no longer engaged in slaveholding and were willing to assist a runaway slave in his quest for manumission.[15]

Of the Verplanck family members in James Brown's life, Daniel's son, Gulian (1786–1870), was the most engaged in civic and public affairs. When he completed college in 1801, the first party system in the country (Federalist v. Democratic-Republican) was still in effect. However, with Thomas Jefferson's election to the presidency in 1800, Democratic-Republican majorities replaced Federalist control of the national government, and Gulian followed his father's example in going with the ascendant political camp. As one biographer explains, "He was educated a federalist, but early in life found himself acting against the federal party."[16] When he was just twenty-five years old and a young lawyer, Gulian returned to his alma mater's (Columbia's) 1811 commencement ceremony. One of the student speakers that day delivered a pro-Republican speech, despite earlier vetting his speech before the Federalist college provost who struck the overtly partisan passages from the text. As a consequence of this defiant act, the student was denied his diploma, which in turn prompted Gulian and others to jump to the platform and rally the audience to support the student. For this act, Gulian was tried and convicted of riot or inciting to riot before New York City Mayor DeWitt Clinton, who was also a Democratic-Republican.[17] Gulian was probably a victim of the Alien and Sedition Acts—Federalist-backed laws designed to suppress Jeffersonian Republicans, particularly in the area of free speech. Still, the fact that both a Federalist faculty member and a Democratic-Republican mayor could find this youthful prank so objectionable illustrates the continuing influence of what may be called a Whiggish sensibility among members of those of Gulian's class—a strict concern for social order, public decorum, and moderation in civic affairs.[18]

Gulian first assumed political office as a member of the New York State Assembly in 1820 (serving until 1823), but according to one biographer, he did nothing in particular to distinguish himself in that office.[19] By 1820, the country had entered "The Era of Good Feelings"—a second party system in which the Federalists disappeared from the scene, having been discredited by their opposition to the War of 1812, and in which the Democratic-Republicans ruled virtually unopposed on the national scene. Certain Federalist leanings never disappeared, particularly those regarding the primacy of commercial and industrial interests in the American economy. These would resurface, but at this time there was a relative lull in partisan feeling and partisan conflict, as potentially divisive issues such as slavery and the tariff were either suppressed or handled amicably between contending groups.[20]

In 1821, the year after Gulian assumed state office, New York state held a constitutional convention to review and revise its constitution—a development that would have great significance for free blacks in the state. Gulian was not a delegate to this particular convention. But it is noteworthy that it was this body that agreed to amend the state constitution to permit all white men over twenty-one access to the vote, regardless of property ownership, but to retain a property qualification for black men—thereby severely limiting black access to the franchise in New York state.[21]

The English precedent of restricting political participation to propertied men during the seventeenth and eighteenth centuries had been transferred to Britain's New World colonies. Even as a revolutionary ideology slowly permeated the ranks of colonial leaders after 1763, never did they consider stretching the boundaries of the voting public to include the poor and landless.[22] Nonetheless, already by then, the uniqueness of America's natural bounty had expanded landholding in the colonies well beyond proportions that could even be hoped for in Europe. Indeed, J. Hector Jean de Crevecoeur, an immigrant who prospered as a farmer in the Hudson Valley's Orange County, praised the opportunities for penniless newcomers to becomes homesteaders in his famous *Letters from an American Farmer* (1782):

> Whenever I go abroad it is always involuntary. I never return home without feeling some pleasing emotion, which I often suppress as useless and foolish. The instant I enter my own land, the bright idea of property, of exclusive right, of independence exalt my mind. Precious soil, I say to myself, by what singular custom of law is it that thou wast made to constitute the riches of the freeholder? What should we American farmers be without the distinct possession of that soil? It feeds, it clothes us, from it we draw even a great exuberancy, our best meat, our richest drink, the very honey of our bees comes from this privileged spot. No wonder we should thus cherish its possession, no wonder that so many Europeans who have never been able to say that such portion of land was theirs, cross the Atlantic to realize that happiness. This formerly rude soil has been converted by my father into a pleasant farm, and in return it has established all our rights; on it is founded our rank, our freedom, our power as citizens, our importance as inhabitants of such a district.[23]

Because so many duplicated de Crevecoeur's experience, the founders of the United States saw no inherent contradiction between the democratic experiment they had launched and property requirements for voters. In fact, borrowing heavily from the political theorist John Locke, they reasoned that democracy would be strengthened by the fact that a multiplicity of enfranchised freeholders would have a literal vested interest—that is, through the very land they held, in the public welfare.[24]

By the 1820s, however, such thinking about the electorate altered, and a consensus emerged from state to state that property qualifications should be lifted for white voting citizens. The impetus behind this change had to do with westward migration and new immigration patterns, coupled with an expanded, optimistic view of democracy per se. Newly arrived people from northern and western Europe, mainly Ireland and Germany, began pouring into the nation's port cities. In the twenty years after 1820 alone, approximately 700,000 people entered the United States. In the 1840s, 1.7 million immigrants arrived; in the 1850s, 2.6 million. In those parts of the country receiving the majority of the newcomers, the Democratic Party especially— always opposed to entrenched elite, commercial political interests—called for an end to property qualifications for the franchise as a way of widening its base by including poor, landless male arrivals and making government more responsive to the broad populace.[25] The results of these political reformulations were significant. Prior to 1800, only South Carolina, Georgia, Kentucky, Vermont, and New Hampshire could claim universal white manhood suffrage. By 1830, these states were joined by Alabama, Mississippi, Louisiana, Illinois, Indiana, Ohio, Maryland, Rhode Island, Massachusetts, and New York. Thirty years later, Florida, Arkansas, Missouri, Iowa, Minnesota, Wisconsin, Michigan, Tennessee, North Carolina, Virginia, Pennsylvania, and Maine had removed property requirements for voting white males.[26]

Democratic expansion of the franchise under Democratic-Republican initiatives was a deeply racialized enterprise in New York state and throughout most of the country. While political citizenship was extended to all adult white males, it was deliberately and severely truncated for African Americans. Democratic-Republicans in the state legislature in 1811 put forth a bill stipulating the presentation of certificates of freedom by would-be black voters. After the defeat of that bill by Federalists, the Democratic-Republicans got behind a similar law that passed on a second try later, and it was the Democratic-Republicans who wrote the property requirements imposed on black voters in 1821.[27]

The prevailing view at the 1821 New York state constitutional convention concerning the black franchise consisted of three arguments. Samuel Young, delegate from Saratoga County, put forth the opinion that equal voting rights for blacks would be inconsistent with the custom of racial inequality in other areas of public life: "We ought to make a constitution adapted to *our* habits, manner, and state of society. Metaphysical refinements and abstract specu-lations are of little use in framing a constitution. No white man will stand shoulder to shoulder with a negro in the train bands or jury room. He will not invite him to a seat at his table, nor in his pew at the church." Young con-tinued his argument for a racially exclusionary suffrage system by cynically constructing an illogical conclusion: "And yet he [the black man] must be placed on a footing of equality in the right of voting and on no other occa-sion whatever, either civil or social."[28] Young further contended that, pos-sessed of suffrage rights, blacks were likely to "sell" their votes to the "richest purchaser":

> In forming a constitution, we should have reference to the feelings, habits, and modes of thinking of the people. . . . And what is the public sentiment in relation to this subject? Are the negroes permitted to a participation in social intercourse with the whites? Are they elevated to public office. No, sir—public sentiment forbids it. This they know; and hence are prepared to sell their vote to the highest bidder. In this manner you introduce cor-ruption into the very vitals of government.[29]

Jacob Radcliffe, former mayor of New York City and representative from New York County, expressed the view that African Americans should be kept from the polling booths because they were "degraded, dependent, and unfit." Young agreed with this too by arguing, "The minds of the blacks are not competent to vote. They are too much degraded to estimate the value, or exercise with fidelity and discretion that important right."[30]

When James F. Brown entered the Verplanck household as a servant in 1827, Gulian was serving in the U.S. House of Representatives as a Jacksonian Democrat, an office he held from 1825 to 1833.[31] Jacksonian Democrats sup-ported western expansion, an expanded electorate, a limited central govern-ment, and the principle of union over states' rights. Although this Demo-cratic Party supported both popular democracy (white male suffrage) and slavery, Gulian nonetheless served as the liaison between Susan F. Williams, James Brown's owner, and James, in the latter's bid for manumission; he assisted James financially in his effort to gain his freedom. Gulian was more of a party man when he was chairman of the House Ways and Means Com-mittee over the issue of the so-called Tariff of Abominations and the result-ing nullification theory put forth by southern opponents of protectionism. He wrote a proposal for a reduced tariff, but in the end it was Henry Clay's suggestion for a gradually reduced tariff that won the peace.[32]

Gulian broke with the Jacksonian Democrats, however, over the matter of the continuation of the Second National Bank. Like many with a Federalist heritage and engaged in commercial pursuits, he saw the utility of that institution as one directed by the national government. During his fourth and last term, he therefore disagreed with President Andrew Jackson's distrust of the bank and his policy of replacing it with so-called pet banks at the state level.[33] It was this issue that led Jackson's opponents to form the Whig Party and to inaugurate the second party system (Whig v. Democratic), which lasted from 1834 to 1854. Many Whigs, in other words, were reinvigorated Federalists, and Gulian was one of them. As a Whig, he ran unsuccessfully for the office of mayor of New York City in 1834, but he served in the New York State Senate from 1838 to 1841.[34]

While the new Whig Party, for all its moderation, would find it hard in the 1830s to avoid the divisive issue of slavery entirely, it does not appear that Gulian was ever publicly outspoken or a leader on this matter, although he seemed to be somewhat open to antislavery advocates. The slavery debate heated up during the decade following the formation of an abolitionist movement led principally by William Lloyd Garrison. In 1837, Garrison's abolitionist paper, *The Liberator*, applauded the appointment to the Board of Regents of the University of New York State of a Reverend Dr. George Cheever, an outspoken opponent of slavery; the paper noted approvingly that Cheever would be joining "such men as . . . Gulian C. Verplanck."[35] Such a statement of approval from Garrison seems to indicate that he anticipated Gulian's support as an antislavery ally, albeit a quiet one. Then, too, Gulian's party, the Whig Party, proved to be the friendlier of the two national parties to pro-abolitionist forces. This was not because the Whigs ever put forth an antislavery party platform at the national level, though. Rather, within the Whig Party, there were strident, individual antislavery voices like those of Gerrit Smith and William Seward. Smith—a wealthy white philanthropist, reformer, and abolitionist—wrote to Gulian in 1837, asking for his backing in the state legislature in securing abolition and full civil rights for free blacks. Smith appealed,

I learn from newspapers and other sources, that great and various benefits are looked for from this ascendancy of the political party [Whig], which has given you so triumphant an election to the Legislature of our state. . . . It may not be proper to put this question to any one member of the Legislature—but if it be, to whom can I put it more suitably than to one, who will carry into the councils of his state an influence proportionate to his high character, as a statesman, and scholar? . . . "[N]othing is prepared" for our colored brother by the laws of this state. And when shall our Legislature remember his wrongs, and his destitution, if it be not at its next session?[36]

In this petition, Smith apparently viewed Gulian as a potential friend of the antislavery cause. Particularly after 1846, Seward led the abolitionist charge in New York state politics, but there does not appear to be any indication that he and Gulian were close.[37] Nor is there any indication that Gulian ultimately supported this cause in the state legislature.

In addition, there is some suggestion that Gulian opposed explicit antislavery politics at the state level. After 1847, some antislavery advocates embarked on a new strategy of linking their cause to the anti-rent movement—efforts to abolish the relics of feudal tenancy in New York state by small farm lessees victimized by the system. Landlords struck back by forming a Freeholders' Committee of Safety, which hired a lobbyist in Albany, one Duncan Pell. Three years later, in 1850, the landlords launched a new journal, the *Albany Evening Journal*, to advertise their cause, hoping that this would become the official voice of the state's Whig Party. Pell was quoted as saying that the publication was the brainchild of the landlords' tightest friends: "[Daniel Dewey] Barnard, [John] Spencer, [Gulian] Verplanck & all that set."[38] Such a statement links Gulian with rather conservative, "aristocratic" elements in the state—people who respected private property and contractual relations concerning it. Slave–master and tenant–landlord relations were alike in that they were both governed by property law. According to these findings, then, there is no record of Gulian's explicit engagement in public antislavery politics, and the evidence for him on this score seems mixed—in true American Whiggish fashion.

By the 1840s, Gulian's commitment to the national Whig Party was vacillating.[39] For instance, Gulian supported the party's choice for the presidency in the 1840 election, William Henry Harrison, which was a logical extension of Gulian's belief in a national bank because Harrison promised to re-establish one. When Harrison died after only one month in office, Brown reported the "melancholy news" and marked the funeral and funeral procession in his diary.[40] But in the next presidential election, in 1844, rather than support the Whig candidate, Henry Clay, with whom he had disagreed over protectionism, Gulian voted for James K. Polk on the Democratic ticket. Polk was a lifelong slaveholder but did not believe in extending slavery to the new territories of Oregon and in the southwest, which became U.S. possessions under his tenure.[41] As a Whig four years later, Gulian opposed the election of Whig candidate Zachary Taylor to the presidency in 1848 even though Brown reported "a Whig supper given at [Fishkill Landing's] Eagle Hotel and rejoicing at General Taylors election" in November 1848.[42] Although Taylor was a Virginian by birth and a slaveholder, he was also a strong nationalist and a critic of southern sectionalism. The Democratic candidate that year, Lewis Cass, believed in popular sovereignty, letting residents of the territories decide for themselves whether to endorse slavery. Was this Gulian's position? Probably so, because in the election of 1852, Gulian seems to have supported the Whig, Millard Fillmore, as a nominee over the party's eventual candidate, Winfield Scott, and over the Democrat Franklin Pierce. Fillmore, who had succeeded President Taylor upon the latter's death, had been chief executive during the enactment of the Compromise of 1850—virtually Cass's position on territorial slavery four years earlier.[43]

By the time of the election of 1856, the Whigs no longer existed. Within the new and third national party system, pitting the Republican Party against the Democratic Party, Gulian returned to the Democratic camp by supporting the election of James Buchanan. Buchanan was probably the most neutral of the other candidates regarding the growing sectional crisis, and Gulian remained a Democrat through the Civil War. But Gulian was an antislavery Democrat, probably believing, like Buchanan, that both secession and going to war to end secession were constitutionally illegal. Most of his energies during the war were spent strenuously decrying arrests made by the federal government during the conflict—arrests he considered arbitrary—and also publishing in various Democratic journals his objections to congressional proposals to issue paper currency (greenbacks) in order to finance the Union war effort. One late-nineteenth-century biographer therefore concluded that Gulian Verplanck was "blind to the great issues involved in our late civil war."[44]

Despite his public stance on abolition, Gulian's *personal* politics regarding slavery tell another story. He aided James F. Brown in his legal manumission, and the knowledge of this is probably why ardent, outspoken abolitionists such as William Lloyd Garrison and Gerrit Smith who wanted to pass antislavery legislation courted him in the first place. Moreover, Gulian employed free blacks within his household in New York City. In 1840, these included one free "colored" male between thirty-six and fifty-five years old, and two free "colored women" also between the ages of thirty-six and fifty-five.[45]

After the election of 1860, the nation's sectional divide was fully exposed, thus making the abstract, pragmatic, and moderate stance on slavery rationalized by Whiggish political philosophy and its adherents like Gulian obsolete and untenable.[46] Following the secession of the southern states a few months later, there was no place for compromise or indecision regarding slavery. Robert Newlin Verplanck (1842–1908)—son of William S. Verplanck (Gulian's son) and the great-grandson of Daniel Crommelin Verplanck—came of age at precisely this moment. He graduated from Harvard College in 1863,[47] a few months after President Abraham Lincoln issued the Emancipation Proclamation. Lincoln's order symbolically expanded the North's purposes in fighting the war from simply that of preserving the union to include the goal of freeing the slaves. African American men who longed to serve in the Union Army from the start of the war were now officially allowed to do so. The timing of the establishment of the Bureau of Colored Troops in May 1863 coincided with Robert's graduation. Like his great-grandfathers Samuel Verplanck and William Samuel Johnson, then, Robert was confronted with the fact of war after a period of protracted political turmoil within the nation. And just as they had had to do, he took a stand on the side of the American republic. But Robert's stance was far more radical than theirs. He joined the army shortly thereafter in October 1863 as an officer with a command over Company H (entering as second lieutenant and later promoted to first lieutenant) and then Company A, U.S. Colored Troops 6th Infantry Regiment. He served until the war's end and was a captain by the time he was mustered out in July 1865.[48] Unlike his male forebears, by serving as a Union officer his was a decidedly public position on the slavery question—a position for which he was willing to risk his life. With Robert, the Verplanck approach to slavery had finally shifted from the cautious progressivism of Whiggery to the radicalism of Frederick Douglass's abolitionism. In no uncertain terms, Whiggery was now dead in the Verplanck family.

What united the politics of Samuel, Daniel, and Gulian was an eighteenth-century, transatlantic, Whiggish sensibility that criticized absolute and corrupt governmental power and championed the rights of the people. Both eighteenth- and nineteenth-century Whigs were proponents of a type of progressive political economy that advanced a system of free market capitalism in which slavery as a form of labor was a costly relic of the past. At the same time, by today's standards, this type of Whiggery had decidedly conservative elements, including a deep belief in traditional social hierarchies and limited democracy. In revolutionary America, this sort of Whiggery was expressed among Patriots who were cautious, though supportive of the break with England. This same Whiggery re-channeled itself after the Revolutionary War mainly into the Federalist Party. Whig principles within Federalist thought can be seen in the Federalist Party's program that supported a strong central government, a controlled form of democracy implemented through an electoral college and a bicameral national legislature, federally sponsored economic development through transportation improvements and a national bank, and the elimination of slavery. Within the nineteenth-century American context, many of the inheritors of Federalist thought—like Gulian— were also Christian humanitarians of various stripes who opposed slavery on moral grounds. But Whiggish morality was also a morality of temperance, moderation, respect for authority deemed worthwhile, and a veneration of private property.[49] With regard to slavery, then, this combination of sentiments meant that Whigs supported private manumissions, opposed the spread of slavery to new territories, but hesitated over the use of violent or other precipitous action toward abolition. And it is this stance that led Daniel and Gulian to aid James in his manumission privately.

And what of James? The former slave probably found Verplanck family politics safe, if not vocal in their condemnation of slavery. The Verplancks' brand of private, not public, antislavery politics coincided with James's appeal to Susan Williams for freedom. The Verplancks, Williams, and James demonstrated their attitudes toward slavery via private acts, valuing decorum and order in public discourse. From his last owner and from his employer, James would not have observed or learned a politics of radical abolitionism. Rather, he would have witnessed and experienced a politics of gradualism and tempered progressivism. Significantly, Robert Newlin Verplanck's role in the Civil War is never mentioned in the diary by a then-elderly, seventy-year-old Brown. Of course, a precipitous drop in diary entries accompanied James's process of aging, particularly after 1860. Still, this silence may have reflected Brown's preference for the complex set of moral, cultural, economic, and political Whiggish sensibilities of his employers rather than the more narrow focus of the Republican Party on a liberal political economy.[50] As a trusted domestic servant, James became intimate with the Whiggery of his employers. Working in the household and on the grounds, he heard stories about the exploits and accomplishments of Verplanck family politicians, past and present. He was familiar with their opinions and their stances on the pressing matters of the day. And, as the next chapters of his life demonstrate, he shared their sense of patrician responsibility, their appreciation for order, their belief in personal and societal improvement. These were the hallmarks of his politics, even as he pressed beyond and more deeply than they in targeting the specific concerns of African Americans for abolition and full citizenship rights.

James F. Brown, Voting Rights Politics, and Antislavery Activism

On November 8, 1837, James F. Brown registered his vote in Fishkill, New York. In typical fashion, Brown's notation of the event was understated: "The election at Fishkill took place this day at which place James F Brown voted for the first time."[1] At the same time, though, the mere fact that he acknowledged the act as an inaugural one, and in the third person, may be taken as an indication that Brown wished to highlight the significance of an African American man's walking into a polling place on an election day anywhere in New York state in 1837. This was a singular event, considering statewide and national developments concerning suffrage rights over the previous fifteen years.

African Americans in the state were well aware of the role of Democrats in keeping them from election polls, and, given the Democrats' racialized take on a widened franchise, African Americans naturally gravitated toward the Whigs after the party's formation in 1834. In New York state, the presence of progressives on black rights within the party—Thurlow Weed, Horace Greeley, and William Seward—was a positive draw as well. In 1837, the year Brown cast his first vote, then, Gulian as a Whig holding a seat in the New York State Senate would have served as a sort of political guidepost for Brown—a political ally by default. Whigs scored great victories at the local, state, and national levels that year and continued to do so the next three years as well.[2] The fact that Brown closely charted these developments along with Whig campaign activities and his own involvement in electoral politics in his diary strongly indicates his support of the Whig ticket during those years. He recorded:

November 9, 1837. The Whigs gained the victory.
November 22, 1837. [T]his day there was a grand sillubration [sic] in the city of N Y in honor of the Whig Triumph.
November 7, 1838. Went to the election at Fishkill—Voted and returned.

November 16, 1838. A grand jubilee supper given at the Star Inn in Triumph of the Whig victory.

November 26, 1838. Went to Newburgh to attend a Whig Jubilee—Eight hundred persons took supper.

November 6, 1839. Came up from N Y—Went to Fishkill Village election.

September 26, 1840. A great Whig meeting at Matteawan.

November 2, 1840. Went up to the election at Myers Corners.

Black opinion in New York state leaned toward the Whigs in 1837, when James first voted, and continued through 1839 despite black dissatisfaction with Whig (and Democratic) resistance to enfranchising black men fully without property qualifications. For instance, following the election in the fall of 1837, the *Colored American*, an African American newspaper established by free black activists Phillip Bell, Samuel Cornish, and Charles Bennett Ray and published in New York City, reported:

Great is the rejoicing of the Whigs in this State. They have gained a victory beyond their most sanguine expectations. The politics of the whole state have been completely revolutionized in their favor, and the interests of the whole people placed in their power. . . . We have voted with the Whigs— their views in politics are measurably our views, yet while we rejoice with them, we rejoice with trembling. We know something of the corruption and the deceitfulness of the human heart. We also have some experience, and know something of the doings of political men, when in power. And if we confine our judgment to past experience, we have nothing to hope for. . . . We have in this Commonwealth [New York State], more than forty thousand colored citizens, disfranchised, oppressed and injured, by legislative enactments. Thousands of our brethren, responsible to God, and made of the same blood, are proscribed and sought to be brutalized, in this enlightened state, and that too, by the very power given of God, for the melioration of the condition of his poor.

Brother Whigs, if you mean that your triumph shall last as long as a morning song, or an evening tale, we warn you, to mete out righteousness to every citizen, whatever be his complexion. Enfranchise, as one of your first acts, the forty thousand colored freeman, illegally robbed of their privileges, and of their rights, by unequal and barbarous laws. The cries and the prayers of these oppressed fellow beings, will come up before you from every part of the State, the ensuing Session of your Legislature.[3]

In March 1838, the *Colored American* proclaimed, "We are a Whig, and vote with the Whigs. . . ."[4] Again displaying political hopefulness regarding the Whig Party, which held the majority in the New York state legislature in 1839, the paper's editors appealed to Whig assemblymen:

> We advise them, then, soon after assembling at Albany, to take into consideration, the rights of the colored people of the State, and as the Constitution of the State will, probably, be amended in some particulars, so to amend that article of the constitution, which provides that no colored man shall be entitled to the exercise of the elective franchise, unless he be possessed of two hundred and fifty dollars worth of real estate, - so to amend it, as that *every male citizen*, without regard to color, above twenty-one years of age, shall possess and have the right to exercise the elective franchise.[5]

As a property owner, Brown held a privileged position among New York state (and national) blacks, in that he could vote. And it was as a property owner that James became somewhat of an activist regarding black suffrage. Beginning in 1836, the year in which he bought his own house, several of Brown's friends—George Knowles, George Washington, William Mitchell, and William Lloyd—began negotiating with white property owners in Fishkill Landing to purchase houses of their own. It is hard not to identify Brown as the central broker of the resulting deals because in at least two cases, the seller was John P. DeWindt, the Verplancks' neighbor to the immediate south of Mount Gulian who had sold him his own house and land. Knowles completed the legalities for his home purchase in 1836. Washington and George "Lott" Jones, another friend of Brown's, acquired full ownership of their properties in 1842 and 1845, respectively, but seemingly had a leasing arrangement on the houses there in the interim after 1836. Lloyd may have acquired property in Newburgh.[6]

Throughout the diary, James's acts of seemingly mundane home ownership duties underscore acts of citizenship. Brown left a record of his diligence in paying tax bills and helping with property maintenance for these friends who owned nearby lots and/or houses in Fishkill Landing. When property taxes were due in January 1845, for instance, he made sure to settle his own account of $1.00 and also paid the twenty cents in taxes owed by African American neighbor George Washington. A year later, he paid land taxes for Washington again, and for another black homeowner, Sarah Bradford. Washington, Bradford, and their spouses were not as fortunate as Julia and

James as to find steady, remunerative employment chiefly in and around Fishkill Landing where they owned their homes. They most frequently worked elsewhere in the Hudson Valley and its environs—Manhattan, Troy, or even New Jersey. So Brown, who maintained contact with them, did them the favor of keeping up with their taxes, informing them of necessary upkeep like painting, and of such legal matters as border disputes with neighbors. In all likelihood, he also helped them find renters when they were away from their premises whereby they received some small profit from home ownership. For example, in the spring of 1845, Samuel Rose "took possession of Mr Washington's house" and in late fall of 1845, Sarah Bradford "hire[d] her house [to] Mr Thompson." Because Rose was one of Brown's black gardening assistants and Thompson was a good friend of James's, it is easy to imagine that James in fact brokered both deals.[7] By such actions, Brown shored up the rosters of local property-owning, vote-eligible blacks.

Brown also assisted Gerrit Smith's free-black land acquisition project in upstate New York. A wealthy white abolitionist and reformer, Smith owned 140,000 acres of family land in the Adirondack Mountains that he gave away in the 1840s to poor blacks—free blacks and newly freed or fugitive slaves—in roughly 40- to 60-acre parcels, leaving them only to pay the taxes needed to retain ownership. His intention regarding African Americans was partly to facilitate their access to the electorate because, with $250 worth of land, black men could vote. In this, he was later joined by other radical white abolitionists, such as John Brown. When Smith announced his plan in August 1846, he had predetermined the number of free blacks per county in New York state who would be eligible to receive this gift. For Dutchess County, the number was 150; by 1849, the number of takers in Dutchess County left only 22 parcels.[8] Yet as early as January 1843, James had "paid eighty two cents to G Smith for Anthony Bradfords tax." This was the Anthony Bradford—Sarah's husband, one imagines—who served as coachman for the Verplancks some eight years earlier. The Smith-Bradford-Brown transaction stands as an early model for the announcement of Smith's eventual Adirondack giveaway scheme. Indeed, four years later, in 1847, James noted, "Deeds was given to the colored people from g Smith, esq for land in Hamilton county." James's access to Smith was probably through Gulian. Smith's 1837 letter to Gulian, cited previously, and a diary entry referring to an incident during which "Gulian Verplanck on a frolic struck G Smith" suggest that Smith and Gulian interfaced politically and socially in the 1830s and 1840s despite Smith's far more aggressive approach to black citizenship rights.[9] James clearly took advantage of these interactions for the benefit of himself and other African Americans.

In 1840, Brown remained loyal to the Whigs—the party of Gulian Verplanck—but the *Colored American* shifted its trust to a new party, the Liberty Party, dedicated solely to the cause of abolition. This was no doubt due to frustration at the Whigs' failure to enact expanded black male voting rights. The Liberty Party's nominee for president that year was James G. Birney and for vice president, Thomas Earle, a former Democrat.[10] That fall, the paper proclaimed:

> Let the colored voters in New York, who are persuaded to vote the *whig* ticket, in *behalf of the slave* and thus refuse to vote for Birney and Earle, pay attention to the facts contained in the article signed Liberty, in the last Colored American; and let them remember that the leading *whig* papers in New York were the most active in getting up the [anti-abolitionist] mobs of 1834. Let them remember the language of Webb's Courier and Stone's Commercial in '34,[11] and then ask themselves whether that party is more favorable, taking their journals as a fair specimen, to our rights than the other party. Let them also remember how Noah, in his Star, croaked against the passage of the jury trial bill, for fear the south would be displeased, and then ask whether a party led on by such men, and drinking in such pro slavery doctrines is fit to be remembered by colored-men. Then look at their arrogance in placing before a free people, a slave holder for Vice President [John Tyler of Virginia], just as the other party have, and, a man by his whole life pledged to the low bidding of the slaveocracy for the Presidency, and then advising honest abolitionists and colored men as did the Chief priests and Elders of old, to vote for Barabas rather than for just and honest man.[12]

Because he voted Whig in this election, it is very likely that Brown, despite his opposition to slavery, considered a vote for Birney, who was bound to lose, to be a wasted one. Indeed, the Liberty Party won only 3 percent of the vote in a hotly contested election—because many Americans considered abolitionists to be radical social destabilizers. Then, too, Whigs in rural, largely white areas of the North—places like Dutchess County—sometimes displayed less overt prejudice against blacks than those in cities with sizable black populations. So Brown may have experienced enough good will and camaraderie from his Whig neighbors to keep him attached to the party in 1840.[13]

The 1840 election does, however, raise the question of the extent of Brown's direct engagement in abolitionist politics. Ending American slavery was the major concern of free northern blacks and particularly those who were privileged enough to vote. Free African Americans had begun holding regular annual national conventions as "The American Society of Free Persons of Colour" in the 1830s to this end and toward the goal of achieving civil rights equality more generally.[14] Because the diary has no entries for the fall of 1833, we do not know how Brown reacted to the abolitionist visitor and agent for the abolitionist publication *The Liberator* who visited Fishkill then. The agent, one Arnold Buffum, reported a very hostile reception from the Dutch Reformed Church in Fishkill: "The minister of the Dutch Reformed Church said he would do all he could to defeat my object: his mother also appeared to take a lively interest in the perpetuation of the slave system. She recommended to me to get a black wife, &c. &c."[15] Here, the pastor in question was Reverend William S. Heyer, and his mother's opposition to Buffum revealed the prevalence of the amalgamationist argument—the view among antebellum white northern defenders of slavery of every class that general emancipation would promote much-dreaded miscegenation between blacks and whites. Yet Brown had no problem attending services at the Dutch Reformed Church in Fishkill that year at least twice.[16] The diary is silent about the Dutchess County Anti-Slavery Society, which was active from at least 1838. Nowhere in the diary did Brown note a major meeting of black abolitionists in Poughkeepsie in July 1840 to choose delegates to an August state convention; or a commemoration of West Indian emancipation held in Poughkeepsie in August 1841; or a "colored citizens' meeting" in Newburgh that same month; or the session of African American abolitionists from Dutchess and adjoining counties held in Poughkeepsie in September 1841; or a gathering of the American Free Mission Society, an antislavery group of mostly white Baptists, in Poughkeepsie in April 1847; or a meeting of "colored citizens" in Poughkeepsie in September 1855 that heard the report of local delegates who had attended the Troy Convention (a state convention of free black activists) and who sought to form a local political suffrage association.[17]

At the same time, there are sporadic hints of possible abolitionist leanings and activities on Brown's part. He took note of the 1837 William Dixon affair in New York City, involving a fugitive slave whose self-proclaimed owners were trying to extradite him to his former southern residence. Although Brown's diary entry is politically neutral and only informational on the matter—"Trying William Dixon in N Y . . . as a runaway slave"—this notation was made roughly nine months after a visit paid him by David Ruggles.[18]

It is very tempting to think that this was David Ruggles the prominent, strident black activist and abolitionist in New York City. Ruggles, along with

William Johnson, George Barker, Robert Brown, and J. W. Higgins, was a founding member of the Committee of Vigilance—a "composite of abolitionist groups, businessmen, and churches to assist bondsmen in need." The fact that this Ruggles may have made a point of visiting specifically with Brown is a possible indication that he hoped to solicit Brown's aid in saving runaway slaves from the South from recapture or kidnapping and/or in helping them to asylum in Canada via New York's Underground Railroad.[19] Naturally Brown's own history would have caused him to sympathize with antislavery forces. Then, too, the timing of this Ruggles visit is somewhat suggestive of its link to abolitionist activity—August 1836, just one year after the establishment of the Committee of Vigilance. Furthermore, Brown was clear that Ruggles "came up from N Y to see me" at a time when the abolitionist Ruggles did, in fact, reside in Manhattan and use it as his political base.[20] Moreover, the insistence of a jury trial for suspected runaways as an essential protection against bogus claims of prior slave status made by kidnappers of free blacks was one hallmark of Ruggles's brand of antislavery activism, so the diary's special note of the Dixon trial might have been a reflection of Brown's communication with Ruggles as well. Presumably, for some or all of these reasons, the historian A. J. Williams-Myers concludes that Brown indeed was connected to major abolitionists in the Hudson Valley.[21]

There is clear evidence that other Manhattan-based black activists and abolitionists campaigned in the Hudson Valley in Fishkill around this time (one year later). Phillip A. Bell, a leading antislavery proponent and black newspaper editor, visited Fishkill in late August 1837 in order to circulate a petition for state legislation allowing adult black men access to the vote. Bell also hoped to gain subscribers to the newly launched *Colored American*. A notice announcing this tour of the mid–Hudson Valley—including Fishkill, Hudson, and Catskill—appeared in the *Colored American* with the following appeal: "Will our brethren in those places, try to have meetings of the colored inhabitants and their friends on those evenings?" Apparently, James was unaware of these events, chose to ignore them, or else decided not to mention anything concerning them, for they do not appear at all in his diary. Instead, for August 28, 1837, the precise day of Bell's Fishkill stopover, James recorded pedestrian business: "Went to Newburgh and got paint for the new gate."[22]

It is possible that in August 1836 Brown met instead with another David Ruggles—David Ruggles, the white horticulturalist who lived across the river just south of Newburgh in New Windsor. The Ruggles homestead reflected its owner's seriousness as a gardener, especially because the cultivated grounds included mulberry trees. In fact, in his day, Ruggles was a pioneer importer of mulberry trees into the United States in the hopes that they would stimulate a domestic silk industry. He sent entries to agricultural fairs sponsored by the American Institute of the City of New York, founded in 1829 and later merged in 1838 with the American Institute of the City of New York for the Encouragement of Science and Invention. He also participated in the Newburgh Horticultural Society, at whose annual exhibitions Brown displayed his gardening successes along with Ruggles's. The fact that the reference to Ruggles in 1836 was a solitary one, never repeated in the diary, also strengthens an argument that he may have been Brown's gardening colleague rather than an abolitionist co-conspirator because David Ruggles, the mulberry tree enthusiast, died in December 1837.[23]

Regardless of whether or not James formed a working relationship with David Ruggles the abolitionist, Williams-Myers's characterization of Brown as a "moral supporter" of the Underground Railroad best captures Brown's political stance on slavery, particularly prior to 1850. During this period, he supported the national political party boasting both a significant antislavery following and an openness toward abolitionism, and he displayed an interest in free black activism on behalf of runaways. As an example of this, James noted "a lecture on slavery at the Five Corners" in Fishkill—a lecture he probably attended.[24]

However, after 1850, James's attention to and public involvement in antislavery activity increased—no doubt prompted by the passage of the Fugitive Slave Act, and by the mounting public character of the national divide concerning slavery's existence in the country. The new law, passed in September 1850 and requiring the return of runaways to their owners, seems to have pushed him to a new level of engagement regarding slavery issues. In his diary entry for October 1, 1850, less than two weeks after the passage of the new act, Brown wrote "Great excitement in N Y concerning the slave law."[25] Perhaps, then, it is not surprising that on October 20, 1850, James "wrote to Mrs. Susan F. Williams [his former owner] of Baltimore." Given the tortured anguish expressed in his parting letter as Anthony Chase/Fisher to Jeremiah Hoffman, and given what we have gleaned of Brown's character, perhaps this new correspondence was to affirm once more the rectitude of his decision to leave; to provide evidence from his autobiography that he had become a useful, productive, free citizen; and to commend Williams for permitting his manumission in the end and not insisting on his return as a runaway.

Brown's antislavery sympathies became more visible in additional ways during the 1850s. On at least two occasions, Brown met with a Mr. Boston "on business" in Poughkeepsie; this was almost certainly Uriah Boston, a regular delegate to the antislavery political Convention of the Colored Inhabitants of the State of New York, held annually in Troy during the 1840s and 1850s and an advocate for expanded African American suffrage.[26] Brown participated in the 1857 commemoration of West Indian emancipation held in the summer of 1857, as indicated by the following diary notation: "Went to Poughkeepsie to see the celubration of the immancipation of the slaves in the West Indies Islands."[27] This was a festive, well-attended occasion. The Poughkeepsie gathering was just one of several occurring at the time throughout the country to mark the seventeenth anniversary of Britain's emancipation of its Caribbean slave population. "Large numbers" of African Americans from the many towns that lined the Hudson River and elsewhere in New York state assembled for a parade, complete with marching bands, that made its way through the major streets of the Queen City. The procession began with a speech by none other than Reverend Henry Highland Garnet—black Presbyterian minister, manumitted ex–fugitive slave from Maryland, outspoken abolitionist, vocal advocate of violent resistance by slaves to their bondage, supporter of black emigration to West Africa, and fiery orator. Church bells sounded as the marchers passed through the streets. The entire event was bookended by an opening prayer and a closing address by Reverend William Goodell—white abolitionist, author of uncompromising antislavery literature, and Liberty Party leader.[28] While Brown's journal notation implies that he was an event onlooker rather than a marcher, a member of the audience rather than a direct participant, one can easily grasp his personal identification with Garnet and his assent to Goodell's stirring words. The entire affair bespoke volumes about James's political style as well as his leanings. The *Poughkeepsie Eagle* commented that "utmost decorum prevailed throughout the entire proceedings, and the colored people in attendance won many friends among the citizens of Poughkeepsie."[29] Decorum. Order. Civility. James deeply believed in these forms of deportment and required them of himself and those with whom he *publicly* associated. At the same time, the message contained by the exemplars of such propriety could be immoderate, progressive, and/or even radical. Two years later, James Brown followed the events surrounding John Brown's siege of Harper's Ferry with three diary entries:

> October 20, 1859. We have news from Harpers Ferry of a great insurrection at that place.
> December 2, 1859. John Brown the Hero at Harpers Ferry insurrection was executed this day at Charlestown Va.
> December 16, 1859. The prisoners was hung today at Charlestown Va.

The depth of James Brown's identification with John Brown, the Harper's Ferry raid, and abolitionism was expressed in the appellation "John Brown the Hero." But that identification was held privately, expressed in his diary and perhaps to Julia and other intimate acquaintances—not in speech making, antislavery society membership, or any other public declaration of political sentiment.

Printed news sources shaped and reveal Brown's politics. There is no explicit indication that Brown subscribed to such antebellum African American newspapers as *Freedom's Journal* (1827–29), the *Colored American* (1837–41), *The National Era* (1847–60), *Mirror of Liberty* (1838–40), the *North Star* (1847–51), the *Weekly Advocate* (January–February 1837), the *Ram's Horn* (1846–48), the *Elevator* (1842), and the *Christian Recorder* (an AME Church publication that began in 1848).[30] But he certainly would have been familiar with them as mostly New York state–based papers and, as will be discussed further below, with at least the last of these publications, given his associations with African American Methodists. Then, too, he cultivated his and Julia's ties to Manhattan's African American community by frequent trips back and forth to the city, and many of the couple's black friends in New York made reciprocal trips up to Fishkill to visit the Browns. These connections kept James abreast of regional and national news affecting African Americans.

Clearly, Brown read the *People's Press,* an African American weekly paper that began publication in New York City in 1841 and lasted less than a year. His diary stated on October 28, 1842, "Wrote a letter to the editor of the peoples press." The editor of the *People's Press,* Thomas Hamilton, was born into a prominent New York black family, influential in African American religious and civic life. His father, William, owed his middle-class and leadership status within the black community to being a skilled craftsman, a carpenter, when most African Americans in the city were unskilled workers; to being a founder with James Varick of the AME Zion church denomination; and to being a regular delegate to black national political conventions in the early 1830s. As a teenager, Thomas Hamilton worked as a carrier for the *Colored American,* as a bookkeeper or mailing clerk for the *Evangelist* (a Baptist publication from 1832 to 1844), and also for the *National Anti-Slavery Standard* (published from 1840 to 1870 as the official organ of the American Anti-Slavery Society). With an early ambition to become an independent publisher, Thomas's first venture, at the age of eighteen, was the short-lived *People's Press.* The paper folded after several months, probably plagued by undersubscription, like so many early African American newspapers. But its pages had apparently championed the antislavery cause with all the fire of its youthful editor. Just what Brown had to say to the publishers of this "spicy little sheet"—so labeled by black abolitionist and a *Colored American* journalist, Charles B. Ray—is lost to the historical record, but in the tradition of antebellum black newspapers, most likely this was a note of support for the newly launched publication and its editor. Perhaps, too, Brown's letter was motivated specifically by its author's respect for the memory of the deceased senior Hamilton and, consequently, was meant as encouragement for Thomas to continue his father's legacy. Elsewhere in the diary, there is evidence that Brown was personally acquainted with various female members of the Varick family. That connection might have extended his circle of friends to include others such as the Hamiltons, who toiled together with the Varicks on race advancement projects in New York City in the 1820s when Brown first arrived in the town, and then again in 1831–32 when he seemingly resided there briefly with Peter Jay. If such connections existed, they would have provided an even more personal reason for the letter to the editor of *People's Press*.[31] There is no record of that letter, but even a tacit, oblique admission of his political sentiments in the diary, as was indicated by such an entry, was uncharacteristic of Brown, and one wonders, alternatively, if the letter was sent anonymously.

Besides a commitment to ending slavery and to equal rights for free blacks, antebellum black newspapers shared a two-pronged didactic message with an implicit politics that accompanied it. For its African American readers, this press promoted racial uplift through adherence to contemporary American middle-class standards of family, hard work, Christian piety, moral rectitude, and social responsibility. For its white readers, the press sought to dispel negative opinions of black intellectual, social, and moral debasement by celebrating black middle-class accomplishments and emphasizing mainstream, antebellum cultural values. According to the historian Joanne Pope Melish, this emphasis on black self-improvement and education represented a new kind of politics within the special context of the North where slavery had been abolished or was being abolished gradually, and where the local memory of slavery had evaporated among whites. In other words, without the conspicuous fact of slavery as an impediment to African American advancement in the North, black leaders interested in race progress could now find a receptive audience among would-be white allies only by adopting two strategies to explain and/or address the debased condition of free blacks—highlighting the flawed perception of whites who devalued black intellectual and moral ability and underscoring the importance of expanded self-uplift efforts by blacks.[32] Both strategies conformed with the life that Brown, as a master gardener, had made for himself and Julia.

Pre–Civil War black newspapers were also optimistic about the American democratic ideal and evinced a patriotic spirit. The journalism historian Frankie Hutton has observed that the "pro-American idealism that was characteristic of the columns of the newspapers and magazines hinged on the editor's belief that democratic values such as liberty and equality could eventually become viable for people of color."[33] Many of Brown's diary entries, notations that may be called patriotic observances, indicate that he shared the black press's hopeful attitude toward the American political system. For instance, virtually every year (with the exception of 1859, when he was down in Manhattan taking care of a personal business matter, and 1860, when Washington's birthday fell on Ash Wednesday), Brown's diary marked the birthday of George Washington by either simply noting it, recording his celebration of it, or by providing a rare personal commentary on it. Thus, on February 22 of the first year of diary keeping, he simply wrote, "Washington's birthday"—a notation he repeated annually each February. For the first time in 1833, that observation was embellished with the information that he participated in Washington birthday celebrations: "I crossed the river in the boat to Newburgh to attend the birth night ball"; there are a total of ten diary years in which Brown feted Washington's birthday, usually by attending a ball in Newburgh held at one of the hotels there.[34] He enjoyed these times immensely, as indicated by his disappointment when such local commemorations did not take place:

February 22, 1842. Nothing said about Washingtons Birthday.
February 22, 1843. Washington's Birthday—Not so much noticed as heretofore.

Brown's veneration of Washington is further underscored by the brief, laudatory commentary he sometimes added to his observations of the birthday: "This is the birthday of George Washington—Father of this country" or "Birthday of the immortal Washington, Father of our country" or "Birthday of Washington—the [G]reat." For Brown, other African Americans, and, indeed, most antebellum Americans, Washington was the embodiment of the American republic. A celebration of his life was a celebration of the democratic principles they hoped would result in expanded opportunities and improved lives for all "people of color" in the new nation. National holidays like Washington's Birthday and the Fourth of July were occasions that assisted all Americans in the new nation through what the historian Sarah J. Purcell calls "the complicated dance of nationalism and politics."[35] But this was especially true of African Americans in their marginalized status as citizens. So Brown's diary also marked Fourth of July celebrations. In a similar vein, Brown charted elections, visits, and deaths involving ideologically diverse presidents, senators, and other important politicians of the day, such as William Henry Harrison, James Polk, Andrew Jackson, Zachary Taylor, Henry Clay, Daniel Webster, Millard Fillmore, and Martin Van Buren. The diary was especially attentive to Clay and Webster—the leading Whigs of his time.[36] Such entries attest to Brown's optimistic embrace of the American political system for its dual ability to contain divergent opinions yet yield eventually to progressive reforms.

In addition to the black press, Brown got his news from the *Fishkill Standard*, the *New York Sun*, and the *Weekly Herald*. On August 4, 1842, he recorded, "The first number of a new newspaper at Fishkill Landing called the *Fishkill Standard* was published on Tuesday morning the 2nd inst. [this month]." Indeed, the *Standard* began publication on August 2, 1842, as a weekly. Its politics were independent, although its editor was a Whig.[37] The fact that Brown became a subscriber at its inception indicates the intensity of his interest in local affairs and his Whiggish opinions.

It is intriguing that Brown's most sustained journal reading seems to have been of the *Sun*, a decidedly conservative publication on matters of race and slavery. On May 14, 1849, Brown "wrote to N Y for the weekly Sun with the subscription inclosed." In early 1851, he complained to his diary, "Received the weekly Sun of the 19th inst and have not received one since the 22nd of January." Roughly one year later, still reading the *Sun*, he recorded, "Received the first number of the Weekly Sun of a new subscription." In January 1855, Brown "paid up for the newspaper on the 26inst." Then in the fall of 1859, he "paid the 'Sun' up to the 24th inst 48 cts" and again at the end of that year, "paid for newspaper."[38] The *Sun* was launched in 1833 by Benjamin Day as a working-class publication. Unlike the older New York newspapers, whose contents—consisting of legal notices, the text of congressional speeches, market reports, and shipping schedules—were aimed at wealthy merchants, Day's paper avoided or sharply abridged such material. Instead, in order to attract a mass readership, the *Sun* included sensational stories of circus accidents, fires, crimes, and hoaxes. It included "helped wanted" advertisements for ordinary laborers—"cooks, maids, coachmen, bricklayers, and men to open oysters in restaurant kitchens." Not surprisingly, given that it cost only a penny per issue, within a year's time the *Sun* claimed more readers than any other paper in the world.[39]

While the *Sun* tended to avoid lengthy political harangues, when it did take partisan stands they were Democratic and therefore critical of antislavery activism. Responding to this, the *Colored American* decried the *Sun's* "gross assertions, that the two races could not live together in freedom and the enjoyment of rights, but must of necessity, be subjected the one to the other or be separated."[40] The *Colored American* upbraided the *Sun* for its support of black emigration to Liberia rather than a program of racial equality within the United States.[41] In a tone similarly critical of the *Sun*, Frederick Douglass's *North Star* reprinted the following piece from the *Boston Whig* in an 1848 issue: "The *New York Sun* states that the underground abolition railway, for stealing slaves, is said to have been exceedingly busy for a few weeks past, as many as 10 or 15 runaways having passed through New York daily. It would have sounded much better had the Sun said, restoring slaves to their natural rights."

James Gordon Bennett's *New York Weekly Herald* was launched a couple of years after the *Sun,* but by 1839, it outsold its rival to claim the widest audience in the world. Its formula for success was a blending of class appeal. The *Herald* covered "the police, court trials and executions, sports and theater, docks and coffeehouses, . . . sermons and church meetings, Wall Street, and international news"—all with "unprecedented accuracy and acumen." But there was also a pioneering "personals" section, society gossip, and ads for all sorts of medical quackery.[42] Everybody read the *Herald*, including James F. Brown. On December 30, 1842, he sent a friend a copy of the *Weekly Herald.*

Yet New York state's antebellum black press also criticized the *Herald* for its disapproval of full racial equality. In the 1840s, when the diary indicates that Brown was a subscriber, the *North Star* vigorously disapproved of the *Herald's* coverage of an interracial event in New York City:

If there is any one thing utterly detested and abhorred by all well regulated and properly constructed minds, it is to hear a man devoid of all sense of moral obligation and religious sentiment, speak upon moral and religious subjects. Not that it is of any consequence what expression of low blackguardism or unfeeling ruffianism he may utter; but that chill of horror, similar to that which one may be supposed to feel when accidentally placed in rather close proximity to a rattlesnake, and hears, for the first time, its angry rattle sounding in his ears, is the result. The two are so incongruous—morality and vice—religion and the utter disregard of God and man; all that is pure, holy sublime, and all that is dark, vicious, vile; benignant love and scowling sin! Oh, the contrast is too hideous; we turn from it with feelings of horror, loathing, and disgust. *The New York Herald* of the 13th inst. has an article under the heading of "The Moral and Religious Anniversaries in New York." From that article the following extract is taken. It is perhaps not the most abominable or profane portion of the article; but it is that in which readers of the north star will be more particularly interested. "We are now in the midst of the moral and religious anniversaries of New York. . . . Yesterday there was a celebration given in the shape of a public breakfast, at the Coliseum, at which all colors and all shades of colors, met together on the common ground of liberty, equality, and fraternity. . . . There they were to be seen, eating and drinking, talking and laughing, rollicking and enjoying themselves at the same board, on the same footing of equality—men and women—black, white mixed, yellow, and all sorts, expecting the 'good time that is coming.' Oh! oh!" Readers will pardon this one infliction. The columns of the North Star are not often disgraced by the hideous trash that is issued from the office of the *New York Herald*. The feelings of this writer, of whose effusions this is a too favorable sample, must be anything but enviable. His face may be whiter than ivory; but his heart!—is the blackness of hell itself to be compared with it?[43]

Frederick Douglass would even later label the *Herald* an "ever-vigilant foe of emancipation."[44]

Brown nonetheless read and subscribed to the *Sun* and the *Herald* despite their opposition to emancipation and full racial equality because these papers were simply the best, readily available sources of information on current events in the 1830s, 1840s, and 1850s concerning New York City, the nation, and the world. Although they did not cover black community news with the depth of the African American press, even black newspapers excerpted their articles of general interest. By reading the *Sun* and the *Herald*, then, James disciplined himself to be an informed political actor.

Although regular participation in the civic sphere through his vote was the most consistent, official expression of Brown's legal citizenship, he also exercised his free status as a witness in court-adjudicated legal cases. The diary records two such instances in the 1850s. For some sort of dispute involving a Fishkill hotelier, Jeremiah Green, and a young clerk, John D. Holden, James was a witness when the case came before the county court in Poughkeepsie. This was in June 1850, and unfortunately, existing court records contain no account of the proceedings, whether civil or criminal. However, it appears that the deliberations favored the sixteen-year-old Holden because two months later, he sent James a gift of Congress water (from Congress Spring in Saratoga Springs).[45] Holden probably was working as a clerk in one of the many hotels there, and perhaps that fact (i.e., that he was free to be gainfully employed) was due to James's earlier testimony in court on his behalf.

In a second case, James appears to have had a part in upholding New York State's Married Woman's Property Act of 1848. A part of a gradual, state-by-state extension of legal rights to women occurring throughout the country at this time, the new statute was a progressive innovation in allowing married women to possess property in their own right and to act in their own property interests (buying, selling, renting, suing, and the like) before courts of law, independent of their husbands.[46] Brown traveled down to Manhattan to testify in February 1855 in the case of a Mrs. Woods before the Supreme Court of New York County. This was a low-level civil case that garnered no coverage by either the African American or the mainstream New York press but that nonetheless had significance in cementing the improved status of women before the law. In the case of *Stephen Woods and Wife v. Susan Thompson and Others*, the defendant sought to forestall Mrs. Woods's action by bringing forth a motion for an appointment of a "next friend" (surrogate) by which to prosecute the case on behalf of Mrs. Woods. The motion apparently assumed that Mrs. Woods and her husband held opposing claims regarding property belonging only to her, in an attempt to invalidate their stance as co-plaintiffs. However, with the help of James's testimony, the motion was defeated; evidently, Brown's word assisted in establishing Mrs. Woods's full concurrence with her husband regarding suit, and the fact that only her opinion mattered regarding the case anyway because the property in question was solely hers. The court decided that "the wife verifies the complaint, signifying not only her full knowledge of its contents, but her consent that the action should be commenced. *She is, therefore, the principal actor in the suit*; . . . the husband is properly joined with the wife as a co-plaintiff; that no next friend is necessary."[47] Brown's knowledge concerning the particulars of the case helped substantiate the fact that Mrs. Woods could join her husband, Stephen, in the action regarding her separate property, and that she also had the right to bring the action alone. In buttressing Woods, Brown was therefore aligned with such leading black and white antebellum abolitionists as Frederick Douglass, Charles Remond, William C. Nell, William Lloyd Garrison, and Wendell Phillips in their support for women's rights.[48]

That Brown's opinion was considered in a New York court of law is significant, not only because he was black but also because Green, Holden, and probably Mrs. Woods were white. Before the Civil War, Illinois, Indiana, Iowa, Ohio, and California had statutes barring black testimony in cases involving white parties. With the exception of Massachusetts, all the other northern states often blocked black testimony "by custom and prejudice" rather than by explicit statute.[49] Brown was heard as a fully credible witness partly because of his association with the prominent Verplanck household, but mainly because of the reputation and stature he had achieved both in Manhattan and the mid–Hudson Valley as a model "colored" citizen—an independent, steady man who knew his own mind and held to his own views, but one with a moderate, mild temperament. He was a Whig in black skin.

The Informal Politics of Association

In addition to agricultural clubs, horticultural groups, and the Whig Party, several other organized causes attracted Brown. These included the Protestant Church, extra-church religious associations (temperance advocates, Bible societies), a firemen's club, children's aid, an African American burial society, and a fraternal order. Such organizations leveraged the collective concerns of individual citizens to influence civic affairs in a number of directions. Participation in such organizations enabled James to experience first-hand the special freedom that de Tocqueville found so striking about democratic life in the young United States—freedom of association.

There is no definitive way of tracking Brown's life as a "joiner." Membership or subscription lists do not exist for most of the groups whose events he attended or followed, and with one exception, there is no record of his being an officer in any organization. But the participation level and participation rate of most antebellum Americans in most civic societies is impossible to ascertain despite de Tocqueville's wonderment at the sheer quantity of voluntary associations in the country engaging mostly ordinary citizens. What is clear is that joining was a mostly middle-class enterprise in the early and mid–nineteenth century, even as that class was being formed and becoming the culturally dominant social group in American society. In the late nineteenth century, African Americans may have been super-joiners compared with whites, according to David Fahey. But the free black antebellum community—impoverished and suffering from economic discrimination—generally did not have the time or income required to maintain formal membership in most associations. So it was the tiny group of steadily employed workers, middling sorts, who constituted the set of African American joiners.[1] Judging by the quantity of organized concerns he mentioned at one point or another in the diary, Brown was part of this group—if not officially, then certainly unofficially. His rural residence made regular participation in Manhattan-based societies with which he sympathized impossible. But appearance on membership rosters was not the only way to be public-spirited.

James was a regular churchgoer who exhibited an antebellum, evangelical Protestant sensibility in the civic sphere. The historian Mark Noll has called the nineteenth century in the United States "the Protestant century" as a way of underscoring the dominance of that branch of Christianity at that time. Certainly the denominational range of Protestant services James attended as a free man—Dutch Reformed, Episcopal, Methodist, African Methodist Episcopal, and African Methodist Episcopal Zion—confirms this point. Noll, Nathan Hatch, Jon Butler, and other historians concur that American Christianity transitioned sharply during the early republican years. From a belief system of tight orthodoxies controlled by an exclusive, educated clergy, the ascendant form of Christianity in the years leading to the Civil War became one of personal piety and reconfigured orthodoxies that were accessible to the ordinary citizen and taught by a less rigidly trained and sometimes unschooled clergy.[2] James embodied this shift by his ability to negotiate seamlessly between the older Episcopal and Calvinist forms (Dutch Reformed) and various newer Methodist or Methodist-influenced groups. But instead of forsaking the established liturgies for emerging worship experiences after moving to New York, James was able to enjoy membership in the older denominations while occasionally "moonlighting" at denominations with eighteenth- and early-nineteenth-century American origins.

While it is true that antebellum Americans were inserting ideas of freedom and democracy into church practice, James went even further than this by literally enacting these ideas in the way he exercised considerable freedom of choice in selecting a place of worship on any given Sunday. To a lesser extent, so did his employers. James was a member of St. Anna's Episcopal Church (renamed St. Luke's after 1868) in Matteawan (today, a part of Beacon), having bought a pew there for the first time in 1841, and is buried in its cemetery alongside his wife. But he also worshiped at the Dutch Reformed Church in Fishkill and occasionally attended Methodist, Baptist, and Presbyterian services as well in Fishkill, Newburgh, Manhattan, and/or Brooklyn.[3] Similarly, James's employees patronized plural churches, although to a far lesser extent than James. Daniel C. Verplanck held pews in the Dutch Reformed Church and at Trinity Church (Episcopal), both in Fishkill Landing, and at St. George's Church (Episcopal) of Newburgh. He was also a vestryman at Trinity-Fishkill when it was reincorporated in 1795. Mary Anna Verplanck "took great interest in church work" at Trinity in Fishkill Landing and later, at St. Anna's (Episcopal) in Matteawan, where the family held a burial vault. Gulian Verplanck attended both Trinity Church (Episcopal) in Manhattan, where he was a warden, and Trinity Church in Fishkill, where he was buried. So in the spread of churches attended, James and his employers were somewhat alike.[4]

But James differed from the Verplancks in his penchant for the antebellum Protestant Church's cutting edge—evangelical churches, especially Methodist—and/or for churches that held to antislavery positions. Indeed, the fastest-growing and largest Christian denomination in antebellum America was the Methodist church.[5] And it was probably with the Methodists that Brown most deeply felt connected emotionally—despite his formal membership in St. Anna's. This was probably due to earlier positive experiences with Methodists as a slave in Maryland, the firmly antislavery position of African American (AME) Methodists, and his attraction to the spiritual vanguard of the era. James recorded attending a Methodist meeting in Fishkill roughly a month after he started the diary in 1829. This was a "class," a small group of approximately ten or twelve individuals who met together weekly, according to Methodist protocol, for the purpose of prayer, to hear a Bible teaching, and to look after one another's spiritual welfare. This particular class was in its infancy, having been formed only that year in the Town of Fishkill by a Reverend Marvin Richardson, and it was probably an all-white group given its location and the fact that James did not indicate that it was "colored"—something he did in the case of African American Methodist gatherings. It would continue to meet in members' homes and the local schoolhouse until a building was erected in 1838–39.[6] During the intervening years, James mentioned attending Methodist services an average of four times per year between 1830 and 1851—the period during which he records Methodist activity of any type in the diary. While this may not seem like much, significantly, these were usually during times of Methodist camp meetings—black or white—or quarterly Methodist meetings, always black, when revivalist services took place. Often, the most prominent denominational preachers such as Reverend William H. Bishop of the AME Zion Church were featured at such times. Hence, James crossed the river in March 1836 to hear "Mr. Bishop" at a Newburgh service.[7]

For all of the otherwise measured approach he took to life, James must have liked the fervor and intensity of revivals and, in this, evinced an affinity for the evangelical spirit of antebellum Protestantism. For example, one of the Methodist services James visited in 1836 services was at an AME Zion Church, and three took place during an annual Methodist camp meeting. Notably, in July of the same year, he visited Broadway Tabernacle in Manhattan, the edifice completed only a few months earlier as "an evangelical cathedral" for Charles Grandison Finney—the foremost preacher of the Second

Great Awakening. When James was at "The Tabernacle," Finney had only just switched his denominational affiliation from Presbyterian to Congregational. But whether Methodist, Presbyterian, or Congregational, revivalist preaching techniques—dramatic and emotional—and the responses they elicited—equally dramatic and emotional—held a special attraction for African Americans drawing upon an African tradition in which the spirit world was real and observable.[8] So in another year, James readily attended camp meeting services held by "the white people" at Low Point, just a few miles north of Mount Gulian on the Hudson River. The AME Zion Church had a twenty-four-member congregation in Fishkill by 1837 and a sixty-one-member congregation in Newburgh the same year. James visited both from time to time.[9] Additionally, for a brief while, he was also drawn to the preaching of Reverend Kingston Goddard, "a gentleman of evangelical views." James recorded a visit to "Mr Godards church" in Brooklyn in November 1841. In all likelihood, this was Christ Church (Episcopal), but Goddard had resigned as rector in April of that year. So, when Brown noted another visit to "Mr Godard's Church" one year later and again in May 1843, he was referring to Emmanuel Church in Brooklyn, where Reverend Goddard served as pastor between the spring of 1842 and early 1844.[10]

The explicit antislavery and/or racially egalitarian stance of the preachers and congregations of many of the "extra" churches James visited was undoubtedly often an important element in their attraction for him. By definition the AME Church and the AME Zion Church fit this description. While the more celebrated AME Church had its beginnings in Philadelphia with Richard Allen as its key founder, the AME Zion Church originated in New York state. Receiving its charter in 1801, the latter denomination was "firmly established in 1820" when, as in the case of the AME Church, "the leaders voted themselves out of the White Methodist Episcopal Church" in pursuit of a racially egalitarian ecclesiastical experience. In addition to the famed homiletic fire of Finney's messages, the fact that the evangelist was an outspoken abolitionist as well surely drew James to the Tabernacle in the summer of 1836. The historian Craig Wilder has called the Tabernacle "the crucible of antislavery in the two cities" of New York and Brooklyn. On a visit to Manhattan in the spring of 1838, James "went to St Philips [sic] Church." St. Phillip's was a black Episcopal church led by Peter Williams Jr.—a radical black abolitionist leader in the city's African American community. Then, too, the fact that the Brooklyn Daily Eagle, a decidedly proslavery newspaper, labeled Reverend Goddard a man of "controversial temper" and "very low church views and pugnacious theological temperament" suggests that in addition to a relaxed, unceremonious approach to liturgy and a tolerance for zealous, passionate expressions of personal faith within services, Goddard may have vocalized antislavery sentiments to his congregation.[11]

It has long been understood that antebellum Methodist Christianity and, more generally, the Protestantism of the Second Great Awakening was a religion of upward mobility, agency, and self-making. Just as each individual with evangelical faith chose the way of salvation, all such individuals were held responsible by this belief system for their own fates in life. The converts' own actions determined whether they were successes or failures. Such a belief system would have provided a powerful incubator for James's thoughts as he considered running away; for his explanation to Jeremiah Hoffman and Susan Williams; for his willingness to attach himself to useful, paternalist connections like those offered by Captain Howland, Peter Jay, and the Verplancks; and for his willingness to apply himself strenuously to the task of improving his gardening through his association with Andrew Jackson Downing and others. For James and other middling antebellum African Americans, while it was true that the American system was blemished by its failure to bestow full citizenship upon them and while it was incumbent upon them to agitate in various ways to remove this stain, it was also incumbent upon them to take every advantage of every honest method available to them to prove themselves worthy of their freedom. For James, then, self-reliance was as much his duty as was advocacy for racial justice. Both supported the ideal of freedom. Self-reliance—accessing legitimate opportunities through diligent effort—was synonymous with the God-given birthright of "all men" intended by "the pursuit of happiness."

James's membership in and/or attendance at Bible society and temperance society meetings was very much about an informal yet critical politics of freedom as well. This was true for him both as an American and as an African American. One of the novel consequences of the Protestant revival of the pre–Civil War years was the institutionalization of evangelicalism through new associations and strategies such as Bible societies, tract societies, the Young Men's Christian Association, female moral societies, and the Sunday School movement. Such methods aimed at social regulation by instilling habits of order, regularity, and self-discipline in the American populace. These self-governing wonts, in fact, resulted in real material success for their devoted practitioners like James and thus wed them to the national political project of individual economic independence. Bible societies, for instance, were ecumenical Christian groups inspired by and/or connected to the American Bible Society, which had been formed in 1816 for the purpose of disseminating Bibles—and, by this, the Christian message—domestically and abroad. Fishkill Landing had its own Bible society, as did Dutchess County. James attended meetings and celebrations held by both societies in the 1830s and 1840s and was clearly convinced of the value they placed on Holy Scripture. In February 1840, Brown purchased two new Bibles—presumably for himself.[12] One was *Scott's Bible*, so named for the annotated commentary provided by Thomas Scott, an Anglican. The special feature of this Bible was its "minute comparison of each passage with others which might illustrate its meaning." A few days later, he bought another annotated Bible, *Henry's Bible*, produced by a Presbyterian minister, Matthew Henry, and valued for its illustrations. Both versions enjoyed enormous popularity in the early nineteenth century.[13] By buying these Bibles and following the activities of Bible societies, James demonstrated his participation in the general revival of Christian belief and piety at this time and his appreciation of the connection between Bible study and realization of the American Dream.

Furthermore, within the context of antebellum America, access to the Bible was tantamount to access to the elusive respectability that mainstream society hesitated to bestow upon African Americans, whether slave or free. For this reason, Frederick Douglass put the following question to readers of the *Liberator*:

> But, there are now in the United States, more than two millions of slaves, who are destitute of the Word of life, and prohibited by law from receiving it. On the week of the last religious Anniversaries in New-York, the American Anti-Slavery Society proposed to the American Bible Society, to put the slaves in possession of God's word, and pledged five thousand dollars, toward the accomplishment of that noble and benevolent object. . . . *What will the Bible Society do?* Will they comply with the proposition of the Anti-Slavery Society, . . . or will they reject the proposition, and decline the generous offer? In the sacred pages of that book, which it is the professed and sole object of the Bible Society to circulate, and put into every family, stands recorded that peremptory and last injunction of our Divine Saviour, "Go ye into all the world, and preach the gospel to every creature."[14]

Here, by linking abolitionism to Bible dissemination, Douglass sought not only to establish the morality of the antislavery cause but also to assert the humanity and citizenship rights of enslaved African Americans. He continued, "This association is called 'The *American* Bible Society'; and yet one *sixth part* of the population of these United States are destitute of the Bible, and, until the late proposition of the Anti-Slavery Society, no step had been taken in order to put it in their possession. Will the Bible Society now *go forward* and supply this one-sixth part of our population with the Word of God? If not, let them blot out the term *American* from their title and Constitution."[15] Likewise, African American leaders considered Bible reading and ownership a boon to the free black population; in their view, it aided intellectual development and encouraged upright moral behavior.[16] In these ways, black Bible promoters hoped to silence detractors who denied the suitability of blacks as full-fledged American citizens and to shore up alliances with white benefactors such as those at the Society for the Encouragement of Faithful Domestic Servants, who distributed Bibles as a reward for job stability.

Similarly, the rise of the antebellum temperance movement and Brown's interest in it coincided with Brown's flight from slavery to freedom and his personal climb from waiter to master gardener. W. J. Rorabaugh has argued that the rise of solo and communal binge drinking, particularly of hard liquor in the 1820s in the United States, was largely symptomatic of a kind of national anxiety. Americans felt great pressure to succeed as they chased a heightened dream of prosperity wrought by an expanding and transforming economy. But they lived in a reality where the possibility and presence of personal failures abounded. Americans who "[b]y working hard and intensely . . . hoped to buy freedom" increasingly retreated into alcohol-induced fantasy when the stress to experience upward mobility became too great. Middle-class industrialists who perceived that such drinking patterns were inimical to their need for a steady labor force and Methodist-influenced evangelicals who believed in a doctrine of self-making and success through self-restraint responded to this situation by combining to organize a temperance movement.[17]

By the late 1830s, when Brown's diary first includes notations about temperance-related activities, there were several national approaches to the cause of self-restraint regarding alcohol. Evangelical reformers—largely middle-class folks worried that declining morality threatened the future of the young republic—labeled all drinking a sin and urged total abstinence. For them, drunkards were hopelessly ruined warnings of the dangers of intemperance, which was synonymous with even moderate consumption of alcohol; for such reformers, the target audience was the moderate drinker. In the 1840s, these voices were joined by those of the unchurched, the working class, and actual reformed alcoholics who similarly argued for abstinence. Most notable among these were the Washingtonians of the Washington Temperance Society and the Sons of Temperance. Unlike evangelical reformers, however, these secular abstainers and reformed drunkards targeted an audience like themselves, and did not consider alcoholism to be a sin that was due to its victims' moral turpitude. They argued instead that heavy, habitual drinkers had not lost all moral sensibilities but only needed to be helped into the land of sobriety and respectability by taking a pledge of total alcohol nonconsumption aside from religious belief.[18] An alternative, perhaps most popular among elites, was a less extreme form of temperance that distinguished between fermented alcohol (beer and wine) as permissible as opposed to hard or distilled liquor (whiskey and rum). Wine consumption was allowed for medical and religious purposes (Holy Communion). These elites also looked past the use of alcohol for celebratory purposes (weddings, balls).[19] Advocates of total abstention, then, whether evangelical or not, represented the radical phalanx among antebellum temperance supporters so that roughly a dozen years after the publication in 1828 of Lyman Beecher's sermons on intemperance had energized these types, their stridency caused them to lose a good part of their former momentum with the general public, although they continued to be a force in antebellum reform.[20]

Leaders and the middle class among African Americans generally supported temperance. In fact, in black circles, drinking was equated with slavery while temperance was likened to freedom.[21] But temperance also had a further racialized dimension. The deep involvement of northern evangelical, abolitionist reformers in the promotion of abstention from alcohol was not lost on southern defenders of slavery. For this reason, southern support for the temperance movement was minimal during the 1830s and blossomed in the early 1840s only through the rise of local chapters of the secular Sons of Temperance below the Mason-Dixon line. There, the message of abstention served to buttress the authority of white males as they strove to keep themselves in check. The historian Douglas Carlson explained this well: "[T]he temperance message affirmed [the white male's] place, arguing that his reputation before his kin, church, and community, his independence, his dominant place in the family, his economic prospects, all could be enhanced or destroyed by his response to alcohol."[22]

During the period when James followed temperance activities in his diary, 1838 to 1846, African Americans were beginning to emphasize their own rationale for teetotalism, one that supplemented but was independent of mainstream, white reformist temperance: For antebellum black American leaders of this period, temperance usually meant total abstinence and in this they joined white middle-class reformers such as Gerrit Smith, who were also often radical abolitionists. The leaders' rationale was political, both pragmatically and philosophically. For one thing, it made sense to form a double-layered alliance with outspoken white critics of slavery. In addition, a radically abstemious approach to alcohol reflected black middle-class leaders' emphasis on personal responsibility and self-discipline as necessary attributes for self- and race advancement. So their advocacy of the complete rejection of alcohol consumption was an essential component of their project of free black community building. In these ways, temperance was not only good for the nation, it was specifically necessary for effective race advancement and moral uplift.[23] The *Colored American* proclaimed:

> Our people came up well under the old pledge. The Temperance cause WAS quite popular among us, but under the new pledge, the only safe and consistent one, there is, we are sorry to say, a hanging back, even among those whose names are still attached to the old pledge. A little wine at weddings, and to greet a friend with, and on other special occasions, is the plea. With as much reason we might say, yes, and a little brandy when cold or wet: the one is just as plausible as the other.—But a radical reform in this respect has commenced among us, and must go on to final conquest.[24]

Here, the newspaper applauded the original white-middle-class reformers who first pledged total abstinence as an example to the poor and working class on the grounds of practicality. They also confirmed the wisdom of the Sons of Temperance's teetotalism. Simultaneously, the editors criticized the exceptions taken by more elite reformers addressing the alcohol consumption problem.

James regularly recorded local temperance gatherings in his journal and, by so doing, his own investment in the contemporary doctrine of self-reliance and self-making. The first such notation recorded a meeting at the Dutch Reformed Church of Fishkill. This one was probably sponsored by loosely abstemious white middle-class reformers—not teetotalers, but those who believed that alcohol consumption was permissible in moderation or on special occasions. The second one, among "the colored people at Newburgh," almost certainly endorsed total abstinence, as did the third meeting in New York City. This last one was sponsored by the Sons of Temperance.[25]

Despite the apparently broad and cross-racial interest in temperance indicated by Brown's journal entries, it is significant that they ceased before the end of the 1840s. By 1850, temperance ideology suffused all reform activity so that the salience of temperance per se as a cause generally waned throughout the country and in the African American community as well. In a similar way, James's enumeration of his church attendance declined in the 1850s. As for so many Americans of his day, the new pressing issue of the day seems to have become slavery.

Still, as sectional divisions intensified during the 1850s, James formed a rather surprising new attachment—one with a local fireman's company. In the early nineteenth century, as volunteer fire companies emerged to replace the old community bucket brigade methods of extinguishing fires, they were exclusively white preserves in the North, often ethnically exclusive to particular immigrant groups. Fire companies became bastions of white working-class masculinity that linked physical prowess and mastery of technology with public service and community protection.[26] Efforts by black communities in cities to form their own volunteer neighborhood fire companies in the North were met with resistance and hostility by established hose companies, which argued that the public good would not be well served by African American companies.[27] Yet James Brown took some interest in firemen's events by helping with setup, for which he may have been paid, and/or by his attendance, as seen in the following diary entries:

December 3, 1849. Went to Newburgh to prepare for the firemens collation [a light meal] at the U S Hotel.
December 31, 1849. Went to Newburgh for a fireman's supper given at Clark & O'Dells.
August 31, 1858. A Firemans parade at the Five Corners.

The racial and class composition of most antebellum firemen's companies makes James's association with local firemen unusual. The ethnic makeup of most antebellum firemen's companies was WASP at first. These were run by prominent, socially elite men who often banned the use of alcohol, as a way of excluding immigrant participation. In response, ethnic groups, especially the Irish, formed their own companies, infused with their own cultural values. By the 1830s, then, the composition and meaning of fire company membership changed substantially in the nation's urban places. No longer "genteel dinner clubs," these fire companies served not only as a badge of status for working class and marginally middle-class men but also as emblems of ethnic pride demonstrated in their parades, balls, and control of neighborhood pubs and taverns. Supporting these crystallizing ethnic identities were new cultural rituals. In the case of the Irish, by the 1850s, St. Patrick's Day celebrations were the sites of such identity formation and solidification. James noted the occasion in 1853 and 1855 as the only "activity" for March 17 in both of those years. Ethnic, and particularly Irish, fire companies were Democratic strongholds to boot, and there was no love lost between the Irish and free African Americans whom the former viewed as competition for personal service, domestic, and unskilled jobs and as potential cheap, scab labor.[28] Indeed, during the presidency of Andrew Jackson (1829–37), the Democratic Party solidified its position as the national party of agrarian interests, the South, and urban immigrant workers such as the Irish in the Northeast. Most assuredly, such forces generally situated themselves squarely within the proslavery camp and/or were inimical to black interests.[29] How can one then explain Brown's attention to and/or involvement in these things?

Place is important here. Brown's association with fire companies occurred in upstate New York. The balls and suppers given by Newburgh firemen at places like Clark and O'Dells, a combination oyster saloon and restaurant, were fundraising affairs.[30] Along with donations and subscriptions for members, fundraising was the main way that antebellum volunteer fire companies acquired monies to purchase new equipment and to pay disability benefits to injured firemen and their families. In the 1840s, such dues ran from $1.00 to $5.00 per year.[31] So when Brown recorded, "Paid up my dues" in Newburgh in 1857, it may have been that these were membership subscription dues for a fire company there.

In Newburgh, the evolution of fire companies reflected national antebellum trends with which James identified. The period from 1825 to 1850, particularly the 1840s, saw a proliferation of fire companies, fire company membership, and intercompany rivalries. Rowdy volunteer companies were replaced by a paid firefighting force as middle-class reformers sought to impose order and discipline in the delivery of fire protection services. Fire insurance companies initially underwrote the lion's share of expenses of fire company maintenance, but they were soon helped and superseded in financial support for local companies as firefighting became more methodical and better organized with the rise of an ideology of professionalism; the introduction of steam fire engines; and the allocation of greater public funds for firemen's salaries, fire stations, and fire equipment.[32] Thus, by the time James took an interest in the fire department across the river, he may have been aligning himself with the discipline, public-spiritedness, and efficient service delivery that had come to characterize such operations.

James also identified with the firemen across the river on a class basis. The chief engineer of the Newburgh Fire Department in 1849, the year James first recorded attending a firemen's event in that town, was Benjamin F. Buckingham, a prosperous harness maker, and his first assistant was Aikman Spier, an iron founder who partnered with James Wilson, another iron founder, as Spier and Wilson. A couple of years later when James attended another firemen's celebration, Newburgh's fire chief was John K. Lawson, a successful young hardware and farm implements dealer. His first assistant was J. A. McCartney—probably James McCartney, a sash and blind maker; the second assistant was John Proudfoot, a tanner who specialized in Moroccan leather.[33] Assuming that these engineers were representative of other firefighters, Brown and Newburgh's firemen were all the middling sort. For the most part, what these workers had in common was their placement in traditional, preindustrial crafts as opposed to large manufacturing outfits and/or in modest retail operations rather than large commercial operations. In an industrializing economy, these men were all holding on to customary ways of earning a living, ways that ensured their independence. Perhaps then, men like Brown and Newburgh's fire engineers, as artisans and agricultural workers in comparison with factory wage earners of their day, felt an affinity for firemen's work because it offered relatively unregimented routines and because it served as a display of their civic commitment as "citizen-craftsmen" to "country, craft, and commercial prosperity."[34]

Finally, fireman's associations provided Brown and other men with opportunities to display their manhood. For Brown, the largely domestic, semi-private displays of restrained manhood he exhibited through church, temperance meetings, and Bible societies were supplemented by his involvement with the firemen's association as a form of martial manhood. Firemen typically displayed this type of manhood through frequent parades. In addition, heads of fire departments—whether they were called fire directors, fire engineers, or fire chiefs—in the antebellum era had the distinction of carrying speaking horns and spanners (wrenches for opening water plugs) to conflagrations in order to direct the firefighting. Fire chiefs ritually and publicly displayed their masculinity in this way both by what they carried and by supervising the activity before scores of onlookers. As firefighters scrambled to follow their chiefs' orders and douse the flames, a spectacle ensued as crowds of curious, concerned, and/or frightened bystanders took in the scene. Fire chief and firefighters were thus confirmed as civic leaders by public witnesses.[35] This was a kind of street theater through which James as a contributor to fire companies vicariously "acted out" the manhood that had proved elusive for him in Maryland; such civic manhood was also confirmed by his presence at fundraising events. This, too, was an expression of freedom. So it only made sense for James to celebrate his fifty-third birthday in 1846 with a group of firemen friends.[36]

Just as support of firefighting was a civic activity for Brown and others like him, road building functioned in the same way. In the early and mid–nineteenth century, public highway construction (as opposed to private toll road and turnpike construction) was a local affair in New York state. Pathmasters or local transportation authorities oversaw road building by community residents who decided when and where construction and/or maintenance was necessary, and who required themselves by law to donate a certain number of days each year to this task.[37] As a Verplanck family employee, James may have been asked to perform this duty for the Verplanck men. But as a taxpaying, able-bodied, voting male in Fishkill Landing, James would have been expected to provide his share of labor independently as well. James referenced his involvement in this practice several times in the diary:

May 19, 1843. Worked my time on the road.
April 19, 1845. Worked one day on the road.
June 23, 1846. Worked this day on the highway.
May 22, 1849. Worked on the highway.

James's support of local firemen was not legally mandated in the way roadwork was, but his decision to chronicle the latter connotes a certain pride in and satisfaction with his contribution to the local public welfare. By exerting time and effort at both activities, he was fulfilling a perceived civic duty.

As a responsible citizen, James also tacitly supported the movement to assist black orphans, particularly as it developed within the African American community in Manhattan. The move in mainstream America to establish a solution to the problem of abandoned children, children of destitute parents, and children of unwed mothers was yet another response to the poverty and dislocations caused by spreading industrialization and antebellum immigration. Middle-class women, generally of an evangelical stripe, spearheaded this effort. In community asylums, which began appearing in the 1830s and proliferating over the next two decades, the parentless received basic survival needs—food and shelter—but also education and religious instruction.[38] In Manhattan, the Association for the Benefit of Colored Orphans was founded in 1836 by a group of white women who served as the overseers of the Colored Orphan Asylum (COA). Solutions to the problem of needy African American children, usually in the form of informal adoptions, had already been implemented by the free black community of New York City. But by 1838, the COA became an important point of intersection for black and white reformers committed to assisting poor, orphaned children. While the city's blacks continued in independent community relief efforts, they also now supported the COA through monetary and clothing donations and/or through adoptions from the COA.[39]

James's connections to orphan work were of the informal and independent type that had become part of the tradition of social responsibility among middling antebellum African Americans. In black circles, aid to children was not limited to those without parents. It included assistance for single parents through unofficial adoptions—sometimes temporary—and the boarding of school-age children of black family friends from good homes in order to further these youngsters' education. In James's case in particular, participation in this work resulted from the coincidence of several things: the fact that he and Julia enjoyed a relatively comfortable living as free blacks, the fact that he and Julia were childless in New York state, connections the Browns had made with the Varick family of New York, and the Browns' general support for antebellum moral reform. The diary provides documentation for at least three informal or temporary "adoptions" or "guardianships." The first was of Aurelia Varick, daughter of Daniel and Mary Varick. James and Julia were friends with Daniel and Mary Varick—eldest son and daughter-in-law of James Varick, AME Zion Church pioneer, and residents of Manhattan. This tie had probably been first formed during James's early days in New York City—before his legal manumission and/or through associations with Manhattan's Bethel AME Zion Church. When the Varicks' daughter, Aurelia, was seven or eight years old, Daniel and Mary put her under the temporary guardianship of James and Julia, who cared for her while she attended one of the Fishkill Landing district schools. Such schools were free, which was not yet the case in 1838 in New York City when Aurelia relocated to the Browns' home. At that time the African schools (for African American children) in Manhattan were supported by parents' tuition along with private and church funds under the supervision of the Manumission Society. This situation would continue until 1841, when the city's "colored schools" were unified by law under the oversight of the New York Public School Society. Still, such schools remained segregated throughout the antebellum period—not by explicit law, but by custom. In contrast, in some rural areas of New York state—in such places as Fishkill Landing, apparently—whites tolerated black attendance at district schools. Because state law required black access to public school after 1827, in rural areas such as those surrounding Mount Gulian where the black population was extremely sparse, simple economics would not have justified the use of tax monies for separate black educational facilities. In fact, the first-known public black school in Fishkill Landing was not built until 1859, probably only as the African American population there expanded. So in settling their daughter, Aurelia, with the Browns for several years, the Varicks ensured their child a free, integrated common school education.[40]

This was an easy enough arrangement to sustain. The Varicks maintained ties through their church network with the AME Zion church in Newburgh, and this in itself was cause for regular visiting. Mary, in fact, brought Methodist devotees from Manhattan to attend Methodist camp meetings in Newburgh. Similarly, Daniel came to check on his daughter. In addition, Julia and James regularly traveled back and forth to Manhattan by steamboat and often took Aurelia along. In February 1840 when she was about ten years old, "Aurelia quit Miss Clark's school" but apparently soon returned to her studies for another three months because Julia took her down to Manhattan in May of that same year. The Browns cared for Aurelia for several years this way, until approximately 1845 when she was fifteen and reestablished in New York City with her mother. This made sense as free school education was typically available in New York state for "colored" children over five and under sixteen.[41]

The Browns may have also taken care of another African American child, Isaac Allaire, whose mother, Mary Allaire, was apparently a family friend in Manhattan—a "mulatto" widow with two "mulatto" children. In the fall of 1846, Julia brought Mary's son, Isaac, up to Fishkill "to board and to go to school." As the Varicks had done for Aurelia, fourteen-year-old Josephine visited her younger brother in early December 1846, in all likelihood to check on him and to relieve his homesickness. In early summer after the school year had ended, Josephine came up to Fishkill Landing to retrieve Isaac. But less than a week later, Mrs. Allaire wrote James to request that he and Julia "keep [her six-year-old] son." This would have been an understandable request from a widowed African American mother with two dependents. She was relegated in all likelihood to domestic service for income, and it would have been all she could do to keep herself housed, clothed, and fed. James responded a few weeks later. Although the diary is not explicit regarding the content of that reply, circumstantial evidence suggests that he and Julia took in Isaac that summer while Aurelia moved out as a young adult worker. For one thing, Aurelia Varick, fifteen years old by then, "left [Fishkill Landing] for N Y to take her place on the steamer Columbia" four days after James's letter of reply. The *Columbia* was a Hudson River steamboat with Manhattan's Harrison Street and Hudson, New York, as its terminal points with several intermediary stops, including Newburgh. Old enough to work for a living, Aurelia was probably put to task on this nearby route—within frequent and daily reach of her Manhattan family and her adopted Fishkill Landing family—in order to work as a steamboat stewardess, someone who attended to female passengers' needs. Given that space was already available in their home for Isaac and even more so with Aurelia gone, the Browns could have easily assented to taking him in for a longer term; after all, their household and perhaps their family budget had included a long-term child boarder for some years. This arrangement lasted four years with Josephine visiting her brother at the Browns' from time to time. By 1850, both Josephine and Isaac were back living with their mother in Manhattan. With Josephine now eighteen years old, the contribution she could now make to the household finances would enable Mrs. Allaire to assume full responsibility for her nine-year old boy.[42]

James and Julia's altruism toward needy black children was reinforced by Aurelia Varick's paternal Aunt Emeline Varick Bastien. According to an AME Zion clergyman and Varick family biographer, Emeline served as a nineteenth directress of the board of the Colored Orphan Asylum.[43] The asylum was founded by two white Quaker women. Initially, black middle-class reformers criticized it for its limited goals for black children. But by the 1840s the COA responded favorably to activist blacks who promoted education for the institution's wards and who felt that the asylum should shelter the children of poor single parents as well as the totally parentless. Emeline Varick, well educated and married well to a public-spirited black Haitian emigré hairdresser, was a reformer in her own right. In 1850 and 1851, she became directress of the newly organized North Star Association of Ladies. This group supported "the emancipation and elevation of the colored people" by fundraising for Frederick Douglass's abolitionist newspaper, the *North Star*, and by soliciting funds and supplies to aid fugitive slaves.[44]

Another child of struggling black friends brought the Browns into direct, formal contact with Manhattan's Colored Orphan Asylum. In August 1854, James learned that William H. Thompson, the son of David and Hester Thompson, was in the COA. James and Julia were friends with Hester and David before their marriage fifteen years earlier, and this association also linked the Thompsons to the Varicks. In the summer of 1838, Hester Purnell worked as a cook or maid for the Verplancks' neighbors the DeWindts. Because of her proximity to the Browns, occasionally Hester chaperoned young Aurelia Varick back and forth to Manhattan to visit her family. At the same time, David corresponded with James and visited the Browns while courting Hester. Two months after her marriage to David in March

1839, Hester moved permanently to Manhattan, presumably to be with or closer to David, but the couple continued to visit and correspond with the Browns over the next three years. Then in the fall of 1844, the Thompsons "sailed for London." A year later, they were back in the United States and probably had at least one child by now, given James's first reference in a diary entry at the time to "David c Thompson and family." The child was William Henry Thompson, born in April 1845, only a few months before his parents' reunion with James and Julia in the United States. David was probably a seaman because in October 1845 he "sailed for London on the ship Mediator"— a packet ship that regularly provided American food provisions to England. This time, David left his wife and son at home, as he would on future trips. A seaman's life exacted a high toll on the family—low sailors' pay, protracted absences, financial hardships for Hester as a black female head of household while David was away, anxieties regarding physical dangers during voyages, emotional readjustments during periods of return, and unemployment during economic downturns. Not surprisingly, in November 1847, the couple separated.[45]

Still, David and Hester retained individual friendships with the Browns and may have experienced intermittent reconciliations. In what must have been a difficult farewell, David visited the Browns in Fishkill Landing on October 30, 1848, before leaving the next day from New York City for a three-year maritime stint in California. No doubt needing emotional and financial support, Hester then moved in with the Browns in their upstate home. She used their residence as a base while she traveled up and down the Hudson, probably working in various households as a domestic. During David's absence, James continued to write to David and assumed the role of surrogate father for little William and caretaker for his mother, Hester. He took the boy to church with him and visited New York City to see about his sick mother in mid-July 1851. But Hester died of consumption (tuberculosis) in Brooklyn one month later in August 1851. James took charge of six-year-old William because his father, David, continued to work at sea. Aurelia Varick, by then married to a one-time seaman, Thomas C. Hoffman, may have also assisted. But the demands of parenting such a young child for fifty-eight-year-old James were too much for him and even the much younger Aurelia because sixteen months after his mother's death, William H. Thompson was admitted to the orphan asylum. This strategy would have made sense and was probably advised by Aurelia's Aunt Emeline. At the time of admission, David, as father, but residing in California, "agreed to pay fifty cents a week for board, tuition and clothing" for his son. Apparently, this arrangement was supposed to be temporary and James probably was to make payments with later reimbursement from David. But eight months later, James informed the asylum that he could no longer pay board for William and "surender[ed] him to the Institution" after providing a letter from David in California declaring the latter's inability to provide for his son's upkeep.[46]

The next year in 1855, David finally returned home after an absence of six years. His reunion with William and the Browns was no doubt bittersweet. He was reunited with his child and his friends, but this happiness was offset by the stark realization of his wife's death, the institutionalization of his son, and the brevity of his reconnection with friends and family. After just two months, in May 1855, he shipped out once more for London on the packet ship *Rhine*. A true friend to the Thompson parents, James continued to look after William from afar. In August 1857, he wrote to the "Superintendent of the colored orphan asylum," probably inquiring after the boy. He soon learned that William had been "put in Raritan Township Monmouth County [New Jersey] In. [that month]" a couple of months earlier. Two weeks later or so, James took the train down to Manhattan, on his way to New Jersey "to see about Wm H Thompson." Young William was now twelve years old in 1857, and the COA evidently had executed the fairly standard practice at the orphanage of indenturing ten- to twelve-year olds, mainly in the surrounding countryside in Westchester County, Long Island, Connecticut, and New Jersey. In fact, William was indentured to David Williamson, a white farmer of some means. According to the standard terms of such indentures, masters would provide for the education and religious instruction of their charges until they turned twenty-one and the indenture was terminated. At this point, boys received one hundred dollars and girls received fifty dollars. At sixty-four years of age, James realized that this was the best he could do to ensure a good future for William.[47] In the tradition of determined agency on the part of black parents whose circumstances forced them to place their children in the care of the COA—a tradition well described by the historian Leslie Harris—James had done his best to remain involved in William's life by working with the COA administration and staff to devise individualized care and visitation plans for their children and/or loved ones.[48]

James and Julia Brown's involvement in the upbringing of the children of their friends may have also had a deeply personal meaning. While still slaves in Maryland, he or they may have had children during their young adult years—children from whom they were separated by the rules of the peculiar institution or by James's flight to freedom. More than twenty years after escaping bondage in Maryland, on February 5, 1848, for the first time James mentioned in his diary receiving a letter from "a sons wife at Williams Port Washington County, Maryland," implying by the use of the singular article that there was more than one son. The letter's author, then, was perhaps a daughter-in-law, the wife of a son sired when he was a young man. The "Williams Port" reference links the son to the extended biological family of James's/Anthony's former owners, William E. and Susan F. Williams, because Williamsport, Maryland owed its beginnings to the farm and lands owned by General Otho Holland Williams, the father of William E. Williams. Whereas William E. had developed a farm at Ceresville near Fredericktown, Otho's second son and William E.'s brother, John Stull Williams, had business interests in both Williamsport and Hagerstown around 1818, two years after James seems to have entered the Williams household.[49] James's services might have then been "legitimately" required in Williamsport and Hagerstown as well as in Ceresville and Baltimore as William E.'s slave. Fredericktown, in fact, was only twenty-four miles from Williamsport and just twenty-two miles from Hagerstown. And after all, William E. had twenty-seven other slave workers on which to rely by 1820.[50] As a young man, perhaps James/Anthony had then fathered one or more children by a female slave in either Williamsport or Hagerstown while he was in either place on loan to John for some task. And if Hagerstown was where his son had been born and lived part of his life, a visit to the child would partly explain his presence there in 1825, the year in which he received a note addressed to him in that place from Reverend Harper in Fredericktown.

Was this the son whose wife wrote to him thirty years later? Just two months after hearing from this daughter-in-law, James learned that a "Mrs. Chase" had drowned herself. Who was she? The same son's wife? Or perhaps the wife of his deceased father, Robert Chase—a stepmother, because he surely would not have referred to his biological mother in such a formal way? In any case, the event shook James deeply—enough for him to mention his attendance at church twice on Sunday, March 26, 1848, alongside his notation of the suicide. Circumstantial evidence certainly suggests that this Mrs. Chase was African American: the shared last name with Anthony and Robert, and the probable marriage to one of James's/Anthony's sons. Approximately one year later, near the anniversary of the suicide, Brown received a letter from "Mrs. Harriot Chase of Williamsport," which he answered the next day. Now, who was *this* woman? The census records a black woman, Harriet Chase, married to a Henry Chase, both living in New Market (Frederick County), Maryland, in 1860. Perhaps this was a new, second wife for son Henry, and perhaps this was her letter of introduction to her new father-in-law. In any event, New Market was in very close proximity to James's old Fredericktown home, in fact just six miles away. Henry was then a forty-five-year-old laborer, born approximately in 1815 when James was a young man of just twenty-two years. Following this line of speculation, perhaps James's emotional tie to Henry's mother was thin. Or, perhaps Julia Williams Brown was Henry Chase's mother. And perhaps James's first romantic and sexual liaisons with her occurred when he was Anthony Chase, and subsequent to these attachments, she had taken the name Julia Chase. This would provide further explanation for why James had recorded in the diary their marriage in 1826 as one between "James F. Brown and Julia Chase." This would supply an additional reason for Julia's hesitation regarding Anthony Chase's plans to run away from Maryland. As a mother, she would have worried about the future not only for James/Anthony and for herself as his wife, but for Henry as their son, still in bondage. Indeed, male fugitive slaves historically far out-numbered female runaway slaves because of the reluctance of slave mothers to leave their children in bondage.[51] If the pair ultimately did leave behind a son or more offspring because of perceived necessity, their willingness to assist the free black children of friends and/or to adopt a child in New York becomes more understandable and even poignant. Through their dependent and orphan work, they hoped to contribute to the building of a future generation of African Americans in the North who were independent by virtue of their training and education, and therefore free. As the historian Lois Horton has well summarized, "[F]reedom and citizenship were considered incompatible with dependence [in antebellum America]. Politicians argued that African Americans, indentured, enslaved, or identified with slavery, were incapable of independence and therefore not entitled to full citizenship."[52] James and Julia intended to disrupt the association of black people with economic and mental dependency—one youth at a time—and by so doing, liberate each for full participation in the civic sphere.

Another set of Brown's public-spirited activities deserves notice—his work to establish "a colored burial ground" in Fishkill. From the colonial period, African Americans had labored to preserve spaces for the burial of their loved ones—places on the national landscape in which they could conduct their own funerary and interment practices. The seventeenth- and eighteenth-century African Burial Ground in lower Manhattan is one of the more widely recognized examples of this. Black insistence on the demarcation of special locations in which to bury their dead continued into the early republican era of the late eighteenth century and the pre–Civil War years of the nineteenth century. After the African Burial Ground was closed to future use in 1790 to make way for the designs of land speculators, Manhattan's African Society, the first-known black religious organization in New York City, petitioned authorities in 1795 for space for a church and burial ground. For free blacks throughout the antebellum period in the United States, African American burial traditions established in the colonial period soon commingled with emergent, mainstream cultural practices regarding death and burial. New public responses to death in the form of tolling church bells, Victorian mourning dress, printed elegies and obituaries, and especially manicured, gardenlike cemeteries helped buttress established African American attention to burial sites. For the general American public, death no longer held grim associations, and graveyards were no longer left unkempt and weed-choked—the haunts of ghosts and goblins. Rather, new kinds of Romantically inspired final resting places like Boston's Mount Auburn Cemetery (1831), Philadelphia's Laurel Hill Cemetery (1836), and Brooklyn's Greenwood Cemetery (1838) were beautifully landscaped, sylvan, pastoral retreats. This would happen as one peacefully meditated on the best memories of the departed, a process that was enabled by the bucolic setting.[53]

Within the antebellum culture of death, mourning, and burial, the concern of African Americans to ensure proper burial spaces took on an additional meaning. For striving blacks, whether working-class, middling, or solidly middle-class, burial grounds—complete with epitaphed gravestones—literally marked the respectability of the deceased for eternity just as their sobriety, industriousness, and steadiness had during their lifetimes. Perhaps it was the fresh pathos of attending Hester Purnell Thompson's funeral that motivated James to participate in a local meeting to buy a black burying ground on August 29, 1851. It was less than ten days after Hester's burial in Brooklyn's Greenwood Cemetery. James and his partners moved swiftly. In less than three days, the group selected a lot and in early September, James began soliciting funds to purchase it on behalf of "the colored people of Fishkill Landing and vicinity." By late October, he and his friends had secured "all the money for the Colored Peoples Union Burying Ground." As one of five black trustees for the association, he registered the deed for the property—bought from John P. DeWindt for $125. On the last day of the month, James recorded with some satisfaction, "J[ohn] Henry Roose was buried in the colored peoples new Burying place It being the first internment in that ground." Just north of the village of Fishkill, east of Fishkill Landing, a black burial ground had been in existence since at least 1832. But James and his friends evidently had considered this location inadequate for their black neighbors for some reason. Perhaps the acreage was too small (as of 2000, only nine gravestones had been found there); perhaps it was too far from the Landing; perhaps its maintenance did not conform to the trustees' standards. Taking matters into their own hands, then, James and his associates ensured that the new Colored People's Union Burying Ground provided a permanent statement of the dignity of the lives of all those who were laid to rest there.[54]

Mutual benefit societies and fraternal orders proliferated in the United States as yet another type of voluntary association appealing to antebellum Americans, including Brown. There is no evidence that James ever formally joined a fraternal order, yet he left clues of an affinity for the Odd Fellows. In 1843, Peter Ogden, a black sailor in New York, received permission from a Manchester, England, Odd Fellows lodge to launch an African American branch of the group. This was called the Grand United Order of Odd Fellows (GUOOF) to distinguish itself from the older, American Independent Order of Odd Fellows (IOOF). The latter was an exclusively white, male club, but both groups were committed to benevolent and charitable work on behalf of their members.[55] Given the occupation of its founder, it is not surprising that Manhattan-based black seamen within James' social circle—specifically Thomas Hoffman (Aurelia Varick's eventual husband) and David C. Thompson (Hester's husband)—both were GUOOF members. In December 1844, a Poughkeepsie branch of the GUOOF, the Olive Branch Lodge, was established. For a while, then, particularly in the 1840s and early 1850s, James charted Hudson Valley and Manhattan Odd Fellows' activities. He noted in October 1845, "The Order of the colored Odd Fellows had their first anniversary celebration," recorded the dedication of a local Odd Fellows Hall, and attended concerts in that venue over the next four years. James identified vicariously with this brotherhood, not only because of his friends' memberships, and not just because of his own benevolent work, but also because perhaps he had once been a seaman.[56]

In practical terms, the GUUOF adhered to the IOOF guiding motto, "Visit the sick, bury the dead, relieve the widow, educate the orphan." And so did James F. Brown. Given Brown's efforts on behalf of ailing Hester Purnell Thompson and other ill friends, his attention to her burial (probably at his own expense), his leadership in securing a black cemetery in Fishkill Landing, his fostering of friends' children, and his solicitousness toward widows such as Josephine Allaire, clearly Brown was an Odd Fellow at heart, if not officially.[57]

Multiple motives fueled Brown's associational life—informal and unofficial as it was. There was his reformist, Methodist-informed sensibility. In its African American refraction, this evangelistic impulse concerned itself not only with individual spiritual improvement but with national progress as well through the attainment of social justice for the black community. Moreover, Brown's sense of manhood prompted his participation in male leisure activities and general acts of social responsibility. In all of this, he demonstrated what the historian Craig Wilder has called an "ethic of mutuality."[58] Certainly, Americans of all types—female and male, working-class and middle- or upper-middle-class, immigrant and native-born, rural and urban—displayed this tendency for civic action through voluntary associations. By such exhibits of citizenship, they hoped to improve life in their young democratic society. This was a national project. Additionally, for Brown, though, as an African American, the exercise of the freedom to associate in numerous ways also furthered a nationalist project—that of race advancement.

Conclusion

Through his escape from bondage, exemption from wage slavery, and rich associational life, James F. Brown contributed to the definition of freedom in the new nation. His letter to his Maryland masters provided a philosophical argument against human slavery and his act of running away declared the untenability of such a system in a democratic country. Brown's successful enterprise supported the claims of proponents of free labor and therefore the commitment of the young republic to democratic capitalism. His engagement with partisan politics and various organized causes confirmed civil society as a legitimate and powerful political realm in the new, free nation. James F. Brown, as a new kind of political actor—the national citizen—therefore helped define by his life the meaning of free citizenship in nineteenth-century America.

Brown's role as a caretaker was probably inspired during his Maryland youth. While James and Julia had no children living in the North, he was a custodial household head of an extended African American family—many with origins in the South. Certainly he functioned as godfather to and guardian of fictive kin—the garden laborers under his supervision, neighbors on his street—but there are also several hints in the diary of strong ties to extended biological family. Levin Huston, Hester Purnell Thompson, William Henry Thompson, George Purnell, Anthony Bradford, Harriott Chase, Comfort Dennis, and Robert Chase were all related by blood or marriage to him. And although at first glance James seems to have spent his slave days in Fredericktown and Baltimore, all of these particular individuals link James to Maryland's Eastern Shore—more specifically, to Worcester and Somerset counties. Levin, Brown's brother-in-law in Salisbury, then, was not the only tie to this area.

To be sure, Levin Huston was the most persistent family connection James held to the region. For nearly thirty years—from October 7, 1830, through April 17, 1859—he recorded his correspondence with Levin. Levin visited James in Fishkill Landing in 1842 and again five years later. But mostly the two exchanged letters, the content of which James never disclosed, but which probably included snippets of everyday life much as the diary itself does.[1] Levin was not just the conduit for money to James's father, but the two apparently shared similar experiences, religious sentiments, political views, and outlooks regarding personal and race advancement as well. Levin and James were legally manumitted by their owners within one year of each other— Levin in 1829 and James, finally, in 1830. Levin and James both purchased their wives' freedom—James in 1826 and Levin in 1849. Huston enjoyed modest material success, as did Brown—Huston by working "as a trader and grocer" and Brown as a gardener. Both men had Methodist leanings and/ or affiliations, and Huston even helped found Salisbury's black John Wesley Methodist Episcopal Church. Just as Brown and others would purchase land for use by Fishkill Landing's African American community (the burial ground), Huston, along with five other freedmen, bought property in Salisbury, Maryland, in 1837 for the erection of Wesley ME Church. It seems, too, that both men favored the Whig Party because in the fall of 1844, James sent his brother-in-law a "representation" of a Whig procession. This was probably a sketch of a huge, pro-Whig parade held in lower Manhattan, "the best ever," a few weeks before the 1844 presidential election, that had appeared in the *New York Herald*. The drawing attempted to depict the size and enthusiasm of the onlooking crowd, the vast number and variety of "Mechanics and Artisans" marching in the procession, and the floral wreath–festooned windows in residences along the route.[2]

But there were several other African Americans from Somerset County or neighboring Worcester County on Maryland's Eastern Shore besides Levin Huston who found their way into James's world and/or consciousness in Fishkill Landing, and, remarkably, all of these were either free blacks or else came from free black families. Worcester, the easternmost county in Maryland, was carved from Somerset County in 1742 and, owing to the labors of Quakers and Methodists, boasted a relatively high proportion of free blacks prior to the Civil War. Robert Chase, James's father, was free on April 9, 1821, when he leased land in Worcester County—some seventeen years before he died. Another probable relative, George Purnell, was a four-year-old slave in Worcester County when his owner set up a gradual manumission plan for him on August 23, 1824: George would be freed at the age of twenty-one, roughly in 1841. Apparently, George made his way to the Hudson Valley and probably worked as a sailor as a very young man because James mentioned a George Purnell in Newburgh, New York, in 1846; a George Purnell sending him some seine twine in 1846; and writing to a George Purnell in 1847.

Perhaps this was Hester Purnell Thompson's brother. Indeed, eight slaves with the last name Purnell were manumitted in Worcester County, Maryland, between August 1824 and July 1834, and while Hester was not listed, George was the first one of these. The records of the New York Colored Orphan Asylum reveal that Hester was, in fact, James F. Brown's cousin. This regional, familial link may also explain James's solicitousness toward "little Hester," as he once called her, and her son, William Henry Thompson. Similarly, Anthony Bradford, for whom James conveniently found a position as a coachman for Mrs. Daniel Verplanck in 1836, may have been related to Esther Bradford, manumitted in Worcester County in 1832 as a grown woman. Likewise, James's sister, Comfort Dennis, with whom he corresponded between December 1830 and July 1857, according to the diary, was probably originally from Somerset County; Linda Dennis, a free black woman, purchased land there for herself and her two daughters—Caroline and Nancy—in June 1826.[3]

But here, the plot truly thickens, for an enterprising "free Negro" named James Brown resided and owned properties in Somerset County, Maryland, in the years before the Civil War. This Brown became a principal landowner in the area by acquiring real estate—"Taylor's Addition," "Baker's Folly," and "Robertson's Swamp"—in the 1820s, 1830s, and 1840s. His holdings attracted other free blacks to the vicinity, and in several instances he directly sold portions of his own parcels in Somerset County to other free African Americans who relocated there from outside the county. The resulting concentration of properties held by free blacks in Somerset County became known as Santo Domingo, a still surviving community in present-day Wicomico County, Maryland.[4] The political self-consciousness behind the naming of this community cannot be overlooked: A group of recently freed African Americans in Somerset County chose to identify their neighborhood with the first independent black nation in the Atlantic world, Haiti on the island of St. Domingue or Santo Domingo—a country where self-liberated, former slaves predominated; a country symbolizing black autonomy and black freedom. Moreover, James Brown was the definite leader of this American community. He enjoyed a "patron–client" relationship between himself and his black neighbors. Not only did he sell land to some of them for their private possession, but he also provided the land for the first African American church in the area.[5]

Another possible layer of the identity for our James F. Brown surfaces with this information, and this one is the most tantalizing of them all. Were James Brown of Somerset County, Maryland, and James F. Brown of Fishkill, New York, one and the same black man, especially given that their ages are off by only one year according to census records, albeit these are rarely precise? There are several reasons to think not. Brown-of-Somerset had children, while Brown-of-Fishkill did not, at least according to federal records. The census clearly listed Brown–of–Santo Domingo as a resident of Somerset County in 1820, 1840, and 1850, and Brown–of–Mount Gulian as a resident of Dutchess County in 1840, 1850, and 1860. In 1820, the Somerset Brown was a farmer whose nine-member household included three free black males under the age of fourteen (sons?); one free twenty-six- to forty-four-year-old male; three free black males over forty-five years old; and one fourteen- to twenty-five-year-old black female. In 1840, the household still contained nine persons, but this time they included one free black male under ten years of age; two ten- to twenty-four-year-old free black males; one thirty-four- to fifty-five-year-old free black male; one free black female under ten years of age; three free twenty- to twenty-four-year-old black females; and one free black thirty-six- to fifty-five-year-old female. Again in 1850, Brown-of-Somerset's household consisted entirely of free African Americans, but in this year there were only seven persons in all. The Somerset Brown was listed as a fifty-eight-year-old farmer owning $800 worth of real estate. No one in the household, including himself, was literate, and in addition to his wife and two daughters, three other black males ranging in age from four to twenty-two years old lived with him as well. Combining county land records and federal census records reveals that the Somerset Brown was married twice; first to a Lydia and then to a considerably younger Isabella (she was twenty-five when he was fifty-eight), probably after Lydia died. In contrast, James F. Brown of Dutchess County was literate and in the census, he and Julia were the only two members of his "official" household in 1840, 1850, and 1860.[6]

Brown–of–Santo Domingo, however, may have been a role model for Brown–of–Fishkill Landing. Young Anthony/James, the quasi-free slave in Baltimore and western Maryland, would have known of Brown–of–Somerset/Santo Domingo through such family members as his father in neighboring Worcester County; Levin Huston in Salisbury, with whom he regularly corresponded; or the Purnells, especially because there was also a George Purnell, a free black man and a probable cousin, who lived in Somerset County in 1820 as one of 105 free African American household heads there—Brown–of–Santo Domingo included. African American Purnells, especially those named George, were indeed ubiquitous in the Somerset–Worcester region—two in one household, apparently father and son, in 1850 and another one living with a white farming family in the same year.[7]

To add to the intrigue, a "coloured woman" named Hettie Fisher living in Somerset County fathered an illegitimate child, evidently by a white man, in 1827. Perhaps Brown–of–Fishkill Landing took one of his earlier names, Anthony Fisher, from her—especially if she was his mother, sister, or some other familial connection. From his father, he probably took his other name, Anthony Chase. Add to the double monikers the strong possibility that the Santo Domingo black community leader James Brown was the inspiration for Anthony Chase/Anthony Fisher to take on the name James F. Brown as he sought to shed his slave identity. Perhaps, upon determining to escape, Anthony Chase/Anthony Fisher attempted simultaneously to confuse, trump, and trounce his Baltimore owner by taking on a name that he associated with freedom, success, and community leadership. The use of aliases by blacks, in fact, was common, if property records in Maryland are any indication. For example, Littleton Purnell was referred to as "alias Bushhead Lit" in two separate Worcester County manumission documents. A deed of sale referred to "Comfort Morris alias Comfort Pollitt free Negro of Worcester County." In yet another land sale, the register said of the same woman: "This deed identifies Comfort Morris with a known alias as Comfort Pollitt and identifies her as a free negro woman of Worcester County."[8] Perhaps, then, owners were not just fooled sometimes by such aliases; rather, masters and whites tacitly accepted, tolerated, and cooperated with them as well in other instances. Perhaps this is why Susan F. Williams, James's former owner, was unconcerned in her correspondence with Daniel C. Verplanck about validating the identity of her former servant despite his triple names mentioned in their exchange of letters—James F. Brown/Anthony/Anthony Fisher.

Speculation that James Brown–of–Somerset County served as role model for James F. Brown–of–Dutchess County is supported by the achievements of both men. As free African Americans, they both encouraged black property acquisition. Just as Brown-of-Somerset donated land for the black church there, James F. Brown helped the local black community acquire a burial ground and may have been instrumental in helping local black Methodists to acquire from John DeWindt land for their first church in Fishkill Landing. Just as Brown-of-Somerset sold lands to free blacks there, James F. Brown apparently facilitated land purchases by his African American friends—again from John DeWindt. Just as Brown-of-Somerset served as patron to several African American clients, the Verplancks and DeWindt operated as patrons for James F. Brown, who, in turn, served as patron-broker for the Fishkill Landing black community through his relationship with the two white community leaders.

In his letter to Susan Williams, Anthony Chase explained his flight to freedom as a necessity in order for him to fulfill his manhood—a restrained manhood that required an avenue for him to pursue his personal ambitions and to provide steadily and securely for his wife, Julia. Having unburdened himself of chattel status and having established a solid economic footing, he widened his paternalism to include extended family, co-workers, and neighbors. The ability to assist them by his own participation in the civic sphere in the achievement of expanded choices and enhanced lives, after having done so for himself and Julia, was perhaps the most satisfying kind of freedom of all.

In the last six years of his journal, years corresponding with momentous times for the nation, James F. Brown recorded fewer and fewer of his days and gave more and more attention to four main subjects in descending order of frequency—the weather, his gardening, the deaths of longtime neighbors and friends, and local misfortunes. A man who had carefully chronicled election results, the visits and deaths of politicians and presidents, major urban riots, and technological firsts—a man who was once a fugitive slave—barely acknowledged the titanic struggle to maintain the Union during the Civil War. The diary mentions nothing about Lincoln's election to the presidency in 1860, or his reelection in 1864. It is silent about the April 1861 firing on Fort Sumter and the advent of North–South hostilities. It offers no summary of major battles. It ignores the Emancipation Proclamation and does not acknowledge Robert Newlin Verplanck's assumption of a United States Colored Troops command. It overlooks the Appomattox treaty, Lincoln's assassination, and the ratification of the Thirteenth Amendment to the U.S. Constitution. The only hints that James was even aware of the great conflict were two entries: one on April 26, 1861—"A company of volentears left Fishkill in the cars for Albany to join the troops at Washington"—and the other on February 3, 1863—"A regiment left Newburgh for N Y."[9]

The tapered and uncharacteristically narrow diary content during these years may be explained in several ways. When Lincoln assumed the Oval Office, James was sixty-eight—twenty years older than the average American expected to live around this point in national history. In 1866 when the diary abruptly stopped, James was seventy-three and showing signs of his age. The years of outdoor work were catching up—damaged hands, recurring back problems, then a sprained shoulder in the fall of 1858 that put him out of commission for a week. In late spring of 1860, he complained of sore eyes "so as not to be hardly able to work." He was more easily distracted and even lost one of his precious timepieces.[10] These ailments made it increasingly difficult for him to keep up the journal with regularity.

Perhaps deaths closer to home had a greater impact than war casualties. The deaths of neighbors and close friends grew as James aged. The list of deaths he recorded in his diary was long between 1860 and 1866: Robert Williams, a black laborer who, with his family, had once rented the upstairs of Brown's house for a year, on March 17, 1860; James Annin, a white laborer who had worked on the Mount Gulian grounds with him, the following week to the day on March 24, 1860, at the age of sixty-five; a month after that, Josephine Washington, only thirteen years old and the daughter of Susan Washington, a widowed African American washerwoman and Maryland native like himself, who lived near his old Division Street house, on April 22, 1860; William Kent, respected local attorney and New York State Supreme Court judge, on January 4, 1861; Samuel Verplanck, Gulian's younger brother, the next month on February 8, 1861; Robert Dewitt, a black laborer who lived near him in the Division Street neighborhood on July 28, 1861—just fifty-six years old; the young white barkeeper Dewitt Campell, on the following day; Charles Williams, the nineteen-year-old son of former tenant Robert, on November 17, 1861; Sarah Mackin, the wife of the merchant–real estate agent–banker James, had paid for the Union Burying Ground, on March 1, 1862; Frederick of the African American Reynolds clan, a boatman and a Division Street neighbor, on November 24, 1863, at only thirty-seven years of age; and Anne Knevels, just twenty-five years old and Gulian's niece through his married sister, Elizabeth, on April 24, 1864.[11] All of these deaths, and even more noted by Brown, occurred in Fishkill. Already suffering from a broken body, James was probably obsessed with the incessant thought that each day might be his last when pelted by such a torrent of losses.

Misdeeds and calamities, too, were all about him, and these captured his mind. Philip Augustus Embury, the fiancé of one of William S. Verplanck's daughters, was murdered in New York City while en route to the train station in order to visit the Fishkill family. A strike during a winter lightning storm damaged the house of Daniel Weed, a white brickmaker, down by the Denning's Point brickyards in February 1862. The next month, a fire destroyed the Newlin gristmill. Two days later, another conflagration demolished John DeWindt's mansion in March 1862. Seven months after that, there were more flames—this time, razing the slaughterhouse and barn of John Bush, the butcher.[12]

With so many troubles assaulting his immediate neighbors and with news of human carnage and bloodshed elsewhere in the country somewhere in his consciousness, James felt himself to be in the deepest winter of his life, literally and figuratively. Not surprisingly, then, that is exactly what he mostly recorded during the national conflict: In April 1862—"Weather very cold and Much Snow on the [Fishkill] Mountains . . . [T]he snow and ice is 2 feet deep." During the next winter—"This morning there began a severe Snow Storm which continued all day and until a late hour in the night leaving a body of snow 18 inches on the ground."[13] Pages upon pages about ice, below-zero temperatures, and blustery winds. Brown's fixation on the cold weather was intermittently relieved by notations on gardening, such as manuring the ground, putting in potatoes, trimming shrubbery, sowing peas, preparing hotbeds. This latter sort of entry, however, stood out for the infrequency of its appearance in comparison with the journal some thirty years earlier and when compared with his present focus on the frigid climate. Decoding the diary, then, suggests that the garden was his refuge, real and imagined, but his visits there in both senses were overshadowed by bleaker happenings on both the local and national levels.

Yet the striking lack of Civil War–related reportage in the diary also had to do with Brown's expectation concerning his future readers. On one of the blank pages at the back of one of the diary volumes, probably some time in the early 1840s, James supplied future readers with a description of himself. He called himself "an old colored man." This is significant because it indicates that he understood and operated within the new, racialized discourse on human difference imposed by whites upon blacks during the antebellum period.[14] Despite the speciousness of the science upon which it supposedly rested, James and antebellum African American leaders like him operated inside the new social construct of race in order to push at its walls and eventually to destroy it. If whites saw them as "colored" or Negro, then that is what they would say they were. But free black activists simultaneously strove to prove to whites (and even misguided blacks) that so-called colored people were no different intrinsically—no different in goals and emotions, no different in strengths or weaknesses, no different in their range of dispositions, and no different in capabilities of achievement—from so-called white people. If reality seemed to suggest otherwise, then that was because most blacks were held in degrading bondage, or prevented from equal employment, or denied education, or cruelly provoked by prejudicial treatment in the social arena.[15] Black leaders would model these truths by their own lives. This ideology informed the content of Anthony Chase's intent-to-run-away letter and it provided the motivation for all of James F. Brown's days as a free man. So it must have been a proud moment when the *Poughkeepsie Eagle* referred to those attending the West Indies Emancipation rally back in 1857, himself included, as "colored *citizens*."[16] As an adult, James F. Brown never forgot his project of modeling exemplary citizenship and, in a directly related way, the purpose of his personal journal. It was literally an account of a colored man's life intended to remediate faulty apprehensions of the African American race—reckoned at the time, of course, in generically male terms.

Whether future readers would be black or white, it was important to counter the prevailing image of blacks as unregulated, passion-driven, and excitable. It was imperative to portray his own steadiness, reason, and well-tempered mind throughout the pages of his life. How, then, would it look to appear biased or extreme about either side of an armed struggle that threatened to render the fabric of the nation, especially when Gulian, the head of the household in which he was employed—someone who had helped to manumit him, someone whose family and connections had enlarged his life chances and those of his friends and loved ones—was committed to the oxymoronic politics of being an antislavery Democrat? If the Democratic southern Confederacy was clearly anathema to James, then in order to live peaceably, respectfully, and honorably within his world at Mount Gulian, he would have to draw deeply from his progressive Whiggish principles of moderation and balance, respect for authority and order. In practical terms, he would have to keep his opinions to himself—rarely, neutrally, and quite dispassionately reporting local war-related happenings—while privately applauding the mustering of Union troops. This, too, would aid his race project and ensure future respect for his life as a colored man, narrated in his own words, by those who had the power to ensure its safekeeping for posterity, the Verplancks. His calculation was spot-on. Following Julia's death, the diary passed into the hands of his employers. Bayard Verplanck and James DeLancey Verplanck presented it to the New-York Historical Society in 1942, seventy-four years after James's death.

Brown's race project intersected a national project. He and middle-class African American leaders were joined by mainstream businessmen, politicians, ministers, writers, and journalists in espousing the doctrine of self-help and self-reliance. But the notion of self-help for African Americans such as Brown, once a fugitive slave, offered a particular twist on the common understanding of the term in the years preceding the Civil War. As drawn by Gayle McKeen, there was a connection between the rhetoric of self-help and the need for self-ownership by antebellum blacks at a time when slavery interfered with a critical element in the emerging concept of freedom—the right to profit from one's own labor.[17] It was imperative for James to loose himself from the chains of legal bondage. Only in that way might he compete in the labor market in order to secure economic independence. And only in that way might he legitimately engage in the public arena to support policies, laws, and practices that promoted prosperity and equal opportunities for the great American bonanza—not merely for himself, not merely for African Americans, but for all citizens of the United States.

James F. Brown died in 1868, but the diary stopped abruptly two years before its author's demise—"The lowest tide that has been for many years in the Hudson River was this day—the flats was bare from the Long Dock down to Denning's Point—So that persons could walk down to get eels and fish with one hand."[18] Such an ending beckons the reader to imagine various closing scenarios for his life. Likewise, the different iterations of young James revealed in the diary invite its audience to consider alternative beginnings for James's story. Choices and options framed James's narrative at its start and conclusion, just as they served as both catalyst and prize for people in antebellum America. Freedom to choose was the epitome of personhood. Freedom to thrive served as both engine and reward for behavior in the marketplace. Freedom to participate in public decision making was the ultimate benefit of life in a democratic society. These freedoms were the flowers that bloomed in James's garden, and it would be up to future generations of Americans to weed and prune freedom's garden after he passed from the scene.

Notes

1. Joyce Appleby, *Inheriting the Revolution: The First Generation of Americans* (Cambridge, Mass.: Belknap Press of Harvard University Press, 2001), p. 5, *passim*.

2. B.V. Brown, James F. (MS 1008), New-York Historical Society, New York, N.Y., 1830, n.d. This entry appears immediately before Brown's entry for 1 January 1830.

3. Brown Diary, 14 January 1841; *Longworth's American Almanac, New-York Register and City Directory for 1839* (New York: Thomas Longworth, 1839), pp. 204, 415, 551. This author measured the dimensions of each of the original volumes held in the collections of the New-York Historical Society. The width of each seemed to be 6.5 to 6.75 inches. The larger measurement reflected age and stretching of the binding or, in some case, the detachment of the front cover from its binding. The binding was brown and the covers were brownish or brown and green in their marbled pattern. A volume labeled "memorandum book 1827 to 1843" had an aged, dark green cover with brown binding. Only this volume was a bit shorter than the others, measuring 6.5 inches by 7 inches long. Information about two of the volumes' retailers was taken from advertisement labels pasted on the inside front cover by the sellers.

4. Molly McCarthy, "A Page, A Day: A History of the Daily Diary in America," Dissertation, Brandeis University, 2004, pp. 1–29; Marilyn Ferris Motz, "Folk Expression of Time and Place: 19th-Century Midwestern Rural Diaries," *The Journal of American Folklore,* Volume 100, Number 396 (April–June 1987), p. 136.

5. McCarthy, "A Page, A Day," p. 76. Robert Aiken, a Philadelphia printer and bookseller, introduced the pocket diary to Americans.

6. Ibid., pp. 29–30, 76, 122–24; Molly McCarthy, "A Pocketful of Days: Pocket Diaries and Daily Record Keeping among Nineteenth-Century New England Women," *The New England Quarterly,* Volume 73, Number 2 (June 2000), pp. 278–84; Motz, "Folk Expression of Time and Place," p. 134. On the expansion of book publishing in early national and antebellum America, see Lawrence C. Wroth, *The Book in America: A History of the Making, the Selling, and the Collecting of Books in the United States* (New York: R. R. Bowker Company, 1939), pp. 60–11; Appleby, *Inheriting the Revolution,* pp. 91–92, 95–96, 99.

7. McCarthy, "A Pocketful of Days," p. 276.

8. Ibid., p. 277; Motz, "Folk Expression of Time and Place," pp. 141–42. On pp. 132–33, however, Motz notes the existence of spiritually introspective diaries dating back to the seventeenth century in Europe and America.

9. McCarthy, "A Pocketful of Days," p. 277.

10. Ibid.; Jane H. Hunter, "Inscribing the Self in the Heart of the Family: Diaries and Girlhood in Late-Victorian America," *American Quarterly*, Volume 44, Number 1 (March 1992), pp. 51–81; Motz, "Folk Expression of Time and Place," pp. 139, 144.

11. Examples include Leslie M. Harris, *In the Shadow of Slavery: African Americans in New York City, 1626–1863* (Chicago: University of Chicago Press, 2003); Craig Steven Wilder, *In the Company of Black Men: The African Influence on African American Culture* (New York: New York University Press, 2001); Graham Russell Hodges, *Root and Branch: African Americans in New York and East Jersey, 1613–1863* (Chapel Hill: University of North Carolina Press, 1999); James Oliver Horton and Lois E. Horton, *In Hope of Liberty: Culture, Community and Protest Among Northern Free Blacks, 1700–1860* (New York: Oxford University Press, 1997); George A. Levesque, *Black Boston, African American Life in Urban America, 1750–1860* (New York: Garland, 1994); Michael Groth, "Forging Freedom in the Mid–Hudson Valley: The End of Slavery and the Formation of a Free African-American Community in Dutchess County, NY, 1770–1850," Ph.D. Dissertation, Binghamton University, 1994; James Oliver Horton and Lois E. Horton, *Black Bostonians: Family Life and Community Struggle in the Antebellum North* (New York: Holmes and Meir, 1979); Edythe Ann Quinn, "*The Hills* Was Home: The History of a Rural African-American Community in Westchester County, New York, 1790s to 1890s," unpublished book manuscript, 2008; Kathryn Grover, *Make a Way Somehow: African-American Life in a Northern Community, 1790–1965* (Syracuse, N.Y.: Syracuse University Press, 1994); A. J. Williams-Myers, *Long Hammering: Essays on the Forging of an African-American Presence in the Hudson River Valley to the Early Twentieth Century* (Trenton, N.J.: Africa World Press, 1994); Gary B. Nash and Jean R. Soderlund, *Freedom by Degrees: Emancipation in Pennsylvania and Its Aftermath* (New York: Oxford University Press, 1991); Shane White, *Somewhat More Independent: The End of Slavery in New York City, 1770–1810* (Athens: University of Georgia Press, 1991); Gary B. Nash, *Forging Freedom: The Formation of Philadelphia's Black Community, 1720–1840* (Cambridge, Mass.: Harvard University Press, 1988); Robert J. Cottrol, *The Afro-Yankees: Providence's Black Community in the Antebellum Era* (Westport, Conn.: Greenwood Press, 1982); Leonard P. Curry, *The Free Black in Urban America, 1800–1850: The Shadow of the Dream* (Chicago: University of Chicago Press, 1981); Daniel Perlman, "Organizations of the Free Negro in New York City, 1800–1860," *The Journal of Negro History*, Volume 56, Number 3 (July 1971), pp. 181–97.

12. Perlman, "Organizations of the Free Negro"; David N. Gellman, *Emancipating New York: The Politics of Slavery and Freedom, 1777–1827* (Baton Rouge: Louisiana State University Press, 2006); Leon Litwack, *North of Slavery: The Negro in the Free States, 1790–1860* (Chicago: University of Chicago Press, 1961), *passim*: Carleton H. Mabee, *Black Education in New York State: From Colonial to Modern Times* (Syracuse, N.Y.: Syracuse University Press, 1979).

13. See, as examples, Joanne Pope Melish, *Disowning Slavery: Gradual Emancipation and "Race" in New England, 1780–1860* (Ithaca. N.Y.: Cornell University Press, 1998); Shane White, *Somewhat More Independent: The End of Slavery in New York City, 1770–1810* (Athens: University of Georgia Press, 1991); Nash, *Forging Freedom*, esp. pp. 172–281.

CHAPTER 1

1. *The Fishkill Standard*, 23 March 1895; "James Brown, Runaway Slave & Journal Keeper," http://www.mountgulian.org/brown.html, accessed 19 February 2009: U.S. Federal Census, 1850; U.S. Federal Census 1860; see, as examples, B. V. Brown, James F. (MS

1008), New-York Historical Society, New York, N.Y. (hereafter Brown Diary), 1 October 1830; Brown Diary, 1 October 1836, Brown Diary, 1 October 1846, 1 October 1858; Brown Diary, 1 October 1859.

2. Brown Diary, 17 January 1829; Brown Diary, 5 December 1832; Brown Diary, 12 January 1833; Brown Diary, 11 January 1846.

3. Edna Agatha Kanely, *Directory of Ministers and the Maryland Churches They Served 1634–1990*, Volume II (Westminister, Md.: Family Line Publications, 1991), p. 227; Kanely incorrectly cites one of Schaeffer's churches as Emmanuel Lutheran when the correct name is Evangelical Lutheran.

4. For mentions of Comfort Dennis, see Brown Diary, 19 January 1851, 27 February 1853, 29 April 1855, and 28 July 1857. James described Levin Huston as his brother-in-law in Brown Diary, 26 December 1842. For information about Esther Huston, sometimes spelled "Ester" or "Easter," and her husband, Levin, see Linda Duyer, *One Kind Favor, See That My Grave's Kept Clean: African American Burial Sites of Dorchester and Wicomico Counties, Maryland*, (Salisbury, Md.: Linda Duyer, 1997) and Linda Duyer, *'Round the Pond: Georgetown of Salisbury, Maryland*, (Salisbury, Md.: Linda Duyer, 2007); the date of Esther's birth is based on the 1870 U.S. Federal Census. For mentions of William Brown, see Brown Diary, 29 March 1829 and 30 April 1829. Under what I assume to be one of his aliases, James Brown recommended Samuel Brown as a replacement worker to an employer he was leaving in Maryland; for this, see Anthony Chase to Jeremiah C. Hoffman, 6 August 1827, Number 1201, Otho Holland Williams Papers, Maryland Historical Society, Baltimore, Md. The 1880 Federal Census reported one black male Samuel Brown in Baltimore; he was a seventy-seven-year-old Maryland native and so would have been born in 1803—ten years later than Brown. The job reference and the age proximity suggest a possible sibling relationship between James and Samuel then.

5. *The Fishkill Standard*, 23 March 1895; 1840 U.S. Federal Census; 1850 U.S. Federal Census; 1860 U.S. Federal Census; 1880 U.S. Federal Census.

6. Brown Diary, 7 October 1830; Brown Diary, 18 August 1838; Somerset County Court Land Records, Maryland State Archives, CE 102–47, JP Liber 2, pp. 96–97; Levin Huston Family Bible, 1816, Nabb Research Center, Salisbury University, Salisbury, Md. Chase acquired his lease on 26 August 1814 from one William W. Polk, perhaps a former owner of both Esther and him.

7. Trevor Burnard, "Slave Naming Patterns: Onomastics and the Taxonomy of Race in Eighteenth-Century Jamaica," *Journal of Interdisciplinary History*, Volume 31, Number 3 (Winter 2001), p. 326.

8. Burnard, "Slave Naming Patterns," pp. 325–27, 330; Darrett B. Rutman and Anita H. Rutman, "'In Nomine Avi'": Child-Naming Patterns in a Chesapeake County, 1650–1750," in Robert M. Taylor Jr. and Ralph J. Crandall, eds., *Generations and Change: Genealogical Perspectives in Social History* (Macon, Ga.: Mercer University Press, 1986), pp. 246–47; Daniel Scott Smith, "Child-Naming Practices, Kinship Ties, and Change in Family Attitudes in Hingham, Massachusetts, 1641–1880," *Journal of Social History*, Volume 18 (1985), p. 543; David Hackett Fischer, "Forenames and the Family in New England: An Exercise in Historical Onomastics," in Taylor and Crandall, *Generations and Change*, pp. 215–41; John C. Inscoe, "Carolina Slave Names: An Index to Acculturation," *The Journal of Southern History*, Volume 49, Number 4 (November 1983), pp. 547–48; Newell N. Puckett, "Names of American Negro Slaves," in George P. Murdock, ed., *Studies in the Science of*

Society (New Haven, Conn.: Yale University Press, 1937), p. 46; Ira Berlin, "From Creole to African: Atlantic Creoles and the Origins of African-American Society in Mainland North America, *William and Mary Quarterly*, Volume 53 (1996), p. 251.

9. James McSherry, *History of Maryland* (Baltimore: The Baltimore Book Company, 1904), p. 91; Ethan Allen and Libertus Van Bokkelen, *History of Maryland* (Philadelphia: E. H. Butler and Co., 1886), p. 149; Barbara J. Fields, *Slavery and Freedom on the Middle Ground: Maryland During the Nineteenth Century* (New Haven, Conn.: Yale University Press, 1985), pp. 1–22, 42, 44. See Reverend A. L. Oerter, *History of Graceham Frederick County Maryland* (Bethlehem, Md.: Times Publishing Co., 1913), pp. 14–15, 19; Abdel Ross Wentz and Francis E. Reinberger, *A History of Evangelical Lutheran Church 1738–1988* (Frederick, Md.: University Publishing Group, 1988), pp. 43–170; James B. and Dorothy S. Ranck, Margaret R. Motter, and Katherine E. Dutrow, *A History of the Evangelical Reformed Church—"Unto Us,"* 1964, pp. 1–75, Historical Society of Frederick County, Maryland, Frederick, Maryland; J. Maurice Henry, *History of the Church of the Brethren in Maryland* (Elgin, Ill.: Brethren Publishing House, 1936), p. 115.

10. Jean Davis, Caroll H. Hendrickson Jr., Arthur Potts, and C. Lynne Price, *History of All Saints' Parish, Frederick, Maryland* (White Plains, Md.: Automated Graphic Systems, 1991), pp. 29–37; Oerter, *History of Graceham Frederick County Maryland*, pp. 141–15; Wentz and Reinberger, *A History of Evangelical Lutheran Church 1738–1988*, pp. 43–170; Ranck, Motter, and Dutrow, *A History of the Evangelical Reformed Church—"Unto Us,"* pp. 1–75.

11. James McSherry and Bartlett B. James, *History of Maryland* (Baltimore: Baltimore Book Company, 1904), p. 339.

12. Paul A. Baglyos, "American Lutherans at the Dawn of the Republic, *Lutheran Quarterly,* Volume 13 (1999), pp. 62–67; Kanely, *Directory of Ministers and the Maryland Churches They Served*, p. 227; Richard M. Chapman, "Just Enough? Lutherans, Slavery, and the Struggle for Racial Justice," *The Cresset* (2008); Anthony B. Pinn, *The African American Religious Experience in America* (Westport, Conn.: Greenwood Press, 2006), pp. 144–45.

13. Joseph Theophilus Singewald, *The Iron Ores of Maryland* (Baltimore: Johns Hopkins University Press, 1911), pp. 193–206; Alan E. Imhoff, "Crossroads and Economic Development: Transportation and Its Effects on Frederick County," in Barbara M. Powell and Michael A. Powell, eds., *Mid-Maryland History: Conflict, Growth, and Change* (Charleston, S.C.: The History Press, 2008), pp. 75–78; McSherry and James, *History of Maryland*, p. 309; *Frederick County, Maryland Directory,* 1878, http://www.newrivernotes.com/md/fred1878.htm, accessed 23 March 2009; Prof. Amos Eaton, "The Gold of the Carolinas in Talcose Slate," *American Journal of Science*, Volume 18, Number 1 (1830), p. 52; Fields, *Slavery and Freedom on the Middle Ground*, pp. 5, 8, 11–12, 18–19; Karen R. Kuff and James R. Brooks, "Building Stones of Maryland," 1985, *Maryland Geological Survey,* http://www.mgs.md.gov/esic/brochures/buildst.html, accessed 23 March 2009; see map and chart of Maryland gold mines in Karen R. Kuff, "Gold in Maryland," 1987, *Maryland Geological Survey*, http://www.mgs.md.gov/esic/brochures/gold.html, accessed 23 March 2009.

14. Tench Coxe, *A Statement of the Art and Manufacture of the United States for the Year 1810* (Philadelphia: A. Cornman, 1814), pp. 80–86.

15. Fields, *Slavery and Freedom on the Middle Ground*, p. 6.

16. Ibid., p. 13; Allen and Van Bokkelen, *History of Maryland*, p. 105; Cheryl Fox, "'I Went Down to the Crossroads': Runaway Slave Strategies of Colonial and Early Federal-

era Maryland, African Americans," in Michael A. Powell and Bruce A. Thompson, eds., *Mid-Maryland: A Crossroads of History*, Volume One (Charleston, S.C.: The History Press, 2005), p. 26; Lacy K. Ford, *Deliver Us from Evil: The Slavery Question in the Old South* (New York: Oxford University Press, 2009), pp. 28–29.

17. Calculated from figures in Fields, *Slavery and Freedom on the Middle Ground*, p. 13. The chart of population statistics provided by Fields here is based on 1790 and 1850 federal census enumerations of the white, "free colored," and slave populations.

18. Federal census figures cited in Thomas J.C. Williams and Folger McKinsey, *History of Frederick County, Maryland*, Volume I (Frederick, Md.: L. R. Titsworth & Co., 1910; reprinted Baltimore: Regional Publishing Co., 1967; reprinted Baltimore: Genealogical Publishing Co., Inc., 1997), p. 219.

19. Williams and McKinsey, *History of Frederick County*, pp. 180, 222; Loren Schweninger, *Black Property Owners in the South 1790–1915* (Chicago: University of Chicago Press, 1990), pp. 52–53. Eugene D. Genovese in *Roll, Jordan, Roll: The World the Slaves Made* (New York: Vintage Books, 1976), pp. 25–48, first developed the notion of "the hegemonic function of the law" in master–slave relationships.

20. 1790 U.S. Federal Census; 1800 U.S. Federal Census.

21. *The Republican Gazette and General Advertiser* (Frederick County, Maryland), 26 October 1816; *The Republican Gazette and General Advertiser*, 14 December 1816; *The Republican Gazette and General Advertiser*, 8 March 1817; *Frederick-Town Herald*, 30 March 1816; *Frederick-Town Herald*, 10 August 1816.

22. *Frederick-Town Herald*, 28 August 1819.

23. See Loren Schweninger, "The Free-Slave Phenomenon: James P. Thomas and the Black Community in Ante-Bellum Nashville" in Darlene Clark Hine and Earnestine Jenkins, eds. *A Question of Manhood: A Reader in U.S. Black Men's History and Masculinity*, Volume I (Bloomington: Indiana University Press, 1999), pp. 340–41. Here, Schweninger tells the story of a mulatto slave, John, who although part of an estate of Charles S. Thomas, took the surname of Richard Rapier—becoming John Rapier, in other words—after being hired out to him.

24. "Focus on the Collection: Fleecy Dale Wool Factory," *Docent News*, Volume 5, Number 1 (March 2006), p. 6, Historical Society of Frederick County, Maryland, Frederick, Md.

25. Arthur Harrison Cole, *The American Wool Manufacture*, Volume I (London: Oxford University Press, 1926), pp. 143–44.

26. Coxe, *A Statement of the Art and Manufactures*, pp. xii, xiii, xxix–xxx.

27. Ibid., pp. 79–80.

28. Cole, *American Wool Manufacture*, pp. 145–54.

29. *The Frederick-Town Herald*, 26 September 1816.

30. William Smith to William Elie Williams, 14 December 1808, Number 987, Otho Holland Williams (OHW) Papers 1744–1839 , MS 908 (Part 5/8), Maryland Historical Society, Baltimore, Md.

31. Otho Holland Williams to Benjamin Williams, 6 May 1794, Number 955, OHW Papers.

32. O. H. Williams to B. Williams, 6 May 1794, OHW Papers.

33. Otho Holland Williams to John Farrell, 20 March 1794, Number 917, OHW Papers; Elie Williams to Otho Holland Williams, 22 March 1794, Number 920, OHW Papers;

Osmond Tiffany, *A Sketch of the Life and Services of Gen. Otho Holland Williams* (Baltimore: John Murphy & Co., 1851), p. 29; Allen and Van Bokkelen, *History of Maryland*, pp. 146–47.

34. Hasell to William Elie Williams, March 1810, Number 994, OHW Papers; Elie Williams to William Elie Williams, 3 October 1810, Number 996, OHW Papers; Elie Williams to William Elie Williams, 14 December 1814, Number 997, OHW Papers; Elie Williams to William Elie Williams, 14 July 1811, Number 999, OHW Papers; Henry R. Warfield to William E. Williams, 15 December 1811, Number 1000, OHW Papers; William Campbell to William Elie Williams, 15 January 1814, Number 1005, OHW Papers; William Hill to William Elie Williams, 24 February 1814, Number 1008, OHW Papers; John Davis to William Elie Williams, 25 July 1814, Number 1014, OHW Papers; Richard Tilghman to William Elie Williams, 4 October 1814, Number 1018, OHW Papers; William Cooke Sr. to William Elie Williams, 24 June 1815, Number 1024, OHW Papers; William Cooke Sr. to William Elie Williams, 27 September 1815, Number 1029, OHW Papers; William Cooke to William Elie Williams, 6 March 1816, Number 1033, OHW Papers; William Cooke to William Elie Williams, 14 May 1816, Number 1035, OHW Papers; Christopher Hughes to William Elie Williams, 13 July 1816, Number 10140, OHW Papers; Edward Greene Williams to William Elie Williams, 27 September 1816, Number 1048, OHW Papers; John Frederick Dorman, *Adventures of Purse and Person, Virginia 1607–1624/5, Fourth Edition* (Baltimore: Genealogical Publishing Company, 2005), pp. 463–64; John F. Porter, *Industries of Western Maryland* (n.p.: Industrial Publishing Co., 1880), pp. 174–75, Historical Society of Frederick County, Maryland, Frederick, Md.; Williams and McKinsey, *History of Frederick County*, pp. 278–79; Suzanne Bohn, "Ceresville Flour Mill," Paper for History 375—Independent Study, Hood College, 14 April 1978, p. 107, Historical Society of Frederick County, Frederick, Md.; Suzanne Bohn, "Ceresville Flour Mill: Nearly 200 Years Old, Still Producing," *The News,* 27 July 1978, pp. C8–C9, Vertical File, "Mills—Ceresville Flour," Historical Society of Frederick County, Frederick, Md.; "The History of Ceresville Mansion," Vertical File—"Historic Buildings, etc.—Ceresville," Historical Society of Frederick County, Frederick, Md.

35. 1820 U.S. Federal Census.

36. William Hill to William Elie Williams, 24 February 1814, Number 1008, OHW Papers; Richard Tilghman to William Elie Williams, 4 October 1814, Number 1018, OHW Papers.

37. For examples, see William Cooke to William Elie Williams, 1 August 1816, Number 1042, OHW Papers; Frank Cooke to William Elie Williams, 18 September 1816, Number 1044, OHW Papers; George Cooke to William Elie Williams, 31 May 1817, Number 1064, OHW Papers; George Cooke to William Elie Williams, 1 July 1817, Number 1075, OHW Papers; Edward Greene Williams to William E. Williams, 10 October 1817, Number 1079, OHW Papers.

38. J. H. Powell to William Elie Williams, 27 September 1815, Number 1030, OHW Papers; Francis Hollingsworth to William Elie Williams, 10 November 1815, Number 1032, OHW Papers.

39. William Cooke Sr. to William Elie Williams, 24 June 1815, Number 1024, OHW Papers.

40. Geoffrey Gilbert, "Maritime Enterprise in the New Republic: Investment in Baltimore Shipping, 1789–1793," *The Business History Review*, Volume 58, Number 1 (Spring 1984), pp. 14–29; "Daniel Howland," Maritime File, The Maryland Historical Society,

Baltimore, Md.; Edward Machett, *The Baltimore Directory and Register, 1816* (Baltimore: Wanderer Office, 1816), p. 86; *Baltimore Directory 1817* (Baltimore: James Kennedy, 1817), p. 94; Samuel Jackson, *Baltimore Directory 1819* (Baltimore: J. Matchett, 1819), n.p.; C. Keenan, *Baltimore Directory 1882–1823* (Baltimore: Richard J. Matchett, 1822), p. 38; Richard J. Matchett, *Baltimore Directory for 1824* (Baltimore: Richard J. Matchett, 1824), p. 157; *Matchett's Baltimore Directory for 1827* (Baltimore: Richard J. Matchett, 1827), p. 137; WG, Book 133, p. 313, 10 November 1815, Land Records, Maryland State Archives, Annapolis, Md.; WG, Book 136, pp. 573–75, 5 July 1816, Maryland Land Records; WG, Book 156, p. 637, 16 August 1820, Maryland Land Records; WG, Book 176, pp. 227, 435, Maryland Land Records; John Thomas Scharf, *The Chronicles of Baltimore* (Baltimore: Turnbull Brothers, 1874), p. 393; Leroy Graham, *Baltimore: The Nineteenth Century Black Capital* (Washington: University Press of America, 1982), p. 45; Richard S. Chew, "Unforeseen Troubles: Baltimore's Atlantic Trade and the Commercial Frustrations of the Confederation Period," p. 35, http://www.librarycompany.org/Economics/2003Conference/papers/htm, accessed 23 February 2009.

41. Loren Schweninger, "The Free-Slave Phenomenon: James P. Thomas and the Black Community in Ante-Bellum Nashville" in Darlene Clark Hine and Earnestine Jenkins, eds., *A Question of Manhood: A Reader in U.S. Black Men's History and Masculinity*, Volume I (Bloomington: Indiana University Press, 1999), pp. 240–53.

42. Fields, *Slavery and Freedom on the Middle Ground*, p. 48.

43. Ibid., p. 62; Christopher Phillips, *Freedom's Port: The African American Community of Baltimore, 1790–1860* (Urbana: University of Illinois Press, 1997), p. 60.

44. Phillips, *Freedom's Port*, pp. 4, 69.

45. Ibid., p. 60; John Hope Franklin and Loren Schweninger, *Runaway Slaves: Rebels on the Plantation* (New York: Oxford University Press, 1999), pp. 33–37; Ford, *Deliver Us from Evil*, pp. 32–35.

46. Phillips, *Freedom's Port*, p. 76.

47. Ibid., p. 81.

48. Loren Schweninger, *Black Property Owners in the South, 1790–1915* (Urbana: University of Illinois Press, 1990), pp. 41–51.

49. Schweninger, *Black Property Owners in the South*, pp. 51–63; Richard C. Wade, *Slavery in the Cities* (New York: Oxford University Press, 1964), pp. 28–54, 143–79, 243–82.

50. See the nonchronological section of the Brown Diary in which the author recorded special events in his life that predated the commencement of the diary itself. See also William R. Quyn, ed., *The Diary of Jacob Engelbrecht*, Volume I (Frederick, Md.: Historical Society of Frederick County, 2001), 10 August 1825. James Harper was indeed an AME preacher who eventually became a deacon and an elder in the church's Canadian conference; in 1856, Harper also became vice president of the church's literary and historical society in Canada. On Harper, see Daniel Alexander Payne, *History of the African Methodist Episcopal Church* (Nashville: A.M.E. Sunday School Union, 1891), pp. 129, 145, 362, 391. Nothing more can be said of Emily Graham and her husband, Thomas, as they don't appear in the census or directories for Hagerstown, Frederick-Town, or Baltimore around this time.

51. Quyn, *The Diary of Jacob Engelbrecht*. There had been a Bethel AME Church in Baltimore since at least 1816, but there was also a Bethel Evangelical Lutheran Church in Frederick County, Maryland, possibly still pastored in 1825 by Reverend Schaeffer, who began his tenure

there in 1808. Because James did not specify a denomination when mentioning Bethel in his diary at this point and in the absence of parishioner rosters for either church from this era, his membership at either place is uncertain. Still, the circumstantial evidence suggests that he belonged to Bethel AME. See Payne, *History of the African Methodist Episcopal Church*, pp. 7–8, 11–14, and Kanely, *Directory of Ministers and the Maryland Churches They Served*, p. 227.

52. James Creighton to William Elie Williams, 15 July 181, Number 1105, OHW Papers; J. W. Patterson to William Elie Williams, 29 July 1818, Number 1109, OWH Papers; Richard Tilghman to William Elie Williams, 29 July 1818, Number 1110, OHW Papers; William Elie Williams to Henry Lee, 10 August 1818, Number 1112, OHW Papers; George Howard to William Elie Williams, 19 August 1818, Number 1114, OHW Papers; William Cooke Jr. to William Elie Williams, 21 August 1818, Number 1116, OHW Papers, George Cooke to William Elie Williams, 22 August 1818, Number 1117, OHW Papers; William Campbell to William E. Williams, 2 September 1818, Number 1122, OHW Papers.

53. Thomas Buchanan to William Elie Williams, 8 February 1819, Number 1139, OHW Papers.

54. Dr. William Bradley Tyler to Dr. Nathaniel Chapman, 30 July 1822, Number 1149, OHW Papers; Dr. William Bradley Tyler to William Elie Williams, 13 August 1822, Number 1152, OHW Papers; Quyn, ed., *The Diary of Jacob Engelbrecht*, 22 November 1822.

55. Regarding administration of the William E. Williams estate see, as examples, James D. Mitchell and James L. Macguire to Henry Lee Williams, 15 March 1826, Number 1171, OHW Papers; Elisha Randall and Paul G. Hands to Henry Lee Williams, 20 April 1826, Number 1173, OHW Papers; James D. Mitchell to Simon Whitney, now the Estate of Wm. E. Williams, Susan F. Williams administrix, 1 July 1826, Number 1177, OHW Papers; James D. Mitchell to William E. Williams Estate, Susan F. Williams, administratrix, 15 September 1826, Number 1180, OHW Papers; Joseph Robinson to H. L. Williams and Susan F. Williams, adminstrators of W. E. Williams, 27 December 1826, Number 1182, OHW Papers.

56. Mrs. Susan F. Williams to the Estate of Henry Lee Williams, Number 1195, OHW Papers.

57. Ibid. The first time that the "Estate of Henry Lee Williams" appears in any of the correspondence constituting the Otho Holland Williams Papers is on March 24, 1827.

58. Henry Lee William to the Executor of his will, 1826, Document 1184, OHW Papers.

59. "News of Old Baltimore," December 17, 1844, reprinted in *Baltimore News*, 1919, Chatsworth File, Maryland Historical Society, Baltimore, Md.; Brantz Mayer, *Baltimore: Past and Present* (Baltimore: Richardson and Bennett, 1871), pp. 295–97.

60. Anthony Chase to Jeremiah Hoffman, Chatsworth House [Baltimore], 8 August 1827, Number 1201, OHW Papers, also partially cited in Robert S. Starobin, ed., *Blacks in Bondage: Letters of American Slaves* (New York: M. Weiner, 1988), p. 120.

61. Henry C. Peden Jr., M.A. *Presbyterian Records of Baltimore City, Maryland 1765–1840* (Westminster, Md.: Family Line Publications, 1995), p. 96. Nevins was an ardent revivalist and reformer who spent his early career as a missionary to South America and then embarked on work in penitentiary reform. Such a man was likely to have been sympathetic to the plight of slaves in Baltimore, and his preaching may have appealed to James, who, as discussed in chapter 9, was an itinerant worshiper. On Nevins's preaching career, see Rev. E. H. Gillett, D.D., *History of the Presbyterian Church in the United States* (Philadelphia: Presbyterian Board of Publication, 1873), pp. 25–26, and J. Thomas Scharf, *History of Baltimore City and County* (Baltimore: Regional Publishing Company, 1971), p. 546.

62. *The Northeastern Reporter,* Volume 44 (St. Paul, Minn.: West Publishing Company, 1896), pp. 294–95.

63. Dr. Christopher Johnson, "The Tilghman Family," *Maryland Historical Magazine,* Volume 1, Number 1 (Baltimore: Maryland Historical Society, 1906), p. 393.

64. Jeremiah Hoffman to William Cooke, 15 August 1827, OHW Papers.

65. Jeremiah Hoffman to Mrs. Susan F. Williams, August 1827, OHW Papers.

66. John Michael Vlach, "Above Ground on the Underground Railroad," in David W. Blight, ed., *The Underground Railroad in History and Memory* (Washington: Smithsonian Books, 2004), pp. 103–5.

67. W. Jeffrey Bolster, *Black Jacks: African American Seamen in the Age of Sail* (Cambridge, Mass.: Harvard University Press, 1997), pp. 1–4, 12, 15, 18, 20–21, 24–25, 28, 32, 36, 73–74, 94, 137–38, 148–49, 185, 191, 211, 232; Franklin and Schweninger, *Runaway Slaves,* pp. 25–27.

CHAPTER 2

1. William Edward VerPlanck, *The History of Abraham Isaacse VerPlanck and His Male Descendants in America* (Fishkill Landing, N.Y.:
John W. Spaight, 1892), pp. 197–98; *Fishkill Standard,* 23 March 1895.

2. Daniel C. Verplanck to Susan F. Williams, 23 March 1828, Verplanck Papers (MS 656), Box 9, Folder 2, Number 57, New-York Historical Society, New York, N.Y.

3. Susan F. Williams to Daniel C. Verplanck, 31 March 1828, Verplanck Papers (MS 656), Box 9, Folder 2, Number 75, New-York Historical Society, New York, N.Y.

4. Daniel C. Verplanck to Mrs. Susan Williams, 23 March 1828, Verplanck Papers, (MS 656) Box 9, Number 54, New-York Historical Society, New York, N.Y.

5. See Daniel C. Verplanck to Mrs. Susan F. Williams, 23 March 1828, Verplanck Papers (MS 656), Box 9, Number 54, New-York Historical Society, New York, N.Y., and Daniel C. Verplanck to "My dear Sir," 23 March 1828, Verplanck Papers (MS 656), Box 9, Number 56 (reverse side), New-York Historical Society, New York, N.Y.

6. Loren Schweninger, *Black Property Owners in the South, 1790–1915* (Urbana: University of Illinois Press, 1997), p. 40.

7. Lacy K. Ford, *Deliver Us from Evil: The Slavery Question in the Old South* (New York: Oxford University Press, 2009), p. 34; Brown Diary, 27 November 1820; Brown Diary, 28 November 1830.

8. Schweninger, *Black Property Owners in the South,* p. 42.

9. Mark E. Kahn, *A Republic of Men: The American Founders, Gendered Language, and Patriarchal Politics* (New York: New York University Press, 1998), pp. 155–77; E. Anthony Rotundo, *American Manhood: Transformations in Masculinity from the Revolution to the Modern Era* (New York: Basic Books, 1993), pp. 10–16.

10. Rotundo, *American Manhood,* pp. 18–20.

11. Amy S. Greenberg, *Manifest Manhood and the Antebellum American Empire* (Cambridge: Cambridge University Press, 2005), pp. 9–14; Rotundo, *American Manhood,* pp. 20–25.

12. Greenberg, *Manifest Manhood,* p. 9; David G. Pugh, *Sons of Liberty: The Masculine Mind in Nineteenth Century America* (Westport, Conn.: Greenwood Press, 1983), pp. xv–xxii, 3–38.

13. Daniel P. Black, *Dismantling Black Manhood: An Historical and Literary Analysis of the Legacy of Slavery* (New York: Routledge, 1997), pp. 99–174; Kathleen M. Brown, *Good Wives, Nasty Wenches, and Anxious Patriarchs: Gender, Race, and Power in Colonial Virginia* (Chapel Hill: University of North Carolina Press, 1996), pp. 107–246, 319–66.

14. Brown to Hoffman, 8 August 1827, OHW Papers; Jeremiah Hoffman to Mrs. [Susan] Williams, August 1827, Number 1152, OHW Papers; J. Hoffman to William Cooke, 15 August 1827, Number 1153, OHW Papers; John Hope Franklin and Loren Schweninger, *Runaway Slaves: Rebels on the Plantation* (New York: Oxford University Press, 2000), pp. 79–80.

15. Darlene Clark Hine and Earnestine Jenkins, "Black Men's History: Toward a Gendered Perspective," in Darlene Clark Hine and Earnestine Jenkins, eds., *A Question of Manhood: A Reader in U.S. Black Men's History and Masculinity* (Bloomington: Indiana University Press, 1999), pp. 13–14; Walter Johnson, *Soul by Soul: Life Inside the Antebellum Slave Market* (Cambridge, Mass.: Harvard University Press, 2001), pp. 79–88.

16. Johnson, *Soul by Soul*, p. 79.

17. Ibid.

18. C. W. Harper, "Black Aristocrats: Domestic Servants on the Antebellum Plantation," *Phylon*, Volume XLVI, Number 2 (1985), p. 124.

19. Dr. George T. Winston, "Relations of Whites and Blacks," address before the American Academy of Political and Social Science on April 13, 1901, "Scrapbook," Mary Norcott Bryan Papers, Southern Historical Collection, University of North Carolina, Chapel Hill, N.C., as cited in Harper, "Black Aristocrats," p. 124.

20. Harper, "Black Aristocrats," p. 125; Eugene D. Genovese, *The Political Economy of Slavery: Studies in the Economy and Society of the Slave South* (Middletown, Conn.: Wesleyan University Press, 1989), pp. 28–34; Eugene D. Genovese, *Roll, Jordan, Roll: The World the Slaves Made* (New York: Vintage Books, 1974), pp. 75–86, 97–98.

21. W. Jeffrey Bolster, "'To Feel Like a Man': Black Seamen in the Northern States, 1800–1860," in Hine and Jenkins, eds., *A Question of Manhood*, p. 363; also see W. Jeffrey Bolster, *Black Jacks: African American Seamen in the Age of Sail* (Cambridge, Mass.: Harvard University Press, 1998), pp. 102–214.

22. William H. Becker, "The Black Church: Manhood and Mission," in Hine and Jenkins, eds., *A Question of Manhood*, pp. 324–25.

23. Daniel Alexander Payne, *History of the African Methodist Episcopal Church* (Nashville: A.M.E. Sunday School Union, 1891), p. 12.

24. Patricia Bradley, *Slavery, Propaganda, and the American Revolution* (Jackson: University Press of Mississippi, 1998), pp. 1–24; James Oliver Horton and Lois E. Horton, *In Hope of Liberty: Culture, Community, and Protest Among Northern Free Blacks, 1700–1860* (New York: Oxford University Press, 1997), pp. 55–76. See also Ira Berlin and Ronald Hoffman, eds., *Slavery and Freedom in the Era of the American Revolution* (Charlottesville: University of Virginia Press, 1983); David Brion Davis, *The Problem of Slavery in the Age of Revolution, 1770–1823* (Ithaca, N.Y.: Cornell University Press, 1975); Paul Finkelman, *Slavery and the Founders: Race and Liberty in the Age of Jefferson* (Armonk, N.Y.: M. E. Sharpe, 1996); Duncan McLeod, *Slavery, Race, and the American Revolution* (Cambridge: Cambridge University Press, 1974); Gary B. Nash, *Race and Revolution* (Madison, Wisc.: Madison House, 1990); Orlando Patterson, *Freedom*, Volume I: *Freedom in the Making of Western Culture* (New York: Basic Books, 1991); Arthur Zilversmit, *The First Emancipation: The Abolition of Slavery in the North* (Chicago: University of Chicago Press, 1967).

25. Ford, *Deliver Us from Evil*, pp. 33–35; Fox, "'I Went Down to the Crossroads,'" pp. 20, 25.

26. On the use of this strategy by James Brown's contemporaries such as Prince Hall, David Walker, and Maria Stewart, see Andrea McArdle, "The Confluence of Law and Antebellum Black Literature: Lawyerly Discourse as a Rhetoric of Empowerment," *Law and Literature*, Volume 17, Number 2 (Spring 2005), pp. 183–223.

27. Elwood L. Bridner Jr., "The Fugitive Slaves of Maryland, *Maryland Historical Magazine*, Volume 66, Number 1 (Spring 1971), pp. 34–49.

28. Leroy Graham, *Baltimore: The Nineteenth Century Black Capital* (Washington: University of Press of America, Inc., 1982), pp. 95–97; Edward Needles Wright, ed., "John Needles: An Autobiography," *Quaker History*, Volume 58, Number 1 (Spring 1969), pp. 3–18.

29. VerPlanck, *History of Abraham Isaacse VerPlanck*, pp. 265–70; *Freedom's Journal*, 9 November 1827. On the sharp drop in the slave population of Delaware in the first two decades of the nineteenth century, making that state a relative haven for freedom-seeking slaves such as Brown, see Ford, *Deliver Us from Evil*, p. 32.

CHAPTER 3

1. VerPlanck, *History of Abraham Isaacse VerPlanck*, pp. 108, 189–207; Joyce D. Appleby, "Commercial Farming and the 'Agrarian Myth' in the Early Republic," *The Journal of American History*, Volume 68, Number 4 (March 1982), pp. 833–36; Drew R. McCoy, *The Elusive Republic: Political Economy in Jeffersonian America* (Chapel Hill: University of North Carolina Press, 1980), pp. 5–12, 76–119; Alice B. Lockwood, *Gardens of Colony and State: Gardens and Gardeners of the American Colonies and of the Republic Before 1840* (New York: Charles Scribner's Sons, 1931).

2. Therese O'Malley, "Appropriation and Adaptation: Early Gardening Literature in America, *The Huntington Library Quarterly*, Volume 55, Number 3, Symposium: "An English Arcadia: Landscape and Architecture in Britain and America" (Summer 1992), p. 425; Joyce Oldham Appleby, Lynn Hunt, and Margaret Jacob, *Telling the Truth About History* (Norton, 1995), p. 31; M. L. Wilson, "Survey of Scientific Agriculture," *Proceedings of the American Philosophical Society*, Volume 86, Number 1, Symposium on the Early History of Science and Learning in America (September 25, 1942), p.52; Benjamin Sexauer, "English and French Agriculture in the Late Eighteenth Century," *Agricultural History*, Volume 50, Number 3. (July 1976), pp. 491–505; T. H. Marshall, "Jethro Tull and the 'New Husbandry' of the Eighteenth Century," *The Economic History Review*, Volume 2, Number 1 (January 1929), pp. 41–60; C. Peter Timmer, "The Turnip, the New Husbandry, and the English Agricultural Revolution," *The Quarterly Journal of Economics*, Volume 83, Number 3 (August 1969), pp. 375–95.

3. Therese O'Malley, "'Your Garden Must Be a Museum to You': Early American Botanic Gardens," *The Huntington Library Quarterly*, Volume 59, Number 2/3 (1996), pp. 212–13; Therese O'Malley, "Appropriation and Adaptation: Early Gardening Literature in North America," *The Huntington Library Quarterly*, Volume 5, Number 3 (Summer 1992), pp. 407–8; Richard Beale Davis, *Intellectual Life in Jefferson's Virginia, 1790–1830* (Knoxville: University of Tennessee Press, 1972), pp. 151–53; Harold T. Pickett, "Early Agricultural Societies in the District of Columbia," *Records of the Columbia Historical Society* (1951–1952), p. 32.

4. VerPlanck, *History of Abraham Isaacse VerPlanck*, p. 189.

5. Field Horne, ed., "The Verplanck Farm Book," unpublished paper prepared for the Department of Interpretation and Education, Sleepy Hollow Restorations, Van Cortlandt Manor, Croton-on-Hudson, N.Y., 15 April 1975 (original book at the New-York Historical Society).

6. VerPlanck, *History of Abraham Isaacse VerPlanck*, pp. 199, 204, 207.

7. See map of Mount Gulian Plantings, Mount Gulian Historic Site, Beacon, N.Y.

8. VerPlanck, *History of Abraham Isaacse VerPlanck*, pp. 206–7.

9. Brown Diary, 11 April 1838, 25 October 1838, 29 May 1839, 3 June 1839; VerPlanck, *History of Abraham Isaacse VerPlanck*, pp. 207, 209.

10. Brown Diary, 1 August 1836, 24 September 1838; Brown Diary, 3 May 1847.

11. Lockwood, *Gardens of Colony and* State, p. 284.

12. David E. Cooper, "Garden, Art, Nature," in Tim Richardson and Noel Kingsbury, *Vista: The Culture and Politics of Gardens* (London: Frances Lincoln Limited, 2005), pp. 5–11; George Carter, "The Garden as Art" in Richardson and Kingsbury, *Vista*, pp. 13–24.

13. John Dixon Hunt, *Gardens and the Picturesque: Studies in the History of Landscape Architecture* (Cambridge, Mass.: MIT Press, 1997), pp. 5–9, 75–102; Samuel H. Monk, *The Sublime: A Study of Critical Theories of XVIII-Century England* (Ann Arbor: University of Michigan Press, 1960), pp. 203–32; John Conron, *American Picturesque* (University Park: Pennsylvania State University Press, 2000), p. 18; Thomas Weiskel, *The Romantic Sublime: Studies in the Structure and Psychology of Transcendence* (Baltimore: Johns Hopkins University Press, 1986), pp. 12–22; Peter de Bolla, *The Discourse of the Sublime: Readings in History, Aesthetics and the Subject* (New York: Basil Blackwell, 1989), pp. 204–5.

14. Richard H. Gassan, *The Birth of American Tourism: New York, the Hudson Valley, and American Culture, 1790–1830* (Amherst: University of Massachusetts Press, 2008), pp. 53–55, 57, 61; Edwin G. Burrows and Mike Wallace, *Gotham: A History of New York City to 1898* (New York: Oxford University Press, 1999), pp. 470–71 .

15. Lockwood, *Gardens of Colony and State*; Brown Diary, 1 November 1836, 12 December 1836, 31 October 1837, 1 November 1837, 21 October 1846, 22 April 1849, 29 April 1849, 10 March 1853, 24 March 1853, 28 October 1858.

16. Brown Diary, 14 December 1832, 25 April 1837.

17. Schuyler, *Apostle of Taste* , pp. 9–15, 17, 241n23.

18. Schuyler, *Apostle of Taste,* pp. 13, 32–34.

19. Brown Diary, 5 April 1830, 23 July 1836, 8 January 1840, 1 April 1841, 6 April 1841, 30 April 1841, 11 June 1841, 25 June 1841, 18 April 1843.

20. Andrew Jackson Downing, "Descriptive Notice of J. W. Knevels Esq's Collection of Exotic Plants at Newburgh, N.Y." in C. M. Hovey and and P. B. Hovey Jr., *The American Gardener's Magazine and Register of Useful Discoveries and Improvements in Horticulture and Rural Affairs*, Volume II (18 November 1836), pp. 96–97.

21. Brown Diary, 20 April 1829, 2 April 1830, 22 July 1836, 14 October 1837, 25 April 1838, 2 June 1838.

22. Schuyler, *Apostle of Taste*, pp. 16–17.

23. Pica, "Wodenethe," *Gardener's Monthly and Horticulturalist.*

24. Cited in Pica, "Wodenethe," *Gardener's Monthly and Horticulturalist*, p. 37.

25. Brown Diary, 2 August 1842, 29 September 1845, 8 December 1845, 16 October 1847, 8 July 1851, 8 September 1852, 23 March 1859.

26. Brown Diary, 16 February 1830, 17 June 1830, 5 July 1830, 10 July 1830, 21 August 1830, 8 October 1830, 12 September 1836, 7 July 1840, 29 March 1842, 20 February 1844.

27. Schuyler, *Apostle of Taste*, pp. 72, 103; Andrew Jackson Downing and Henry Winthrop Sargent, *Treatise on the Theory and Practice of Landscape Gardening*, (New York: A. O. Moore and Co., 1859), p. i; Arthur G. Adams, *The Hudson: A Guidebook to the River* (Albany: State University of New York Press, 1981), p. 208. On Sargent, see the 1850 U.S. Census and the 1880 U.S. Census.

28. Brown Diary, 17 October 1830, 11 November 1848, 2 March 1849, 15 February 1851, 1 July 1852. See William Bennett listed in the 1850 U.S. Census.

29. Brown Diary, 13 March 1849, 11 November 1852, 1 January 1855. See the 1850 U.S. Census for listing of B. Manning.

30. Brown Diary, 25 September 1852; the 1850 U.S. Census listed two gardeners, Michael Ross and William Lucas, in the A. J. Downing household. There was also a local "Professor Davis" whose gardeners—"Mr. Hopkins" and "Mr. Dixion" or "Mr. Dexion"—James consulted; these also supplied Brown with plant cuttings and the botanical bounty from their respective employers' gardens; on this see Brown Diary, 19 August 1852, 11 November 1852, 30 March 1858, 12 April 1860.

31. Brown Diary, 9 March 1854, 16 March 1854. The pickup was probably in the southernmost end of the town of Poughkeepsie. James Deacon is listed as a gardener in Poughkeepsie living with his wife, Elizabeth, and their children in the 1860 U.S. Census. He may have died shortly after that date, leaving his widow to carry on the business, because in 1854, James explicitly mentioned collecting the plants from her. Elizabeth Deacon's probable widowhood is also suggested by the fact that she is listed as the head of her household with no husband present in the 1860 U.S. Census of Poughkeepsie.

32. George F. Lemmer, "Early Agricultural Editors and Their Farm Philosophies," *Agricultural History*, Volume 31, Number 4 (October 1957), *passim*. Also see Stephen C. Luntz, *List of the Agricultural Periodicals of the United States and Canada Published During the Century July 1810–July 1910*. (Washington: U. S. Department of Agriculture Miscellaneous Publication 398, 1941); Robert Buist, *The Family Kitchen Gardener* (New York: C. M. Saxton, 1850).

33. Tamara Plakins Thornton, "The Moral Dimensions of Horticulture in Antebellum America," *The New England Quarterly*, Volume 57, Number 1 (March 1984), p. 5; Anthony Ramirez, "Where There's a Plant, She's Got an Answer," *New York Times*, 16 January 2007); *New-York Farmer and Horticultural Repository*, Volume 1, Number 2 (February 1828), pp. 30–32, 41; *New-York Farmer and Horticultural Repository*, Volume 1, Number 11 (November 1828), p. 264; *New-York Farmer and Horticultural Repository*, Volume 1, Number 12 (December 1828), pp. 273–75.

34. *New-York Farmer and Horticultural Repository*, Volume 1, Number 12 (December 1828), p. 287–88; *New-York Farmer and Horticultural Repository*, Volume 1, Number 9 (September 1828), pp. 206–7; *New-York Farmer and Horticultural Repository*, Volume 1, Number 6 (June 1828), pp. 137–38; *New-York Farmer and Horticultural Repository*, Volume 1, Number 7 (July 1828), p. 156; *New-York Farmer and Horticultural Repository*, Volume 1, Number 8 (August 1828), p. 186.

35. Lemmer, "Early Agricultural Editors and Their Farm Philosophies," pp. 3–22; Lake Douglas, "'To Improve the Soil and the Mind': Content and Context of Nineteenth-Century Agricultural Literature," *Landscape Journal*, Volume 25, Number 1 (2006), pp. 67–79.

36. Brown Diary, 4 October 1830; Schuyler, *Apostle of Taste*, pp. 18–19.

37. Brown Diary, 1 June 1830, New-York Historical Society; Brown Diary, 18 June 1830, 13 June 1830, 15 June 1830.

38. *Schuyler, Apostle of Taste, p. 37; William A. Mann, Landscape Architecture: An Illustrated History in Timelines, Site Plans and Biography (New York: Wiley, 1993), pp. 51, 212, 226, 360–61; Proceedings of the New-York Horticultural Society at the Celebration of Its Tenth Anniversary, August 26, 1828 (New York: E. Conrad, 1828), pp. 3, 5.*

39. *New-York Farmer and Horticultural Repository*, Volume 1, Number 2 (February 1828); *New-York Farmer and Horticultural Repository*, Volume 1, Number 4 (April 1828).

40. Burrows and Wallace, *Gotham*, p. 179.

41. Alice Morse Earle, *Old Time Gardens, Newly Set Forth* (New York: Macmillan, 1901), p. 26.

42. Burrows and Wallace, *Gotham*, p. 179; Earle, *Old Time Gardens*, pp. 26–27. As examples, see *New-York Farmer and Horticultural Repository*, Volume 1, Number 2 (February 1828), p. 36; *New-York Farmer and Horticultural Repository*, Volume 1, Number 5 (May 1828); "Proceedings of the New-York Horticultural Society," *New-York Farmer and Horticultural Repository*, Volume 1, Number 10 (October 1828).

43. Brown Diary, 6 April 1835, 28 April 1836.

44. *New-York Farmer and Horticultural Repository*, Volume 1, Number 7 (July 1828); *New-York Farmer and Horticultural Repository*, Volume 1, Number 8 (August 1828); *New-York Farmer and Horticultural Repository*, Volume 1, Number 9 (September 1828); *New-York Farmer and Horticultural Repository*, Volume 1, Number 10 (October 1828); *New-York Farmer and Horticultural Repository*, Volume 1, Number 11 (November 1828); *New-York Farmer and Horticultural Repository*, Volume 1, Number 12 (December 1828).

45. Brown Diary, 6 July 1837, 25 February 1841, 22 March 1852, 1 February 1853, 24 March 1854, 11 February 1858, 13 February 1858, 19 December 1858, 7 Mary 1858, 25 July 1859.

46. *New-York Farmer and Agricultural Repository,* Volume 1, Number 7 (July 1828); *New-York Farmer and Agricultural Repository,* Volume 1, Number 8 (August 1828), *New-York Farmer and Agricultural Repository,* Volume 1, Number 9 (September 1828); *New-York Farmer and Agricultural Repository,* Volume 1, Number 10 (October 1828).

47. Brown Diary, 24 April 1838.

48. See Thomas Bridgeman, *The Fruit Cultivator's Manual* (New York: A. Hunford, 1847); Thomas Bridgeman, *The American Gardner's Assistant* (Philadelphia: Porter and Coates, 1850).

49. Brown Diary, 12 October 1852, 9 December 1852.

50. *New York Times*, 24 March 1895; Daniel Crommelin Verplanck, Mary Anna's father, sold the family town residence on Wall Street in New York City in 1822, but Gulian, Mary Anna's brother, owned a house on 14th Street there. On this, see VerPlanck, *History of Abraham Isaacse VerPlanck*, pp. 193, 198, 244.

51. *Proceedings of the New-York Horticultural Society at the Celebration of Its Tenth Anniversary, August 26, 1828 (New York: E. Conrad, 1828), pp. 3–5l. Burrows and Wallace, Gotham, pp. 585–86. On the Dutchess County origins of the Ash family, see The Settlers of the Beekman Patent (Online database: NewEnglandAncestors.org, New England Historic Genealogical Society, 2003), orig. published as Frank J. Doherty, The Settlers of the Beekman Patent, Dutchess County, New York: An Historical and Genealogical Study of All the*

18th Century Settlers in the Patent, six volumes (Pleasant Valley, N.Y.: Frank J. Doherty, 1990–2001).

52. Schuyler, *Apostle of Taste*, pp. 9–15. 17, 241n23.

53. Brown Diary, 30 July 1830, 6 August 1830. The familial Walton connection is surmised from the fact that Mary Anna's mother was a Walton by birth; her maiden name was Anne Walton; on this, see VerPlanck, *History of Abraham Isaacse VerPlanck*, pp. 190–95.

54. Hovey, ed., *The Magazine of Horticulture*, 1839, p. 452.

55. Brown Diary, 19 October 1848, 20 October 1848, 21 October 1848, 4 January 1849, 6 April 1849.

CHAPTER 4

1. VerPlanck, *History of Abraham Isaacse VerPlanck*, pp. 197–98.

2. VerPlanck, *History of Abraham Isaacse VerPlanck*, p. 198.

3. Brown Diary, 6 May 1829, 26 May 1829.

4. See examples in Brown Diary, 26 April 1830, 3 May 1830, 18 May 1830, 23 May 1830, 5 June 1830, 7 June 1830, 25 October 1830, 1 December 1830, 5 December 1830, 15 February 1831.

5. Brown Diary, 4 March 1831; Gellman, *Emancipating New York*, pp. 39, 125, 133–34, 209, 212; Leslie M. Harris, *In the Shadow of Slavery: African Americans in New York City, 1626–1863* (Chicago: University of Chicago Press, 2003), pp. 61, 118; John Jay, *Memorials of Peter A. Jay—Compiled for His Descendants* (Holland: G. J. Thieme, 1905), p. 161 and *passim*; Graham Russell Hodges, *Root and Branch: African Americans in New York and East Jersey 1613–1863* (Chapel Hill: University of North Carolina Press, 1999), pp. 166–68.

6. Gellman, *Emancipating New York*, p. 209; Jay, *Memorials of Peter A. Jay*, pp. 64, 65, 93, 104, 161; Burrows and Wallace, *Gotham*, p. 514.

7. John L. Rury, "Philanthropy, Self-Help, and Social Control: The New York Manumission Society and Free Blacks, 1875–1810," *Phylon*, Volume 46, Number 3 (3rd quarter, 1985), pp. 231, 233–37, 240–41; Charles E. Knowles, *History of the Bank for Savings in the City of New York 1819–1929*, n.p., as researched, prepared, and transcribed by Miriam Medina, http://www.bklyn-genealogy-info.com/Business/BankSavings.NYC.html. Accessed 11 November 2009.

8. *First Annual Report of the Society for the Encourgement of Faithful Domestic Servants in New-York* (New York: Dan Fansahw, 1826), pp. 14, 16, 30; *Second Annual Report of the Managers of the Society for the Encouragement of Faithful Domestic Servants in New-York* (New York: D. Fanshaw, 1827), pp. 1, 12, 21, 32; *Third Annual Report of the Society for the Encouragement of Faithful Domestic Servants in New-York* (New York: D. Fanshaw, 1828); *Fifth Annual Report of the Society for the Encouragement of Faithful Domestic Servants in New-York* (New York: Daniel Fanshaw), 1830, pp. 7–8; Hodges, *Root and Branch*, pp. 200–4, 217–18.

9. In 1833, there were twelve entries on gardening and twenty-seven on other kinds of work. In 1834, there were ten gardening entries and twenty-one about nongardening work.

10. Brown Diary, 1 April 1835, 6 April 1835.

11. Brown Diary, 28 May 1836, 8 July 1836, 24 August 1836, 22 February 1838, 14 July 1838, 15 July 1838, 16 July 1838, 2 May 1839, 29 September 1839.

12. Schuyler, *Andrew Jackson Downing*, p. 17. For Hunt's position as an important editor, see Burrows and Wallace, *Gotham*, p. 847, and *Hunt's Merchants' Magazine and Commercial Review*, Volume XXX (1845), pp. i, 17.

13. Schuyler, *Andrew Jackson Downing*, pp. 20–27; New York Agricultural Society, *The Cultivator* (Albany: Luther Tucker, 1847), p. 101.

14. Alice Morse Earle, *Home Life in Colonial Days* (New York: Macmillan, 1898), pp. 436–37; Alice Morse Earle, *Old Time Gardens*, with an introduction by Virginia Lopez Begg (Lebanon, N.H.: University Press of New England, 2005; originally published in 1901 by Macmillan), p. 12.

15. Brown Diary, 14 September 1840.

16. Brown Diary, 12 September 1840, 14 September 1840; Edward Manning Ruttenber and Charles A. Tice, *A History of Newburgh* (Newburgh, N.Y.: E. M. Rutter and Company, 1859), pp. 180–81.

17. C. M. Hovey, ed., *The Magazine of Horticulture, Botany, and All Useful Discoveries and Improvements in Rural Affairs*, Volume VI (Boston: Hovey & Co., 1840), p. 348.

18. *Transactions of the Pennsylvania Horticultural Society* (Philadelphia: William Stavely & Company, 1840), p. 108. There is no hard evidence of a collaboration other than the longstanding association between Brown and Downing on horticultural matters, as discussed below, and the timing of Brown's trip with the praise for Downing's contribution to the Philadelphia exhibit in 1840.

19. *Transactions of the Pennsylvania Horticultural Society*, pp. 90, 95.

20. For examples of James's nongardening work after 1836, see Brown Diary, 19 May 1850. On James's public road work, see, as examples, Brown Diary, 12 May 1842, 28 June 1842; also see http://www.tfhrc.gov/pubrds/summer96/p96su2.htm and http://www.cato.org/pubs/journal/cj9n1/cj9n1-9.pdfnd. Accessed 7 July 2009.

21. For examples, see Brown Diary, 8 February 1837, 17 October 1838, 5 January 1839, 13 June 1840, 10 September 1847, 12 September 1854.

22. Virginia E. Verplanck, "The Verplanck Garden at Mount Gulian, Fishkill-on-Hudson," in Lockwood, *Gardens of Colony and State*, p. 286.

23. Brown Diary, 23 December 1841, 27 May 1836, 10 July 1837, 17 November 1841, 1 March 1842, 20 June 1844, 5 January 1849, 28 March 1849, 24 January 1851. John Bloomer is listed as a Fishkill resident in the 1840, 1850, and 1860 U.S Censuses; for the last two of these, he is described as a "carman" and teamster, respectively.

24. Various Reynolds family men are listed in the 1850 U.S. Census and in the 1870 U.S. Census as black residents of Fishkill. John Annin is listed in the 1840 U.S. Census as a white resident of Fishkill. The Brown Diary suggests that Montgomery, New York, was Ephraim Chancelor's birthplace because of his trips there to visit relatives, but he is not listed in any federal census. The diary mentions Amelia Chancelor, probably Ephraim's wife, on 11 November 1840, 4 October 1849, and 9 March 1850, and she is listed in the 1850 U.S.Census as a black woman with her last named spelled "Chancellor" living in Fishkill. Ephraim died of cholera during the epidemic of 1849; on this, see several entries in the diary: 12 July 1849, 25 July 1849, 29 July 1849, 1 August 1849, 6 August 1849, 10 August 1849, 13 August 1849, 14 August 1849, 27 August 1849, 7 September 1849, 4 October 1849. Lott Jones is listed as a "free, colored" resident of Fishkill in the 1840 U.S. Census. Brown mentions Jones in several entries, for example 20 September 1842, 24 December, 1843, 28 March 1845. Robert Williams is listed in the 1820 and 1830 U.S. Censuses as a black resi-

dent of Fishkill, based on who resided in his household—free colored persons only. (He is also listed in the 1830 U.S. Census, but no one else is indicated in his household that year.) Brown Diary, 15 April 1841. Edward Bush is listed as a black laborer and resident of Fishkill in the 1850 U.S. Census. Cornelius Jacocks is listed in the 1830 and 1860 U.S. Censuses—as a resident of Fishkill in the former enumeration and as a black driver living in Poughkeepsie in the latter enumeration. Brown Diary, 24 November 1840, 19 March 1840, 27 April 1840. For some of the less frequently mentioned garden workers, see Brown Diary, 13 September 1845, 13 April 1847, 28 June 1851, 23 March 1852, 13 September 1852, 30 March 1857, 18 March 1858. Stanford Rose is listed as black and residing in Fishkill in the 1850 and 1860 U.S. Censuses; in 1850, he is listed as a boatman. In the diary, Brown noted a Larie Slavens as a garden worker on 12 April 1859, a Leara Slavien as a garden worker on 16 March 1860, and a Leara Slavin as a garden worker on 8 April 1861. These were undoubtedly the same individual despite Brown's confusion about the spelling. The 1860 federal census of New York state lists a Lawrence Slavin residing in Fishkill that year. "Lawrence" is spelled with an asterisk, an indication that the census indexer was unsure of the spelling from the manuscript. Coleman, mentioned in the Brown Diary on 1 March 1842 as a garden worker, was probably Martin Coleman, listed as an African American laborer living in Fishkill in the 1850 U.S. Census.

25. Brown Diary, 15 November 1838, 18 November 1839, 10 December 1845, 20 January 1847. On the seasonal rhythms of agricultural work in nineteenth-century Dutchess County more generally, see William P. McDermott, *Dutchess County's Plain Folks: Enduring Uncertainty, Inequality, and Uneven Prosperity, 1725–1875* (Clinton Corners, N.Y.: Kerleen Press, 2004), pp. 153–55.

26. Examples of this abound in the diary. For a sampling, see 26 February 1836, 27 May 1836, 4 January 1837, 27 March 1837, 10 April 1837, 12 April 1837, 10 July 1937, 25 March 1838, 4 April 1839, 6 September 1839, 25 September 1839, 2 October 1839, 10 October 1839, 18 November 1839, 26 February 1840, 12 March 1840, 24 November 1840, 22 December 1840, 17 November 1841, 1 March 1842, 14 March 1842, 15 March 1842, 11 April 1842, 26 April 1842, 5 January 1849, 24 January 1851, 23 March 1853, 15 June 1854, 19 May 1859, 18 August 1859, 24 March 1860, and 26 March 1860.

27. Brown Diary, 23 January 1838, 29 January 1840, 19 February 1840, 25 February 1841, 25 February 1844, 8 January 1845, 19 January 1847, 8 February 1847, 3 January 1850, 6 February 1850, 6 January 1851, 26 January 1851, 5 March 1852, 26 January 1855, 6 February 1855.

28. Brown Diary, 26 October 1841, 25 February 1843; 1850 U.S. Census.

29. Brown Diary, 20 April 1836, 24 August 1836, 14 June 1837, 4 April 1838, 25 April 1838, 2 November 1838, 24 November 1838, 22 June 1839, 13 November 1839, 21 January 1840, 15 March 1840, 21 April 1840, 16 May 1840, 3 December 1840, 25 June 1841, 28 June 1841, 5 March 1842, 11 March 1842, 8 December 1845, 25 November 1848, 22 March 1853, 26 March 1859.

30. Brown Diary, 26 June 1839, 29 September 1840, 16 September 1847, 20 June 1848, 27 September 1849, 24 September 1850, 27 September 1852.

31. Myra B. Young Armstead, *"Lord, Please Don't Take Me in August": African Americans in Newport and Saratoga Springs, 1870–1930* (Urbana: University of Illinois Press, 1999), pp. 100–5; James Oliver Horton and Lois E. Horton, *In Hope of Liberty: Culture, Community, and Protest Among Northern Free Blacks, 1700 to 1860* (New York: Oxford University Press, 1997), pp. 114–19; Graham Russell Hodges, *Root and Branch: African Americans in New*

York and East Jersey, 1613–1863 (Chapel Hill: University of North Carolina Press, 1999), pp. 200–3; Robert Roberts, *The House Servant's Directory, or a Monitor for Private Families: Hints on the Arrangement and Performance of Servants' Work with General Rules for Setting Out Tables and Sideboards,* Graham Russell Hodges, ed. (Armonk, N.Y.: M. E. Sharpe, 1998); Shane White, *Somewhat More Independent: The End of Slavery in New York City, 1770–1810* (Athens: University of Georgia Press, 1991), pp. 156–63.

32. Joseph Smith, *Reminiscences of Saratoga or Twelve Seasons at the "States"* (New York: Knickerbocker Press, 1897), *passim*; Anna R. Bradbury, *History of the City of Hudson, New York with Biographical Sketches of Henry Hudson and Robert Fulton* (Hudson, N.Y.: Record Printing and Publishing Co., 1908), p. 179; www.oldindustry.org/MA_HTML/MA_Novisit.html.

33. Smith, *Reminiscences of Saratoga*, pp. 1–2, 4–7.

34. The literature on this subject is large, but some excellent examples include Bruce Laurie, *Artisans into Workers: Labor in Nineteenth Century America* (Urbana: University of Illinois Press, 1997); Sean Wilentz, *Chants Democratic: New York City and the Rise of the American Working Class, 1788–1850* (New York: Oxford University Press, 1984); Bruce Laurie, *Working People of Philadelphia 1800–1850* (Philadelphia: Temple University Press, 1983); Paul G. Faler, *Mechanics and Manufacturers in the Early Industrial Revolution: Lynn, Massachusetts, 1780–1860* (Albany: State University of New York Press, 1981); Paul E. Johnson, *A Shopkeeper's Millennium: Society and Revivals in Rochester, New York, 1815–1837* (New York: Hill and Wang, 1979); and Howard B. Rock, *Artisans of the New Republic: Tradesmen of New York City in the Age of Jefferson* (New York: New York University Press, 1979).

35. Brown Diary, 17 June 1848, 18 June 1848, 21 June 1848; VerPlanck, *History of Abraham Isaacse VerPlanck*, pp. 273–76.

36. Brown Diary, 23 February 1833, 4 February 1836, 15 February 1836, 2 August 1836, 16 January 1837, 6 February 1839, 4 February 1840, 7 January 1842, 11 January 1843, 26 January 1843, 9 May 1844, 10 January 1845, 21 January 1846, 4 February 1846, 31 December 1847, 25 January 1847, 19 January 1848, 29 February 1849, 30 January 1850, 22 January 1851, 21 January 1852, 15 January 1853, 25 January 1853, 20 January 1853, 7 January 1857, 20 June 1857, 20 August 1860, 1 September 1860, 20 December 1861, 26 February 1863; Dutchess County Land Records, Liber 58, pp. 92–93 (21 January 1836), Dutchess County Clerk's Office, Poughkeepsie, N.Y. Brown is listed as a real estate owner in the 1850 U.S. Census; he is listed with no real estate in the 1860 U.S. Census. Jane Neal of Fishkill is listed in the 1850 and 1870 U.S. Censuses.

37. Brown Diary, 14 January 1833, 23 February 1833, 30 April 1836, 7 February 1838, 2 February 1839, 13 July 1839, 26 September 1839, 21 January 1840, 6 February 1841, 25 March 1842, 17 October 1842, 24 January 1843, 23 August 1843, 21 April 1844, 24 February 1846, 26 February 1846, 22 October 1846, 28 December 1846, 6 January 1847, 11 January 1847, 6 December 1850; Adams, "The Standard of Living During American Industrialization," pp. 903, 911; Adams, "Prices and Wages in Maryland, 1750–1850, pp. 635. Other examples of Julia's jobs are indicated in the Brown Diary, 14 June 1843, 1 September 1843, and 22 July 1845. Julia often took out-of-town temporary work as a domestic or cook.

38. Brown Diary, 28 May 1833, 18 March 1834, 12 October 1834, 24 April 1837, 27 June 1837, 20 October 1837, 7 February 1838, 7 April 1838, 7 August 1839, 26 September 1839, 1 June 1840, 30 September 1841, 21 April 1841, 14 June 1841, 6 August 1841, 7 August 1841, 8 August 1841, 9 August 1841, 9 August 1841, 12 August 1841, 2 August 1841, 2 September 1843, 4 July 1845, 16 June 1846, 19 January 1847, 18 October 1847, 8 November 1847,

5 February 1851, 7 May 1851, 10 May 1851, 22 October 1851, 24 October 1851, 5 February 1852, 20 September 1852, 13 May 1854, 9 August 1858, 17 August 1858, 2 August 1858; David Lewis Hammarstrom, *Fall of the Big Top: The Vanishing American Circus* (Jefferson, N.C.: McFarland Press, 2007), pp. 29–43; Myra B. Young Armstead, "*Lord, Please Don't Take Me in August*," pp. 18–34; Cindy S. Aron, *Working at Play: A History of Vacations in the United States* (Chicago: University of Chicago Press, 1999), pp. 15–44; Robert Bogdan, *Freak Show: Presenting Human Oddities for Amusement and Profit* (Chicago: University of Chicago Press, 1988), pp. 25–35; Mark Irwin West, "A Spectrum of Spectators: Circus Audiences in Nineteenth Century America," *Journal of Social History,* Volume 15, Number 2 (Winter 1981), pp. 265–70; Edward Harold Mott, "*Between the Ocean and the Lakes*": *The Story of Erie* (New York: Ticker Publishing Co., 1908), pp. 371, 386–87; *New York Times,* 6 August 1858, p. 4; *New York Times,* 7 August 1858, p. 5; *Brooklyn Daily Eagle,* 21 May 1851.

39. J. C. Loudon, Allen Robert Branston, and Jane Webb Loudon, *An Encyclopedia of Gardening* (London: Longman, Green, Longman, and Roberts, 1835), pp. 1222–24. See Richard Drayton, *Nature's Government: Science, Imperial Britain, and the "Improvement" of the World* (New Haven, Conn.: Yale University Press, 2000), pp. 139–46 for a discussion of the high and low ends of botany and horticulture as occupations in Britain.

40. Loudon et al., *An Encyclopedia of Gardening,* pp. 1222–24.

41. David Schuyler, *Apostle of Taste: Andrew Jackson Downing 1815–1852* (Baltimore: Johns Hopkins University Press, 1996), pp. 220–21; Brown Diary, 4 February 1839, 10 February 1839, 19 February 1841, 15 January 1844, 16 January 1844, 30 January 1842, 30 January 1847, 21 July 1849, 18 July 1859, 14 June 1860.

42. Brown Diary, 16 June 1849, 12 July 1849, 4 October 1849, 28 July 1852, 29 July 1852, 6 May 1853, 8 May 1853, 13 May 1853, 26 May 1853, 27 May 1853, 6 November 1856, 27 November 1856, 28 November 1856, 30 November 1856, 3 December 1856; VerPlanck, *History of Abraham Isaacse Verplanck,* p. 206; Brown Diary, 11 October 1858.

43. Brown Diary, 17 March 1860, 28 March 1860, 10 April 1861, 24 November 1863, 26 November 1863. Haight is identified as a farmer in the 1880 U.S. Census and specifically as the Verplanck family farmer in the Brown Diary, 15 July 1852.

44. Brown Diary, 25 December 1856.

CHAPTER 5

1. On this, see Rozsika Parker, "Unnatural History: Women, Gardening and Femininity" in Tim Richardson and Noel Kingsbury, eds., *Vista: The Culture and Politics of Gardens* (London: Frances Lincoln Limited, 2005), pp, 87–95; Jennifer Bennett, *The Historical Relationship Between Women and Plants* (Camden East, Ont.: Camden House, 1991), pp. 11–38; Susan Broag Bell, "Women Create Gardens in Male Landscapes: A Revisionist Approach to Eighteenth-Century English Garden History," *Feminist Studies,* Volume 18, Number 3 (Autumn 1990), pp. 471–74; Leigh Ann Whaley, *Women's History as Scientists* (Santa Barbara, Calif.: ABC-CLIO, 2003). Mary Anna's temporary, unofficial admission to the NYHS network in order to show her lima beans, celery, and melons in the summer of 1830 was necessarily facilitated by men close to her—her cousin and her brother—and by another man as well, her gardener, James F. Brown. So James continued to exhibit through 1840, although his diary contains no mention of a similar course for Mary Anna in the ten years following her presentations in 1830.

2. James E. DeKay, *Natural History of New York* (New York: D. Appleton & Co., 1842), pp. 135; Robert Wilson Hoge, "A Doctor for All Seasons: David Hosack of New York," *American Numismatic Society Magazine* (Spring 2007), accessed at http://ansmagazine. com/spring07/hosack.html, 19 July 2008; Burrows and Wallace, *Gotham*, pp. 345, 498, 548–49; Jerry Cheslow, "If You're Thinking of Living In/Murray Hill: A Quiet Enclave Close to Midtown," *New York Times*, 5 December 1999; Charles Monaghan, "Lindley Murray and the Enlightenment," *Paradigm*, Number 19 (May 1996), accessed at http://faculty. ed.uiuc.edu/westbury/paradigm/monaghan2.html, 19 July 2008; *Proceedings of the NYHS at the Celebration of the Tenth Anniversary*, p. 3.

3. David Schuyler, *Apostle of Taste: Andrew Jackson Downing 1815–1852* (Baltimore: Johns Hopkins University Press, 1996), pp. 13–15.

4. Tamara Plakins Thornton, "The Moral Dimensions of Horticulture in Antebellum America," *New England Quarterly*, Volume 57, Number 1 (March 1984), p. 9; Tamara Plakins Thornton, *Cultivating Gentlemen: The Meaning of Country Life among the Boston Elite, 1785–1860* (New Haven, Conn.: Yale University Press, 1989), *passim*.

5. *American Quarterly Review*, Volume 21 (June 1837), pp. 366–67.

6. *New-York Farmer and Horticultural Repository*, Volume 1, Number 1 (January 1828), pp. 1–2.

7. *New-York Farmer and Horticultural Repository*, Volume 1, Number 1 (January 1828), p. 1.

8. Ibid.

9. Ibid.

10. McCarthy, "A Page, A Day," p. 30; Marilyn Ferris Motz, "Folk Expression of Time and Place: 19th-Century Midwestern Rural Diaries," *The Journal of American Folklore*, Volume 100, Number 396 (April–June 1987), p. 139.

11. E. P. Thompson, "Time, Work-Discipline and Capitalism," *Past and Present*, Volume 38 (December 1967, pp. 56–97; David S. Landes, *Revolution in Time: Clocks in the Making of the Modern World* (Cambridge, Mass.: Belknap Press of Harvard University Press, 1983), p. 72; Michael O'Malley, *Keeping Watch: A History of American Time* (New York: Viking, 1990), pp. 5, 9, 55–72; Lewis Mumford, *Technics and Civilization* (New York: Harcourt, Brace and Company, 1934), pp. 13–14, 23.

12. Martin Bruegel, "'Time That Can Be Relied Upon': The Evolution of Time Consciousness in the Mid-Hudson Valley, 1790–1860," *Journal of Social History*, Volume 28, Number 3 (Spring 1995), pp. 547–64.

13. Brown Diary, 24 March 1838, 4 February 1846, 18 December 1850, 15 April 1853, 31 July 1861.

14. Brown Diary, 17 May 1839.

15. Benjamin Franklin, "Advice to a Young Tradesman" in Bliss Perry, ed., *Little Masterpieces* (New York: Doubleday and McClure Company, 1902), p. 153; Daniel T. Rodgers, *The Work Ethic in Industrial America 1850–1920* (Chicago: University of Chicago Press, 1978), *passim*; Appleby, *Inheriting the Revolution*, pp. 56–89.

16. Motz, "Folk Expressions of Time and Place," pp. 145–46; Arthur Ponsonby, *English Diairies: A Review of English Diaries from the Sixteenth to the Twentieth Century with an Introduction on Diary Writing* (London: Methuen & Co., Ltd., 1923), p. 6.

17. Cited in Molly McCarthy, "A Pocketful of Days: Pocket Diaries and Daily Record Keeping among Nineteenth-Century New England Women," *The New England Quarterly*, Volume 73, Number 2 (June 2000), pp. 284–85.

18. "Finding Aid Information," Brown Diary, New-York Historical Society.

19. Motz, "Folk Expressions of Time and Place," pp. 136, 143–44; Brown Diary, 10 July 1837, 6 July 1843.

20. Brown Diary, 30 January 1839, 6 February 1839, 11 February 1839.

21. Brown Diary, 18 February 1841, 8 February 1842. It is not clear how often and when exactly Brown was paid, but the diary records one instance of his receiving a year's "settlement" from Mary Anna Verplanck, on 8 February 1841. This could have been an actual cash payment for the previous year's work or an agreement on salary between James and Mary Anna for the next year. For general information on hiring and payment practices for farm laborers in nineteenth-century Dutchess County, N.Y., see William P. McDermott, *Dutchess County's Plain Folks: Enduring Uncertainty, Inequality, and Uneven Prosperity* (Clinton Corners, N.Y.: Kerleen Press), pp. 152–57.

22. Brown Diary, 23 August 1843, 5 December 1850, 9 September 1851.

23. Brown Diary, 6 January 1847, 11 January 1847, 29 March 1853, 3 May 1853; E. M. Ruttenber, *History of the Town of Newburgh* (Newburgh, N.Y.: E. M. Ruttenberg & Co., 1859), pp. 151–52. On Mace, see the 1850 U.S. Census.

24. McCarthy, "A Pocketful of Days," p. 277; Jane H. Hunter, "Inscribing the Self in the Heart of the Family: Diaries and Girlhood in Late-Victorian America," *American Quarterly*, Volume 44, Number 1 (March 1992), pp. 51–81; Motz, "Folk Expressions of Time and Place," p. 143–44.

25. Brown Diary, 14 October 1857, 21 October 1857.

26. *Freedom's Journal*, 20 April 1827.

27. *The North Star*, 28 April 1848.

28. *The National Era*, 24 April 1851.

29. Richard Drayton, *Nature's Government: Science, Imperial Britain, and the "Improvement" of the World* (New Haven, Conn.: Yale University Press, 2000), pp. 183–84; Lucile H. Brockway, *Science and Colonial Expansion: The Role of the British Royal Botanic Gardens* (New York: Academic Press, 1979), pp. 84–86; Mary Louise Pratt, *Imperial Eyes: Studies in Travel Writing and Transculturation* (London: Routledge, 1992), pp. 15–37.

30. Londa Schiebinger, *Plants and Empire: Colonial Bioprospecting in the Atlantic World* (Cambridge, Mass.: Harvard University Press, 2004), *passim*.

31. Franz Broswimmer, "Botanical Imperialism: The Stewardship of Plant Genetic Resources in the Third World," *Critical Sociology*, Volume 18, Number 1 (April 1991), pp. 3–17; Schiebinger, *Plants and Empire*, pp. 194–225; Pratt, *Imperial Eyes*, pp. 24–36, 123; Staffan Muller-Wille, "Walnuts at Hudson Bay, Coral Reefs in Gotland," in Londa Schiebinger and Claudia Swan, eds., *Colonial Botany: Science, Commerce, and Politics in the Early Modern World* (Philadelphia: University of Pennsylvania Press, 2005), pp. 44–48.

32. Beatrice Scheer Smith, "Jane Colden (1724–1766) and Her Botanic Manuscript," *American Journal of Botany*, Volume 75, Number 7 (July 1988), pp. 1090–96.

33. Schuyler, *Apostle of Taste*, *passim* but especially pp. 85–106, 212–30.

34. Brown Diary, 20 April 1833.

35. As examples, in the year in which it first appeared, 1832, *Lander's Travels* was advertised by booksellers in the *Baltimore Gazette and Daily Advertiser* (7 August 1832, p. 4; 8 August 1832, p. 4; 15 August 1832, p. 1); the *Connecticut Mirror* (18 August 1832, p. 3); the *Southern Patriot* (18 September 1832, p. 3.); the *Rhode-Island American and Gazette* (1 September 1832, p. 4); *American Advocate* (28 September, p. 3); *The Age* (24 October

1832, p. 4); and the *Ohio State Journal* (5 December 1832, p. 4). On The Family Library and early nineteenth-century self-help literature aimed at the British working class, see John Feather, *A History of British Publishing*, pp. 140–43; R. W. Church, *The Oxford Movement: Twelve Years 1833–1845* (Whitefish, Mont.: Kessinger Publishing, 2004, originally published 1892), p. 13.

36. For a listing of the Family Library titles, see Charles Boileau Elliott, *Travels in the Three Great Empires of Austria, Russia, and Turkey* (London: R. Bentley, 1838), p. 6.

37. Richard Lander and John Lander, *Landers' Discovery of the Termination of the Niger* (New York: J. & J. Harper, 1832), n.p. (unnumbered first pages).

38. Robert Huish, *The Travels of Richard and John Lander into the Interior of Africa, for a Discovery of the Course and Termination of the Niger* (London: John Saunders, 1836), pp. 488, 1069–70, (http://tiny.cc/1tm2h), accessed 15 June 2009.

39. Richard Westmacott, *African-American Gardens and Yards in the Rural South* (Knoxville: University of Tennessee Press, 1998), pp. 14–20, 87–108; "The South: Letters on the Production, Industries, and Resources of the Slave States, *New York Times*, 22 September 1853, p. 2; *New York Times*, 24 March 1865, p. 4; *New York Times*, 25 June 1871, p. 5; *New York Times*, 29 March, p. 5.

40. Judith Carney and Richard Nicholas Rosamoff, *In the Shadow of Slavery: Africa's Botanical Legacy in the Atlantic World* (Berkeley: University of California Press, 2010), pp. 16, 112–17, 140–44, 177–79; Judith Carney, *Black Rice: The African Origins of Rice Cultivation in the Americas* (Cambridge, Mass.: Harvard University Press, 2001); Daniel C. Littlefield, *Rice and Slaves: Ethnicity and the Slave Trade in Colonial South Carolina* (Urbana: University of Illinois Press, 1981), pp. 74–113; Robert L. Hall, "Food Crops, Medicinal Plants, and the Atlantic Slave Trade," in Anne L. Bower, ed., *African American Foodways: Explorations of History and Culture* (Urbana: University of Illinois Press, 2007), pp. 17–44; Kenneth F. Kiple, *A Moveable Feast: Ten Millennia of Food Globalization* (Cambridge: Cambridge University Press, 2007), pp. 13, 38–40; Peter Wood, *Black Majority: Negroes in Colonial South Carolina from 1670 through the Stono Rebellion* (New York: Norton, 1996), pp. 35–62.

41. Westmacott, *African-American Gardens and Yards*, p. 15.

42. Brown Diary, 16 September 1839, 10 September 1847.

43. According to Motz, "Folk Expressions of Time and Place," p. 134, "recipes and medical cures" were often included in nineteenth-century American rural diaries. In this respect too, then, the Brown diary conformed to contemporary conventions.

44. G. Gundaker, "Tradition and Innovation in African-American Yards," *African Arts*, Volume 26, Number 2 (April 1993), pp. 58–71; Timothy Ruppel, Jessica Neuwirth, Mark P. Leone, and Gladys-Marie Fry, "Hidden in View: African Spiritual Spaces in North American Landscapes," *Antiquity*, Volume 77 (June 2003), pp. 321–35; Clare Rishbeth, "Gardens of Ethnicity," in Tim Richardson and Noel Kingsbury, eds., *Vista: The Culture and Politics of Gardens* (London: Frances Lincoln Limited, 2005), pp. 47–48; E. E. Lemaistre, "African Americans and the Land in Piedmont, Georgia from 1850 to the Present," M.A. Thesis, University of Georgia, 1988; Westmacott, *African-American Gardens and Yards*, pp. 87–108.

45. Barbara Bulison Mooney, "The Comfortable Tasty Framed Cottage: An African-American Architectural Iconography," *The Journal of the Society of Agricultural Historians*, Volume 61, Number 1 (March 2002), pp. 48–67.

46. Brown Diary, 11 May 1840, 17 April 1838, 7 May 1833, 14 May 1836.

47. Brown Diary, 16 November 1839.

48. Brown Diary, 5 March 1840.

49. Brown Diary, 18 May 1850.

CHAPTER 6

1. Eric Foner, *The Story of American Freedom* (New York: Norton, 1998), pp. 58–68.

2. Alan Dawley, *Class and Community: The Industrial Revolution in Lynn* (Cambridge, Mass.: Harvard University Press, 1975; 2nd ed. 2000); Sean Wilentz, "Artisan Origins of the American Working Class," *International Labor and Working-Class History*, Volume 19 (Spring 1981), pp. 1–3; Sean Wilentz, *Chants Democratic: New York City and the Rise of the American Working Class, 1788–1850* (New York: Oxford University Press, 1984), pp. 61–107; Daniel Jacoby, *Laboring for Freedom: A New Look at the History of Labor in America* (Armonk, N.Y.: M. E. Sharpe, 1998), pp. 13–32.

3. Alan Taylor, *American Colonies: The Settling of North America* (New York: Penguin, 2002), p. 172.

4. Seth Rockman, *Scraping By: Wage Labor, Slavery, and Survival in Early Baltimore* (Baltimore: Johns Hopkins University Press, 2009), pp. 2–4, 53, 77, 132–93, 243.

5. Charles G. Steffen, *The Mechanics of Baltimore: Workers and Politics in the Age of Revolution* (Urbana: University of Illinois Press, 1984), pp. 53–170.

6. Rockman, *Scraping By*, p. 42.

7. Ibid., pp. 41–44.

8. Wilentz, *Chants Democratic*, p. 102.

9. Ibid., pp. 61–103.

10. Martin Hoyles, "The Garden and the Division of Labour," in Tim Richardson and Noel Kingsbury, eds., *Vista: The Culture and Politics of Gardens* (London: Francis Lincoln, Ltd., 2005), pp. 21–38.

11. In the early twentieth century, the director of the Brooklyn Botanical Garden wrote a couple of pieces about "professional" gardening but seemed to be addressing wealthy women who sought training in horticulture, not those who were contemplating paid serious employment in the field of gardening. See C. Stuart Gager, "Horticulture as a Profession," *Science*, Volume 9, Number 1265 (March 28, 1919), pp. 293–300; and C. Stuart Gager, "The School of Horticulture in Perspective, *Science*, Volume 84, Number 2182 (October 23, 1936), pp. 357–65.

12. Maarten Park, Catharina Lis, Jan Lucassen, and Hugo Soly, eds., *Craft Guilds in the Early Modern Low Countries: Work, Power, and Representation* (Burlington, Vt.: Ashgate, 2006), pp. 36, 42, 62–64, 157–73; Ann Lancashire, *London Civic Theatre: City Drama and Pageantry from Roman Times to 1558* (Cambridge: Cambridge University Press), *passim*; John M. Wasson, *Devon (Records of Early English Drama)* (Toronto: University of Toronto Press, 1984), pp. xvii–xviii; Edward Waite Miller, "The Church and Medieval Trade Unions," Papers of the American Society of Church History (Second Series), Volume 32 (1910), pp. 175–86.

13. Wilentz, *Chants Democratic*, pp. 87–97.

14. Norman Simms, "Ned Lumm's Mummers Play," *Folklore*, Volume 89, Number 2 (1978), pp. 166–78.

15. *Baltimore Gazette and Daily Advertiser,* 4 February 1832, p. 4.

16. Walter B. Smith, "Wage Rates on the Erie Canal, 1828–1881," *The Journal of Economic History,* Volume 23, Number 3 (September 1963), pp. 304, 309; Donald R. Adams Jr., "Wage Rates in the Early National Period: Philadelphia, 1785–1830," *The Journal of Economic History,* Volume 28, Number 3 (September 1968), p. 408; Donald R. Adams Jr., "Prices and Wages in Maryland, 1750–1850," *The Journal of Economic History,* Volume 46, Number 3 (September 1986), pp. 633, 638; Brown Diary, 1 March 1841, 23 March 1852; William P. McDermott, *Dutchess County's Plain Folks: Enduring Uncertainty, Inequality and Uneven Prosperity, 1725–1875* (Clinton Corners, N.Y.: Kerleen Press, 2004), pp. 153, 156; *Boston Daily Courier,* 2 April 1840, p. 1. Several East Coast papers carried this politically charged story about White House expenses.

17. *Baltimore Gazette and Daily Advertiser,* 4 February 1832, p. 4; Smith, "Wage Rates on the Erie Canal, 1828–1881," p. 304; McDermott, *Dutchess County's Plain Folks,* p. 153. Using the Consumer Price Index to translate Brown's purchasing power in 1850 into contemporary (2010) terms, Brown's salary in 1850 (figured at $400) provided him with a disposable income of $11,500 in cash for household items, according to calculation formulas provided by "Measuring Worth" (see http://www.measuringworth.com/aboutus.php) through EH.net, the Economic History Association's Web site. In understanding this figure, it is important to note that Brown's house was paid off by that year and he had owned it free and clear since 1839. In addition, households in the mid–nineteenth century spent far less on consumer goods than today's families. Furthermore, the concept of consumer credit in modern terms was unknown in the nineteenth century. Using the Gross Domestic Product Per Capita calculator at the same Web site, Brown's status or rank in earnings in current (2010) terms would be the equivalent of $172,000. These figures are approximations at best and should not be taken literally. For this reason, it is best to consider Brown's income in relation to that of other farm and artisanal workers of his time living in a still largely agricultural economy.

18. For examples, see *The Liberator,* 9 August 1834, for a trenchant report of an auction of a slave who was recommended as "a good Hostler, Coachman, a Body or House Servant, or Gardener"; *Colored American,* 11 May 1839, for a caustic listing of various laborers, including gardeners, advertised as property; *Frederick Douglass' Paper,* 30 July 1852, for a report on the late Henry Clay's estate, which included a slave gardener; *Douglass' Monthly,* June 1860, regarding a fugitive slave from Maryland, "once regarded as the lawful property of a gentleman, whom he served in the capacity of a gardener."

19. *The Southern Patriot,* 9 March 1832, p. 3.

20. *Baltimore Gazette and Daily Advertiser,* 4 March 1836, p. 3.

21. Rockman, *Scraping By,* p. 52.

22. *Colored American,* 14 July 1838, 28 July 1838, 13 July 1839, 29 May 1841; *National Era,* 22 May 1851; *Frederick Douglass' Paper,* 23 September 1853; *The Liberator,* 2 April 1859, 17 May 1861.

23. J. C. Loudon, Allen Robert Branston, and Jane Webb Loudon, *An Encyclopedia of Gardening* (Loudon: Longman, Green, Longman, and Roberts, 1835), pp. 132, 1223.

24. Daniel E. Meades, "South Carolina Fugitives as Viewed Through Local Colonial Newspapers with Emphasis on Runaway Notices 1732–1801," *Journal of Negro History,* Volume 60, Number 2 (April 1975), p. 308; Clifford K. Shipton, "Immigration to New England, 1680–1740," *Journal of Political Economy,* Volume 44, Number 2 (April 1936), p. 233; Loudon, Branston, and Loudon, *An Encyclopedia of Gardening,* pp. 132, 267, 1223–24;

The Farmer's Cabinet, 31 March 1827, p. 2; *Barre Gazette,* 16 May 1845, p. 2; *National Era,* 1 September 1853; Alice B. Neal, "The Gardener's Daughter," *Godey's Lady's Book,* September 1856; *National Era,* 27 January1859.

25. *New York Herald,* 25 September 1856; *New York Herald,* 20 June 1857; *New York Herald,* 22 September 1857; *New York Herald,* 24 March 1858, pp. 6–7; *New York Herald,* 28 March 1858, p. 6; *New York Herald,* 3 August 1860, p. 6.

26. Ibid., 6 March 1857, p. 6.

27. Ibid.

28. *The Public Ledger,* 19 March 1840, p. 3.

29. Sean Wilentz, *The Rise of American Democracy: Jefferson to Lincoln* (New York: Norton, 2005), pp. 721–22.

30. Wendell Phillips, "The Question of Labor," *The Liberator,* 9 July 1847. For additional examples of the discussion of "wage slavery" in the antebellum African-American press, see *The Liberator,* 2 April 1847; "The Pleasures of Industry," *Colored American,* 19 October 1839.

CHAPTER 7

1. Alexis de Tocqueville, *Democracy in America,* Volume II, translated by Henry Reeve, Esq. (New York: J. & H. G. Langley, 1841), pp. 114–17; Theda Skocpol and Morris P. Fiorina, eds., *Civic Engagement in American Democracy* (Washington: Brookings Institution Press, 1999), p. 9; Theda Skocpol, "The Tocqueville Problem: Civic Engagement in American Democracy," *Social Science History,* Volume 21, Number 4 (Winter 1997), pp. 456–57.

2. L. Marx Renzalli, *Maryland: The Federalist Years* (Cranbury, N.J.: Associated University Press, 1972), pp. 319–20.

3. Edmund S. Morgan, *Inventing the People: The Rise of Popular Sovereignty in England and America* (New York: Norton, 1989); Gordon Wood, *The Creation of the American Republic 1776–1787* (Chapel Hill: University of North Carolina Press, 1969).

4. Bernard Bailyn, *The Ideological Origins of the American Revolution* (Cambridge, Mass.: Belknap Press of Harvard University Press, 1992, 1967), pp. 94–159.

5. Gordon Wood, *The Radicalism of the American Revolution* (New York: Vintage, 1993), pp. 11–94.

6. Lawrence E. Klein, *Shaftesbury and the Culture of Politeness: Moral Discourse and Cultural Politics in Early Eighteenth-Century England* (Cambridge: Cambridge University Press, 1994), pp. 121–12; Lorinda B.R. Goodwin, *An Archeology of Manners: The Polite World of the Merchants Elite of Colonial Massachusetts* (New York: Kluwer Academic/Plenum Publishers, 1999), *passim.*

7. Joseph S. Tiedeman and Eugene R. Fingerhut, eds., *The Other New York: The American Revolution Beyond New York City, 1763–1787* (Albany: State University of New York Press, 2006), pp. 107–54; Joseph S. Tiedeman, *Reluctant Revolutionaries: New York City and the Road to Independence, 1776–1783* (Ithaca, N.Y.: Cornell University Press, 1997), pp. 223–31, 238–40, 246–47; Leopold S. Launitz-Schurer, *Loyal Whigs and Revolutionaries: The Making of the Revolution in New York 1765–1776* (New York: New York University Press, 1980), p. 160.

8. William Cullen Bryant, *A Discourse on the Life, Character, and Writings of Gulian Crommelin Verplanck* (New York: New-York Historical Society, 1870), pp. 7–9.

9. *The American Revolution Beyond New York City, 1763–1787* (Albany: State University of New York Press, 2006), pp. 107–54; Tiedeman, *Reluctant Revolutionaries*, pp. 223–31, 238–40, 246–47; Launitz-Schurer, *Loyal Whigs and Revolutionaries*, p. 160; Bryant, *A Discourse on the Life*, p. 7.

10. The Office of the State Comptroller, *New York in the Revolution as Colony and State, Volume* II (Albany, N.Y.: J. B. Lyon Company, 1904), pp. 63–67.

11. VerPlanck, *The History of Abraham Isaacse Verplanck*, pp. 149, 152–59; Patrick Ruckert, "Image of the American Patriot: The Fight for the American Public, James Fenimore Cooper and the Society of the Cincinnati," The Schiller Institute, November 2007, http://www.schillerinstitute.org/educ/hist/patriot_image_toc.html, accessed 29 June 2009.

12. Gellman, *Emancipating New York*, pp. 56–77; Hugh Barbour, Christopher Densmore, Elizabeth H. Moger, Nancy C. Sorel, Alson D. Van Wagner, and Arthur J. Worrall, eds., *Quaker Crosscurrents: Three Hundred Years of Friends in the New York Yearly Meetings* (Syracuse, N.Y.: Syracuse University Press, 1995), pp. 68–71.

13. L. Lloyd Stewart, *A Far Cry from Freedom: Gradual Abolition (1799–1827): New York State's Crime Against Humanity* (New York: AuthorHouse, 2006), pp. 120–34; Leslie M. Harris, *In the Shadow of Slavery: African Americans in New York City, 1626–1683* (Chicago: University of Chicago Press, 2003), pp. 56–71; Shane White, *Somewhat More Independent: The End of Slavery in New York City, 1770–1810* (Athens: University of Georgia Press, 1991), pp. 24–55; Burrows and Wallace, *Gotham*, pp. 285–87; Rogers M. Smith, *Civic Ideals: Conflicting Views of U.S. Citizenship in U.S. History* (New Haven, Conn.: Yale University Press, 1999), pp. 142–44; U.S. Census, 1800; Gellman, *Emancipating New York*, p. 170; Eugene A. Hoffman, *Genealogy of the Hoffman Family: Descendants of Martin Hoffman, with Biographical Notes* (New York: Dodd, Mead, 1899), pp. 499–500.

14. E. Edwards Beardsley, *The Life and Times of William Samuel Johnson* (New York: Hurd and Houghton, 1876), pp. 108–17, 129–45; Elizabeth Peterkin McCaughey, *From Loyalist to Founding Father* (New York: Columbia University Press, 1980), pp. 179–94; William Givens Andrews, *William Samuel Johnson and the Making of the Constitution* (Bridgeport, Conn.: Standard Association Printers, 1887). Daniel married Elizabeth Johnson in 1785 and completed his education at Columbia College in 1788. On this, see VerPlanck, *The History of Abraham Isaacse VerPlanck*, p. 189; see Gordon S. Wood, *Empire of Liberty: A History of the Early Republic, 1789–1815* (New York: Oxford University Press, 2009), pp. 95–139, and Wilentz, *The Rise of American Democracy*, pp. 28, 32, for brief summaries of the restraining impulses of Federalists toward popular democracy. Johnson was college president. Like his own father, Johnson had hoped for a reasonable accord with the British that would forestall the necessity of war for independence. In 1775, in fact, Johnson was sent as part of a delegation from his home state of Connecticut to General Gage to forge some sort of agreement regarding the Anglo-American discord over British taxes. Again in 1779, the people of his town, Stratford, sent him to convince British General Tryon not to burn it down. Johnson was so placating in his approach to the British that colonial dissidents in Connecticut for a while considered him an enemy of the state, literally, and ordered his imprisonment as such. Johnson was able to get himself paroled, and then, through the good offices of Connecticut Governor Trumbull, Johnson was allowed to return to his rural home for the war's duration because he, like Samuel Verplanck, had contributed some of his own property to the war effort and helped the Continental Army (in this case, by encouraging enlistments). Like Samuel Verplanck, too, Johnson removed

himself from public affairs during the war to pass this period in relative quietude. Later, at the Constitutional Convention of 1787, he was an especially articulate and effective spokesman for the strong central government crafted by this document. During the partisan debates and conflict spurred by the Jay Treaty of 1794, Johnson took a decidedly Federalist stance in support of the settlement with Britain. According to his biographer, E. Edwards Beardsley, he told the graduating class that year, "Make yourselves well acquainted with the true nature of civil liberty. . . Study the true industry of your country. Examine its present situation and what will be the effect of union, order, harmony, a firm government of laws and an energetic execution of them. See whether true Liberty does not consist in an exact obedience to law, a submission to the public will, a surrender of all individual, inferior, partial subordinate interests, emoluments, and objects to general, public, and universal welfare." This was a clear expression of Federalist thinking, tinged by Old Whig concerns for political stability. So Daniel received such a political education from his father and his father-in-law that reinforced this approach to civic life, particularly because Daniel was a student at Columbia College during Johnson's tenure as its president.

15. "Daniel Crommelin Verplanck," *Biographical Dictionary of the United States Congress, 1774–2005*, http://search.ancestry.com. Accessed 1 July 2009; 1810 U.S. Census; Wood, *Empire of Liberty*, pp. 508–42; Gellman, *Emancipating New York*, p. 206. See Wilentz, *The Rise of American Democracy*, pp. 49–62, for a summary of the emergence of Democratic-Republican societies. Gellman, *Emancipating New York*, pp. 127–28, makes it clear that Democratic-Republicans sometimes produced antislavery literature while Federalists were not above expressing disdain for "black social pretensions" so that, although it was unusual, it was not unheard of for a Democratic-Republican such as Daniel C. Verplanck to feel comfortable endorsing a private manumission.

16. Bryant, *A Discourse on the Life*, p. 47; Wood, *Empire of Liberty*, pp. 90–140.

17. Bryant, *A Discourse on the Life*, pp. 16–18; VerPlanck, *History of Abraham Isaacse VerPlanck*, pp. 226–27.

18. John C. Miller, *Crisis in Freedom: The Alien and Sedition Acts* (Boston: Little, Brown, 1952); David Walker Howe, *The Political Culture of the American Whigs* (Chicago: University of Chicago Press, 1979), pp. 29–30.

19. "Daniel Crommelin Verplanck," *Biographical Dictionary of the United States Congress*; Bryant, *A Discourse on the Life*, p. 23.

20. Daniel Walker Howe, *What God Hath Wrought: The Transformation of America, 1815–1848* (New York: Oxford University Press, 2007), pp. 91–124.

21. Nathaniel H. Carter, William L. Stone, and Marcus T.C. Gould, *Reports of the Proceedings and Debates of the Convention of 1821, Assembled for the Purpose of Amending the Constitution of the State of New York* (Albany, N.Y.: E. and E. Rosford, 1821), pp. 178–204; Gellman, *Emancipating New York*, pp. 207–13.

22. See Bernard Bailyn, *The Ideological Origins of the American Revolution* (Cambridge, Mass.: Belknap Press of Harvard University Press, 1992).

23. J. Hector Jean de Crevecoeur, "Letter II," *Letters from an American Farmer* (London: T. Davies, 1782), http://avalon.law.yale.edu/18th_century/letter_02.asp, accessed 7 November 2008.

24. Joyce Appleby, *Capitalism and a New Social Order* (New York: New York University Press, 1984).

25. Wilentz, *The Rise of American Democracy*, pp. 182, 186–90, 195, 199, 201; James West Davidson, Brain DeLay, Christine Leigh Heyrman, Mark H. Lytle, and Michael B. Stoff, *Nation of Nations: A Narrative History of the American Republic, Volume I: To 1877* (Boston: McGraw-Hill Higher Education, 2007), pp. 296, 411–13.

26. Ibid., p. 305.

27. Gellman, *Emancipating New York*, p. 202; Litwack, *North of Slavery*, pp. 80–81.

28. *Reports of the Proceedings and Debates of the Convention of 1821*, pp. 28, 191; Gellman, *Emancipating New York*, pp. 207–8; Wilentz, *The Rise of American Democracy*, pp. 189–94.

29. *Reports of the Proceedings and Debates of the Convention of 1821*, pp. 28, 190, 191.

30. Ibid.

31. "Daniel Crommelin Verplanck," *Biographical Dictionary of the United States Congress*; Walter Barrett, *The Old Merchants of New York City* (New York: Thomas R. Knox, 1885), p. 256.

32. Howe, *What God Hath Wrought*, p. 493; Robert V. Remini, *The Legacy of Andrew Jackson: Essays on Democracy, Indian Removal, and Slavery* (Baton Rouge: Louisiana University Press, 1990); Richard E. Ellis, *The Union at Risk: Jackson Democracy, States' Rights, and the Nullification Crisis* (New York: Oxford University Press, 1989), pp. 99–100, 147, 150–51, 165–66, 168; Bryant, *A Discourse on the Life*, pp. 25–28; Wilentz, *The Rise of American Democracy*, p. 385.

33. Bryant, *A Discourse on the Life*, p. 32.

34. "Daniel Crommelin Verplanck," *Biographical Dictionary of the United States Congress*; Bryant, *A Discourse on the Life*, pp. 33–36; Burrows and Wallace, *Gotham*, pp. 573–75; Michael F. Holt, *The Rise and Fall of the American Whig Party: Jacksonian Politics and the Onset of the Civil War* (New York: Oxford University Press, 1999), pp. 23–32; Wilentz, *The Rise of American Democracy*, pp. 391–402; Howe, *What God Hath Wrought*, p. 493.

35. *The Liberator*, 15 April 1859.

36. Letter of Gerrit Smith to Hon. Gulian C. Verplanck, 12 December 1837, New-York Historical Society, New York, N.Y.

37. Reeve Huston, *Land and Freedom: Rural Society, Popular Protest, and Party Politics in Antebellum New York* (New York: Oxford University Press, 2000), pp. 182–83; Harris, *In the Shadow of Slavery*, pp. 215–23.

38. Huston, *Land and Freedom*, pp. 185–88; Holt, *The Rise and Fall of the American Whig Party*, p. 241.

39. Bryant, *A Discourse on the Life*, pp. 33–47.

40. Wilentz, *The Rise of American Democracy*, p. 522; Howe, *What God Hath Wrought*, pp. 588–89; Brown Diary, 4 March 1841, 5 April 1841, 7 April 1841, 9 April 1841.

41. Bryant, *A Discourse on the Life*, pp. 25–28; Walter R. Borneman, *Polk: The Man Who Transformed the Presidency and America* (New York: Random House, 2008), pp. 231, 323–25; Wilentz, *The Rise of American Democracy*, pp. 577–86; Howe, *What God Hath Wrought*, pp. 701–81; David M. Potter, *The Impending Crisis, 1848–1861* (New York: Harper Perennial, 1976), pp. 64–65; Eugene Irving McCormac, *James K. Polk: A Political Biography* (Berkeley: University of California Press, 1922), pp. 612, 618–20. Gulian was not a protectionist, but in the interest of compromise during the Nullification Crisis of 1832, as chair of the House Ways and Means Committee he had proposed a substantially reduced tariff—yet one "so framed as to cause as little inconvenience as might be to the manufacturers." Again, Gulian preferred the kind of measured approach to contentious issues that his grandfa-

ther and father had displayed. In the end, Congress adopted Henry Clay's plan for a tariff that would be gradually reduced over a ten-year period. So with this memory, Gulian supported the Democratic candidate, James K. Polk, over Clay as the Whig nominee in 1844.

42. Brown Diary, 16 November 1848.

43. Howe, *What God Hath Wrought*, pp. 828–31; Wilentz, *The Rise of American Democracy*, pp. 616–17; Potter, *The Impending Crisis, 1848–1861*, pp. 70, 72, 110; Holt, *The Rise and Fall of the American Whig Party*, pp. 127, 247–49; Bryant, *A Discourse on the Life*, p. 47.

44. Bryant, *A Discourse on the Life*, p. 47. On federal arrests by executive order and suspension of *habeas corpus* during the Civil War, see Timothy H. Donovan and Thomas E. Greiss, *The American Civil War* (Garden City Park, N.Y.: Square One Publisher, 2002), p. 16, and Irwin Unger, *The Greenback Era: A Social and Political History of American Finance* (Princeton, N.J.: Princeton University Press, 1964), pp. 13–40.

45. 1840 U.S. Census.

46. Howe, *The Political Cutlure of the Whigs*, pp. 263–98.

47. "Captain Robert Newlin Verplanck," Mount Gulian Web site, http://www.mountgulian.org/newlin.html. Accessed 7 July 2009.

48. Samuel P. Bates, *History of Pennsylvania Volunteers, 1861–5*, Vol. 1 (Harrisburg, Pa.: B. Singerly, 1871), p. 959; James M. Paradis, *Strike the Blow for Freedom: The 6th United States Colored Infantry in the War* (Shippensburg, Pa.: White Mane Publishing, 2000); "Captain Robert Newlin Verplanck"; Robert Newlin Verplanck, U.S. Civil War Records and Profiles, http://tiny.cc/aj33o. Accessed 2 July 2009.

49. Howe, *The Political Culture of the Whigs*, pp. 96–122, 150–80.

50. Wilentz, *The Rise of American Democracy*, pp. 490–99. Compare the moral philosophy of the Whigs as summarized in Howe, *The Political Culture of the Whigs*, pp. 23–42, with the Republican Party presidential campaign strategy in 1860 as discussed in Wilentz, *The Rise of American Democracy*, pp. 760–62, 764–65. At their respective cores, Whigs were far more values-driven than the relatively pragmatic Republicans.

CHAPTER 8

1. Brown Diary, 7 November 1837.

2. Michael F. Holt, *The Rise and Fall of the American Whig Party: Jacksonian Politics and the Onset of the Civil War* (New York: Oxford University Press, 1999), pp. 41, 46–47, 99–100, 109; Howe, *What God Hath Wrought*, pp. 511–12, 577–78; Wilentz, *The Rise of American Democracy*, pp. 490–91.

3. *The Colored American*, 18 November 1837.

4. Ibid., 29 March 1838.

5. Ibid., 16 November 1839.

6. Brown Diary, 29 May 1836, 19 June 1836, 26 June 1836, 2 August 1836, 13 August 1836, 3 September 1836, 22 September 1836, 7 June 1837, 8 July 1837, 2 May 1838, 24 August 1838, 21 April 1842, 22 July 1842, 23 July 1842, 14 January 1845; Dutchess County Land Records, Liber 58, p. 92–93 (21 January 1836), Dutchess County Clerk's Office, Poughkeepsie, N.Y.; Dutchess County Land Records, Liber 60, p. 241 (13 August 1836), Dutchess County Clerk's Office, Poughkeepsie, N.Y.; Dutchess County Land Records, Liber 74, p. 257 (20 July 1842), Dutchess County Clerk's Office, Poughkeepsie, N.Y.; Dutchess County Land Records, Liber 79, pp. 442–443 (1 April 1845), Dutchess County Clerk's Office, Pough-

keepsie, N.Y. No deed was found in the name of William Lloyd in the Dutchess County, New York, Land Records, but a William Lloyd is listed as a porter in Newburgh in the Newburgh City Directory, 1858–59, p. 33

7. Brown Diary, 10 January 1845, 21 January 1846. On George Washington, see 27 November 1845, 11 April 1846, 7 December 1846, 11 March 1847, 8 October 1847, 9 October 1847, 24 November 1847. On Anthony and Sarah Bradford, see Brown Diary, 14 February 1842, 15 March 1842, 12 November 1845, 9 April 1846, 6 May 1847. On Samuel Rose, see Brown Diary, 12 May 1845.

8. John Stauffer, *The Black Hearts of Men: Radical Abolitionists and the Transformation of Race* (Cambridge, Mass.: Harvard University Press, 2002), pp. 81–82, 102–4, 127–38; Paul Schneider, *The Adirondacks: The History of America's First Wildnerness* (New York: Henry Holt, 1997), p. 105–14; Octavious Brooks Frothingham, *Gerrit Smith: A Biography* (New York: G. P. Putnam, 1879), pp. 102–8; "Tale of Gerrit Smith Behind Adirondack Suit," *New York Times*, 19 November 1904; Howe, *What God Hath Wrought*, p. 654.

9. Brown Diary, January 1843, 27 September 1843, 15 April 1847; *The National Era*, 15 April 1847; Wilentz, *The Rise of American Democracy*, pp. 592, 620, 647.

10. Howe, *What God Hath Wrought*, p. 652; Wilentz, *The Rise of American Democracy*, pp. 532, 547–54; Holt, *The Rise and Fall of the American Whig Party*, pp. 155–57.

11. These are references to James Watson Webb, a proponent of African colonization for blacks in his journal, *Courier and Enquirer*, and William Leete Stone, secretary of the New York Colonization Society and editor of the *Commercial Advertiser*. As advocates of black colonization, these two considered abolitionists to be extremists and used their publications to spread this view during the New York City anti-abolitionist riots of July 1834. On this, see Mike Wallace, *Gotham: A History of New York City to 1893* (New York: Oxford University Press, 1999), pp. 556–59.

12. *Colored American*, 10 October 1840.

13. Holt, *The Rise and Fall of the American Whig Party*, p. 118; William Nestbit Chambers, "Election of 1840," in Arthur M. Schlesinger Jr., ed., *History of American Presidential Elections, 1789–1968* (New York: Chelsea House Publishers, 1971).

14. Horton and Horton, *In Hope of Liberty*, p. 208.

15. *The Liberator*, 5 October 1833. For another reference to Buffam's work, see Daniel R. Biddle and Murray Dubin, *Tasting Freedom: Octavius Catto and the Battle for Equality in Civil War America* (Philadelphia: Temple University Press, 2010), p. 48.

16. Brown Diary, 3 February 1833, 28 March 1833, 23 June 1833; James H. Smith, *History of Dutchess County, New York 1683–1882* (Syracuse, N.Y.: D. Mason & Co., 1882), p. 524; James Brewer Stewart, "Modernizing 'Difference': The Political Meanings of Color in the Free States, 1776–1840" in Michael A. Morrison, and James Brewer Stewart, *Race and the Early Republic: Racial Consciousness in Nation-Building in the Early Republic* (New York: Rowman and Littlefield, 2002), p. 122; Leslie M. Harris, *In the Shadow of Slavery: African Americans in New York City, 1626–1863* (Chicago: University of Chicago Press, 2003), pp. 195–98.

17. Minutes of the Executive Committee of the Dutchess County Anti-Slavery Society, 29 May 1838–11 April 1840, Manuscripts and Archives Division, New York Public Library, New York, N.Y.; *Colored American*, 25 July 1840, 14 August 1841, 21 August 1841, 18 September 1841; *The National Era*, 22 April 1847; *North Star*, 3 December 1847; *Frederick Douglass's Paper*, 5 October 1855.

18. *Colored American,* 15 July 1837, 12 August 1837; Brown Diary, 5 August 1836; 15 April 1837; Hodges, *Root and Branch,* p. 245; *Harris, In the Shadow of Slavery,* pp. 210–13.

19. In his recent biography of David Ruggles, black abolitionist, Graham Russell Hodges makes no mention of a connection to Dutchess County, N.Y. On this Ruggles, see Graham Russell Gao Hodges, *David Ruggles: A Radical Black Abolitionist and the Underground Railroad* (Chapel Hill: University of North Carolina Press, 2010); Hodges, *Root and Branch,* pp. 245–48, 251; Fergus M. Bordewich, *Bound for Canaan: The Epic Story of the Underground Railroad: America's First Civil Rights Movement* (New York: Harper Paperbacks, 2006), pp. 166–86; Graham Russell Hodges, "David Ruggles: The Hazards of Anti-Slavery Journalism," *Media Studies Journal,* Volume 14, Number 2 (Spring/Summer 2000); Dorothy B. Porter, "David Ruggles: An Apostle of Human Rights," *Journal of Negro History,* Volume 28, Number 1 (1943), pp. 23–50.

20. Leslie M. Harris, *In the Shadow of Slavery: African Americans in New York City, 1626 to 1865* (Chicago: University of Chicago Press, 2003), p. 206.

21. Hodges, *David Ruggles,* pp. 1, 5, 93, 99, 103–5, 117, 161; A. J. Williams-Myers, "The Underground Railroad in the Hudson River Valley: A Succinct Historical Composite," *Afro-Americans in New York Life and History,* Volume 27, Number 1 (January 2003), pp. 55–73.

22. *Colored American,* 26 August 1837; Brown Diary, 28 September 1837; Harris, *In the Shadow of Slavery,* pp. 154, 182; Timothy Shortell, "The Rhetoric of Abolitionism: An Exploratory Analysis of Antislavery Newspapers in New York State," *Social Science History,* Volume 28, Number 1 (Spring 2004), p. 83.

23. Sarah C. Ruggles to C. H. Ruggles, 11 August 1824, C. H. Ruggles Papers, New-York Historical Society (NYHS), New York, N.Y.; Sarah C. Ruggles to C. H. Ruggles, 1 June after 1824 before 1831 [*sic*], C. H. Ruggles Papers, NYHS; Sarah C. Ruggles to C. H. Ruggles, after 1837 [*sic*], C. H. Ruggles Papers, NYSH; Sarah C. Ruggles to C. H. Ruggles, probably 1838 [*sic*], C.H. Ruggles Papers, NYSH; Sarah C. Ruggles to C. H. Ruggles, December perhaps 1837 David died 12/19/1837 [*sic*], C. H. Ruggles Papers, NYHS; C. H. Ruggles to Sarah C. Ruggles, 25 December 1838, C. H. Ruggles Papers, NYHS; Accounts of Aaron Belknap, Treasurer of the Newburgh Horticultural Society, 1829–1834, Aaron Belts Belknap Correspondence, Belknap Family Papers, New-York Historical Society, New York, N.Y.; *Journal of the American Institute of the City of New York,* Volume 2, Number 3 (December 1836), p. 121; *Journal of the American Institute of the City of New York,* Volume 2, Number 5 (February 1837), pp. 229–31; *Albany Register*; Edward Manning Ruttenber and Charles W. Tice, *History of the Town of Newburgh* (Newburgh, N.Y.: E. M. Ruttenber and Co., Printers, 1859), pp. 146–47.

24. Brown Diary, 1 August 1842; Brown's mentions of "Five Corners Fishkill Landing " and of "Eagle Hotel, five corners" in his diary entries for June 20, 1845, and February 11, 1848, respectively, confirm that there was a Five Corners in Fishkill Landing (there was also one in New Windsor, N.Y.—just south of Newburgh—but the Eagle Hotel was in Fishkill Landing).

25. Brown Diary, 1 October 1850.

26. Brown Diary, 11 January 1853, 15 January 1855; *Colored American,* 12 September 1840, 2 October 1841; *Frederick Douglass' Paper,* 3 February 1854, 5 October 1855; Mid-Hudson Antislavery History Project, June 2007 Research Report, http://www.hudsonrivervalley.net/presscenter/newsClippings/MHAHP_UGRRreport.pdf, accessed 10 July 2009.

27. Brown Diary, 4 August 1857.

28. *The Liberator,* 7 August 1857, 14 August 1857; *Poughkeepsie Journal,* 8 August 1857, p. 2; W. M. Brewer, "Henry Highland Garnet," *The Journal of Negro History,* Volume 13, Number 1 (January 1928), pp. 36–52; Steven H. Shiffrin, "The Rhetoric of Black Violence in the Antebellum Period: Henry Highland Garnet," *Journal of Black Studies,* Volume 2, Number 1 (September 1971), pp. 46–54; Joel Schor, *Henry Highland Garnet: A Voice of Black Radicalism in the Nineteenth Century* (Westport, Conn.: Greenwood Press, 1977); Foner, *The Rise of American Democracy,* pp. 556, 627. See also Reverend William Goodell, *Slavery and Anti-Slavery: A History of the Great Struggle in Both Hemispheres; With a View of the Slavery Question in the United States* (New York: William Harned, 1852), and William Goodell, *The American Slave Code in Theory and in Practice* (New York: American and Foreign Anti-Slavery Society, 1853).

29. *Poughkeepsie Journal,* 8 August 1857, p. 2.

30. Frankie Hutton, *The Early Black Press in America* (Westport, Conn.: Greenwood Press, 1993), pp. 165–66; I. Garland Penn, *The Afro-American Press and Its Editors* (Springfield, Mass.: Willey, 1891), pp. 25–51, 55–56, 61–70; Penelope Bullock, *The Afro-American Periodical Press, 1838–1909* (Baton Rouge: Louisiana State University Press, 1981), p. 55.

31. Brown Diary, 28 October 1842; *Colored American,* October 30, 1841; Penn, *The Afro-American Press,* pp. 55–56; Bullock, *The Afro-American Periodical Press,* p. 55, 57; Donald Franklin Joyce, *Black Book Publishers in the United States: A Historical Dictionary of the Presses, 1817–1990* (Westport, Conn.: Greenwood, 1991), pp. 117–21; Stafford North, "The Evangelist," in Douglas A. Foster, Anthony L. Dunnavant, Paul M. Blowers, and D. Newell Williams, eds., *The Encyclopedia of the Stone-Campbell Movement* (Grand Rapids, Mich.: William B. Eerdmans, 2005), pp. 322–23; "Antislavery Journalism in the United States and Great Britain," in Peter P. Hinks, John R. McKivigan, and R. Owen Williams, eds., *Encyclopedia of Antislavery and Abolition* (Westport, Conn.: Greenwood Press, 2006), pp. 51–53; Aldon Morris, "Centuries of Black Protest: Its Significance for America and the World," in Herbert Hill and James E. Jones Jr., eds., *Race in America: The Struggle for Equality* (Madison: University of Wisconsin Press, 1993), p. 31.

32. Hutton, *The Early Black Press in America,* p. xiv, 36–39; Bullock, *The Afro-American Periodical Press,* p. 15; Joanne Pope Melish, "The 'Condition.' Debate and Racial Discourse in the Antebellum North," in Michael A. Morrison and James Brewer Stewart, eds., *Race and the Early Republic: Racial Consciousness and Nation-Building in the Early Republic* (Lanham, Md.: Rowman and Littlefield, 2002), pp. 75–94.

33. Hutton, *The Early Black Press in America,* p. 26.

34. Brown Diary, 22 February 1833, 22 February 1834, 22 February 1836, 22 February 1837, 22 February 1838, 22 February 1848, 22 February 1849, 22 February 1850, 22 February 1851, 22 February 1861.

35. Sarah J. Purcell, *Sealed with Blood: War, Sacrifice, and Memory* (Philadelphia: University of Pennsylvania Press, 2002), p. 99.

36. Brown Diary, 4 March 1841, 7 April 1841, 4 March 1845, 24 June 1845, 4 July 1846, 22 June 1849, 4 July 1849, 4 July 1850, 12 July 1850, 23 July 1850, 30 June 1852, 4 July 1852, 5 July 1852, 19 July 1852, 27 October 1852, 29 October 1852, 4 March 1853, 14 June 1857, 16 October 1859; Holt, *The Rise and Fall of the American Whig Party,* pp. 1–2, 25; Howe, *The Political Culture of the Whigs,* pp. 123–49; Potter, *The Impending Crisis,* p. 96.

37. Brown Diary, 4 August 1842; James H. Smith, *History of Dutchess County, New York, 1683–1882* (Syracuse, N.Y.: D. Mason & Co., 1882), pp. 522–23.

38. Brown Diary, 14 May 1849, 25 February 1851, 18 January 1851, 18 January 1852, 30 January 1855, 21 September 1859, 8 December 1859.

39. Wallace, *Gotham*, pp. 522–25.

40. *Colored American*, 13 July 1839; *North Star*, 12 May 1848.

41. *Colored American*, 25 September 1841.

42. Wallace, *Gotham*, pp. 525–27.

43. *North Star*, 19 May 1848.

44. *Frederick Douglass' Paper*, 20 August 1852.

45. Brown Diary, 8 June 1850, 2 August 1850, 8 August 1850, 10 August 1850; 1850 U.S. Census. The Dutchess County Clerk's Office does have microfilm of nineteenth-century convictions, but the "Index of Convictions 1820–1862" (actually in two volumes—Volume 1, Series 76: 1820–62 and Volume 2, Series 77: 1859–1889) does not list Green or Holden. Similarly, the index to the County Clerk's Minutes for civil cases in 1850 does not list either Green or Holden as either a plaintiff or a defendant.

46. On this, see Norma Basch, *In the Eyes of the Law: Women, Marriage and Property in Nineteenth-Century New York* (Ithaca, N.Y.: Cornell University Press, 1982), *passim*.

47. 11 How., Pr. 184, *Woods v. Thompson* (1855).

48. Husband and Wife 210 (1), *Abbott New York Digest,* Volume 19 (St. Paul, Minn.: West Publishing Company, 1955), pp. 164–65; Brown Diary, 13 February 1855, 14 February 1855, 18 February 1855, 7 March 1855. Although Brown gives no specifics concerning the case, his siding with Woods in opposing the motion can be surmised from the fact that this was the position in the case taken by E. R. Bogardus, of Manhattan in 1855 but originally from Fishkill and a longtime legal adviser to and counsel for James and his friends; for this, see Brown Diary, 22 January 1851, 21 January 1851, 19 February 1855; the 1850 U.S. Census, which has Edwin R. Bogardus practicing law in Fishkill, and the 1860 U.S. Census, which shows him practicing in Manhattan. See also Nancy A. Hewitt, "Origin Stories: Remapping First Wave Feminism," Proceedings of the Third Annual Gilder Lehrman Conference at Yale University—Sisterhood and Slavery: Transatlantic Antislavery and Women's Rights," 25–28 October 2001, pp. 3–9, 14, 16, 19–20; *The Liberator*, 28 October 1853; Sally Gregory McMillen, *Seneca Falls and the Origins of the Women's Rights Movement* (New York: Oxford University Press, 2008), pp. 73, 75–119, 147; Sara M. Evans, *Born for Liberty: A History of Women in America* (New York: 1989), pp. 67–92; Elizabeth R. Varon, "Tippecanoe and the Ladies, Too: White Women and Party Politics in Antebellum Virginia," pp. 498–503.

49. Leon F. Litwack, *North of Slavery: The Negro in the Free States 1790–1860* (Chicago: University of Chicago Press, 1961), pp. 93–94.

CHAPTER 9

1. For various views of voluntarism in the nineteenth century according to gender, class, and race and for participation rates, see Angela G. Ray, "The Permeable Public: Rituals of Citizenship in Antebellum Men's Debating Clubs," *Argumentation and Advocacy*, Volume 41 (Summer 2004); David M. Fahey, *Temperance and Racism: John Bull, Johnny Reb, and the Good Templars* (Lexington: University Press of Kentucky, 1996), pp. 3–4, 9–10; Paula Baker, "The Domestication of Politics: Women and American Political Society, 1780–1920," *American Historical Review*, Volume 89, Number 3 (June 1984), pp. 620–33;

Mary P. Ryan, "The Power of Women's Networks: A Case Study of Female Moral Reform in Antebellum America," *Feminist Studies* Volume 5, Number 1 (Spring 1979), pp. 66–70; and Don H. Doyle, "The Social Functions of Voluntary Associations in a Nineteenth-Century American Town," *Social Science History*, Volume 1, Number 3 (Spring 1977), pp. 333–55. On African-American voluntarism in the nineteenth century, see Joe William Trotter, "African American Fraternal Organizations in American History: An Introduction," *Social Science History*, Volume 28, Number 3 (Fall 2004), pp. 355–66; Theda Skocpol and Jennifer Lynn Oser, "Organization Despite Adversity: The Origins and Development of African American Fraternal Associations," *Social Science History*, Volume 28, Number 3 (Fall 2004), pp. 367–437; Fahey, *Temperance and Racism*, p. 107.

2. Mark A. Noll, *A History of Christianity in the United States and Canada* (Grand Rapids, Mich.: William B. Eerdmans, 1992), pp. 163–64; Jon Butler, *Awash in a Sea of Faith: Christianizing the American People* (Cambridge, Mass.: Harvard University Press, 1992), pp. 257–88; Nathan O. Hatch, *The Democratization of American Christianity* (New Haven, Conn.: Yale University Press, 1990), pp. 3–48.

3. As examples, see Brown Diary, 21 March 1830, 2 May 1830, 14 April 1833, 3 July 1836, 18 June 1837, 1 January 1841, 26 June 1842, 30 May 1843; Brown Diary, 17 August 1845.

4. VerPlanck, *A History of the Male Descendants of Abraham Isaacse VerPlanck*, pp. 206–7, 242; Edward M. Ruttenber and Charles W. Tice, *History of the Town of Newburgh* (Newburgh, N.Y.: E. M. Ruttenber and Co., 1859), pp. 196–98; Smith, *History of Dutchess County*, p. 518.

5. Noll, *A History of Christianity*, pp. 164, 167, 171, 173, 176, 220.

6. Brown Diary, 15 February 1829; Dennis Bratcher, ed., "The General Rules of the Methodist Class Meetings," 1808, 1848, 1868; http://www.crivoice.org/creedclass.html. Accessed 13 August 2009; Smith, *History of Dutchess County*, p. 518.

7. A sampling of references to Methodist service attendance includes those for Brown Diary, 14 April 1833, 9 June 1833, 23 June 1833, 21 July 1833, 28 July 1833, 13 March 1836, 25 August 1836, 28 August 1836; Moore, *History of the A.M.E. Zion Church*, pp. 384–85.

8. Frank Lambert, "'I Saw the Book Talk': Slave Readings of the Great Awakening, *Journal of African American History,* Volume 87 (Winter 2002), pp. 1, 16–17, 19; Milton C. Sernett, ed., *African American Religious History: A Documentary Witness* (Chapel Hill, N.C.: Duke University Press, 1999), p. 13; Horton and Horton, *In Hope of Liberty*, pp. 132–36, 139–40, 144–46.

9. Brown Diary, 13 March 1836, 25 August 1836, 28 August 1836, 29 August 1836, 24 September 1841; Charles E. Hamrick-Stowe, *Charles G. Finney and the Spirit of American Evangelicalism* (Grand Rapids, Mich.: William B. Eerdmans, 1996), pp. 161–64; Garth M. Rosell and Richard Dupuis, eds., *The Original Memoirs of Charles G. Finney* (Grand Rapids, Mich.: Zondervan, 2002, 1876), pp. 269–83; Noll, *A History of Christianity,* pp. 174–76; Hatch, *The Democratization of Christianity,* pp. 67, 196–201; Butler, *Awash in a Sea of Faith,* p. 163.

10. *Colored American,* No. II, 21 October 1837; *Brooklyn Eagle,* 6 April 1884, p. 6; J. Alexander Patten, *Lives of the Clergy of New York and Brooklyn: Embracing Two Hundred Biographies of Eminent Living Men in All Denominations* (New York: Atlantic Publishing, 1874), pp. 31–32, http://www.archive.org/stream/livesofclergyofnoopatt/livesofclergyofnoopatt_djvu.txt, accessed 17 August 2009; Henry Reed Stiles, *A History of the City of Brooklyn*, Vol. III (Brooklyn: Published by Subscription, 1870), pp. 665–66, 668.

11. *African Methodist Episcopal Zion Church*, "About Our Church," http://www.amez. org/news/amezion/aboutourchurch.html, accessed 18 August 2009; Christopher Rush, "Rise of the African Methodist Episcopal Zion Church," in Sernett, ed., *African American Religious History*, pp. 155–63; Albert J. Raboteau, *Canaan Land: A Religious History of African Americans* (New York: Oxford University Press, 1999), pp. 21–41; "Communications: Letters from Henry C. Wright Warrington," 22 April 1843; *The Liberator*, Volume XIII, Issue 30 (July 28, 1843), p. 120; Craig Steven Wilder, *A Covenant with Color: Race and Social Power in Brooklyn* (New York: Columbia University Press, 2000), pp. 52–53, 82–85; Harris, *In the Shadow of Slavery*, pp. 83–84; *Brooklyn Eagle*, 23 January 1869, p. 2; *Brooklyn Eagle*, 6 April 1884, p. 6. Brooklyn, after all, was also the home of two of the era's most prominent evangelical radical abolitionists—Arthur and Lewis Tappan.

12. Hatch, *The Democratization of American Christianity*, pp. 141–45; Noll, *A History of Christianity*, pp. 223, 227–30; Paul S. Boyer, *Urban Masses and Moral Order in America, 1820–1920* (Cambridge, Mass.: Harvard University Press, 1978), pp. 3–53, 77–80, 108–22; Isaac Ferris, *Jubilee Memorial of the American Bible Society, 1816–1866* (New York: American Bible Society, 1867), Appendix, p. 3; *Annual Report of the American Bible Society, Volume 1* (New York: Daniel Fanshaw, 1838), p. 180; Brown Diary, 6 February 1840, 8 February 1840.

13. S. L. Greenslade, ed., *The Cambridge History of the Bible: The West from the Reformation to the Present Day* (Cambridge: Cambridge University Press, 1975), p. 493–94.

14. *Liberator*, 31 May 1834.

15. Ibid. Similar views were expressed in other black newspapers. See, for example, *The National Era*, 30 March 1848.

16. *North Star*, 27 July 1849; *Frederick Douglass' Paper*, 23 December 1853.

17. W. J. Rorabaugh, *The Alcoholic Republic: An American Tradition 1800–1830* (New York: Oxford University Press, 1979), pp. 147–222. For a slightly different take on alcohol consumption in the first decades of the nineteenth century, see Ian R. Tyrrell, *Sobering Up: From Temperance to Prohibition in Antebellum America 1800–1860* (Westport, Conn.: Greenwood Press, 1979), pp. 137–38; Tyrrell argues that although hard liquor consumption had increased through 1810, for the next two decades it was rivaled and bested by beer, cider, and wine consumption.

18. Katherine A. Chavigny, "Reforming Drunkards in Nineteenth Century America: Religion, Medicine, Therapy," in *Altering American Consciousness: A History of Alcohol and Drug Use in the United States* (Amherst: University of Massachusetts Press, 2004), pp. 109–13; Ann-Marie E. Szymanski, *Pathways to Prohibition: Radicals, Moderates, and Social Movement Outcomes* (Durham, N.C.: Duke University Press, 2003), pp. 24–36; Tyrrell, *Sobering Up*, pp. 8–9, 12, 110–13.

19. Tyrrell, *Sobering Up*, pp. 146–50; Fahey, *Temperance and Racism*, p. 8; *Colored American*, 6 March 1841.

20. Chavigny, "Reforming Drunkards in Nineteenth Century America," p. 110; Szymanski, *Pathways to Prohibition*, p. 31; Fahey, *Temperance and Racism*, p. 8; Lyman Beecher, *Six Sermons on Intemperance* (Boston: T. R. Marvin, 1828). Tyrrell, in *Sobering Up*, pp. 150–51, argues that the decline in temperance converts in the 1830s was short-lived and temporary, reflecting only the loss of financial backing in the short term for the cause following the Panic of 1837.

21. Tyrrell, *Sobering Up*, p. 5; Fahey, *Temperance and Racism*, p. 105; Daniel Yacavone, "The Transformation of the Black Temperance Movement, 1827–1854: An Interpretation,"

Journal of the Early Republic, Volume 8, Number 3 (Autumn 1988), p. 290; Denise Herd, "The Paradox of Temperance: Blacks and the Alcohol Question in Nineteenth-Century America," in Susanna Barrows and Robin Room, eds., *Drinking: Behavior and Belief in Modern History* (Berkeley: University of California Press, 1991); Patricia A. Schechter, "Temperance Work in the Nineteenth Century," in Darlene Clark Hine, ed., *Black Women in America* (Brooklyn: Carlson, 1993); Kenneth Christmon, "Historical Overview of Alcohol in the African American Community, *Journal of Black Studies*, Volume 25, Number 3 (January 1995), p. 328.

22. Douglas W. Carlson, "Temperance Ideology in the Deep South," *Journal of the Early Republic*, Volume 18, Number 4 (Winter 1998), pp. 690–91.

23. Yacovone, "The Transformation of the Black Temperance Movement," pp. 290–97; Craig Steven Wilder, *In the Company of Black Men: The African Influence on African American Culture in New York* (New York: New York University Press, 2001), p. 88; Fahey, *Temperance and Racism*, p. 105. On Gerrit Smith's teetotalism, see Tyrrell, *Sobering Up*, pp. 128, 138–39, 145.

24. *Colored American*, 6 March 1841.

25. Brown Diary, 6 March 1838, 6 September 1845, 9 June 1846, p. 2; "Temperance Celebration in New York," *Albany Evening Journal*, 6 June 1846, p. 2.

26. Mark Tebeau, *Eating Smoke: Fire in Urban America, 1800–1850* (Baltimore: Johns Hopkins University Press, 2003), pp. 13–53; Robyn Cooper, "The Fireman: Immaculate Manhood," *Journal of Popular Culture*, Volume 28, Number 4 (Spring 1995), pp. 139–70.

27. Tebeau, *Eating Smoke*, pp. 37–38.

28. Bruce Laurie, "Fire Companies and Gangs in Southwark," in Allen F. Davis and Mark Haller, eds., *The Peoples of Philadelphia: A History of Ethnic Groups and Lower Class Life, 1790–1840* (Philadelphia: Temple University Press, 1973), pp. 75–81; J. J. Lee and Marian Casey, eds., *Making the Irish American: History and Heritage of the Irish in the United States* (New York: New York University Press, 2006), pp. 354–56; Kenneth Moss, "St. Patrick's Day Celebrations and the Formation of Irish-American Identity, 1845–1875," *Journal of Social History*, Volume 29, Number 1 (Autumn 1995), pp. 125–48.

29. See, as examples, Frederick M. Binder and David M. Reimers, *All the Nations Under Heaven: An Ethnic History of New York City* (New York: Columbia University Press, 1995), pp. 62–63; Noel Ignatiev, *How the Irish Became White* (New York: Routledge, 1995); David R. Roediger, *The Wages of Whiteness: Race and the Making of the American Working Class* (New York: Verso, 1999), pp. 71–76, 140–43.

30. *Newburgh Directory for 1858–1859* (Newburgh, N.Y.: Turnbull & Mears, 1859), pp. 20, 46, as compiled by the Orange County Historical Society, Local History Room, Newburgh Library, Newburgh, N.Y.

31. Tebeau, *Eating Smoke*, p. 22; Edward Manning Ruttenber, *History of the Town of Newburgh* (Newburgh, N.Y.: E. M. Ruttenber, 1859), pp. 172–76; Laurie, "Fire Companies and Gangs," p. 75.

32. Amy S. Greenberg, "The Origins of the American Municipal Fire Department: Nineteenth Century Change from an International Perspective," in Michele Dagenais, Irene Maver, and Pierre-Yves Saunier, *Municipal Services and Employees in the Modern City: New Historic Approaches* (Burlington, Vt.: Ashgate, 2003), pp. 47–65; Ruttenber, *History of the Town of Newburgh*, pp. 172–76; Amy S. Greenberg, *Cause for Alarm: The Volunteer Fire Department in the Nineteenth Century City* (Princeton, N.J.: Princeton University Press, 1998).

33. 1850 U.S. Census; 1860 U.S. Census; *Newburgh Directory for 1858–59*, pp. 22, 33, 45.

34. Laurie, "Fire Companies and Gangs," p. 83; Wilentz, *Chants Democratic*, pp. 23–24.

35. Laurie, "Fire Companies and Gangs," pp. 77–78; Amy S. Greenberg, *Manifest Manhood and the Antebellum Empire* (New York: Cambridge University Press, 2005), p. 140.

36. Brown Diary, 1 October 1846.

37. Michael R. Fein, *Paving the Road: New York Road Building and the American State, 1880–1956* (Lawrence: University Press of Kansas, 2008), pp. 18–21. See also Brown Diary, 19 January 1844. On private roads, see Daniel B. Klein and John Majewski, "Turnpikes and Toll Roads in Nineteenth Century America," *EH.net* (http://eh.net/encyclopedia/article/klein.majewski.turnpikes), accessed 20 December 2010.

38. Timothy A. Hacsi, *Second Home: Orphan Asylums and Poor Families in America* (Cambridge, Mass.: Harvard University Press, 1997), pp. 11, 13–53, 76–81, 133, 149–52, 174–77.

39. Wilder, *In the Company of Black Men*, pp. 124–25, 128, 140, 150; Harris, *In the Shadow of Slavery*, pp. 6, 82, 128–29, 136–37, 145–69; Anne M. Boylan, "Benevolence and Antislavery Activity among African American Women in New York and Boston, 1820–1840," in Jean Fagin Yellin and John C. Van Horne, eds., *The Abolitionist Sisterhood: Women's Political Culture in Antebellum America* (Ithaca, N.Y.: Cornell University Press, 1994), pp. 131–32.

40. Brown Diary, 22 July 1838, 24 July 1838; B. F. Wheeler, *The Varick Family* (s.n.: Mobile, Ala., 1906), pp. 5–8, 17–20; Davison M. Douglas, *Jim Crow Moves North: The Battle Over Northern School Segregation, 1865–1954* (New York: Cambridge University Press, 2005), pp. 12–40; Carleton Mabee, *Black Education in New York State from Colonial to Modern Times* (Syracuse, N.Y.: Syracuse University Press, 1979), pp. 70–72, 79, 288, 290; William Oland Bourne, *History of the Public School Society of the City of New York* (New York: William Wood & Co., 1870), pp. 156, 164–65; Harris, *In the Shadow of Slavery*, pp. 130–32, 134–35, 137–39, 142–44; S. S. Randall, *A Digest of the Common School System of the State of New York* (Albany, N.Y.: C. Van Benthuysen & Co., 1844), pp. 235–36; Smith, *History of Dutchess County*, pp. 506–7. The 1840 U.S. Census confirms a free black female under ten years of age living in the James F. Brown household.

41. Brown Diary, 9 January 1838, 2 September 1838, 19 March 1839, 3 May 1839, 13 February 1840, 15 April 1841, 14 February 1842, 11 March 1842, 1 May 1842, 28 October 1842, 11 November 1842, 24 January 1845; Mabee, *Black Education in New York State*, pp. 71–72; Randall, *A Digest of the Common School System*, pp. 235–36; U.S. Census 1850.

42. Brown Diary, 31 October 1846, 1 December 1846, 19 May 1847, 21 May 1847, 16 June 1847, 22 June 1847, 10 July 1847, 13 November 1849, 17 September 1851, 22 September 1851; *New York Times*, 27 June 1855; Young Armstead, *"Lord, Please Don't Take Me in August,"* p. 70. The U.S. 1850 Census and U.S. 1880 Census contain information on the Allaires.

43. Wheeler, *The Varick Family*, p. 26. A Miss M. A. Varick, a Miss E. M. Verplanck, several members of the Jay family, and a Mrs. James Brown are all listed as subscribers of the COA in 1856; on this, see *Twentieth Annual Report of the Association for the Benefit of Colored Orphans* (New York: John F. Trow, 1856), pp. 18–19, 21. One M. A. Varick is listed as a manager of the COA and a Miss Varick is listed as a member of the Executive Committee of the COA for 1858 and 1859, respectively; on this, see *Twenty-first Annual Report of the Association for the Benefit of Colored Orphans* (New York: John F. Trow, 1858), p. 3, and *Twenty-second Annual Report of the Association for the Benefit of Colored Orphans* (New York: John F. Trow, 1859), p. 4. A Miss E. M. Verplanck was a COA subscriber in

1858, according to the association's annual report, p. 20. A Mrs. James Brown is listed as a subscriber of the COA in 1859, as is a Miss E. M. Verplanck on pp. 14 and 21 of that society's report for that year. See *Twenty-third Annual Report of the Association for the Benefit of Colored Orphans* (New York: "Home" Printing Office, 1860), p. 17, for a listing of Mrs. James Brown as a life member of the COA for having donated $25 within the previous five years, and p. 20 of the same report for a listing of Miss E. M. Verplanck as a COA subscriber. From COA records, it is not clear whether "Miss Varick" is Emeline Varick or whether "Mrs. James Brown" is the wife of African American James F. Brown of Fishkill. But circumstantial evidence suggests a cross-racial sisterhood of benevolent work through the COA involving Emeline Varick, Julia Brown, several female relatives of Peter Jay, and a female member of the Verplanck family.

44. Harris, *In the Shadow of Slavery*, pp. 145–69; *Freedom's Journal*, 11 January 1828; *The Liberator*, 19 April 1834; *Colored American*, 12 April 1850; *North Star*, 23 January 1851; *The Liberator*, 7 February 1851; *North Star*, 3 April 1851.

45. Brown Diary, 30 August 1838, 30 September 1838, 8 October 1838, 30 November 1838, 4 March 1839, 9 March 1839, 14 March 1839, 12 May 1839, 22 July 1840, 1 August 1840, 3 August 1840, 20 October 1840, 1 July 1842, 25 February 1843, 19 September 1844, 1 October 1844, 26 September 1845, 1 October 1845, 13 January 1846, 28 January 1846, 2 February 1846, 10 December 1846, 24 November 1847; Joseph A. Scoville, *The Old Merchants of New York City*, Volume 2 (New York: Carleton, 1864), p. 262; *Merchant's Magazine and Commercial Review*, Volume 19 (July–December 1848), p. 345. On black mariners' work and its effect on black family life, see W. Jeffrey Bolster, *Black Jacks: African American Seamen in the Age of Sail* (Cambridge, Mass.: Harvard University Press, 1997), pp. 5, 161, 165, 169.

46. Brown Diary, 5 December 1847, 30 October 1848, 8 April 1849, 11 May 1850, 14 May 1849, 28 October 1849, 4 November 1849, 9 June 1851, 17 July 1851, 20 August 1851, 22 August, 1851, 16 February 1853, 29 August 1854.

47. Brown Diary, 19 March 1855, 20 March 1855, 21 March 1855, 25 March 1855, 26 March 1855, 2 May 1855, 11 August 1857, 18 August 1857, 19 August 1857, 4 September 1857; "Days of the Old Packet," *New York Times*, 13 December 1891; Harris, *In the Shadow of Slavery*, pp. 163–67; Association for the Benefit of Colored Orphans, "Admissions (with Some Indentures and Short Histories 1837–1866)," Records, Volume 23, New-York Historical Society, New York, N.Y. David Williamson was a farmer used to using black and white farm hands. The 1850 federal census lists David Williamson as a farmer in Raritan, Monmouth County, New Jersey, with $20,000 worth of real estate and a thirty-year-old African American, a fourteen-year-old African American boy, and a fifteen-year-old white boy all living in the household as laborers. In the 1850 New Jersey slave schedules, David Williamson is listed as having a fifty-five-year-old "female slave" (although in 1846, slavery had officially ended in the state). In the 1860 federal census, the David Williamson household contained four black servants, including William H. Thompson, born in New York state and fourteen years old.

48. Brown Diary, 23 September 1845, 3 October 1845, 13 January 1846; Harris, *In the Shadow of Slavery*, pp. 159–60. In 1845, just as Aurelia was shifting into young adulthood and away from the Browns' supervision into young adulthood and before sealing their childcare arrangement with the Allaires, James and Julia had intended to take in yet another dependent. In September 1845, James had informed his diary, "[B]rought up a girl to live with us." One month later, again he had written, "Taken a girl Julia to live and

be brought up by myself and wife as ours or as our own child." But roughly three months later, he had entered, "D C Thompson and Julia Attire, a girl, [w]ent to NY." With that notation, there was no further mention of this attempted adoption or of this particular Julia.

49. Brown Diary, 5 February 1848; Thomas Scharf, *History of Maryland: From the Earliest Period to the Present Day* (Baltimore: John B. Piet, 1879), pp. 330–35; Osmond Tiffany, *A Sketch of the Life and Services of Gen. Otho Holland Williams* (Baltimore: John Murphy & Co., 1851), pp. 29–30; John Stull Williams to William Elie Williams, 23 July 1818, #1106, Otho Holland Williams Papers (OHWP), Maryland Historical Society; John Stull Williams to William E. Williams, 16 October 1818, OHWP.

50. 1820 U.S. Census.

51. Brown Diary, 26 March 1848, 21 April 1849; 1860 U.S. Census; John Hope Franklin and Loren Schweninger, *Runaway Slaves: Rebels on the Plantation* (New York: Oxford University Press, 2000), pp. 210–12.

52. Lois E. Horton, "From Class to Race: Northern Post-Emancipation Racial Reconstruction," *Journal of the Early Republic*, Volume 19, Number 4 (Winter 1999), p. 646; Eric Foner, "Free Labor and Political Ideology," in Melvyn Stokes and Stephen Conway, eds., *The Market Revolution in America: Social, Political & Religious Expressions, 1800–1830* (Charlottseville: University of Virginia Press, 1996), pp. 99–127.

53. Ross W. Jamieson, "Material Culture and Social Death: African-American Burial Practices," *Historical Archeology*, Volume 29, Volume 4 (1995), pp. 39, 41–43, 46–50; Harris, *In the Shadow of Slavery*, pp. 1–2, 41, 74, 83–84; "Green Wood Cemetery," *New York Times*, 7 June 1868; Gary Laderman, "Locating the Dead: A Cultural History of Death in the Antebellum, Anglo-Protestant Communities of the Northeast," *American Journal of Religion*, Volume 63, Number 1 (Spring 1995), pp. 30–52; Philip Pregill and Nancy Volkman, *Landscapes in History: Design and Planning in the Eastern and Western Traditions* (New York: Wiley, 1999), pp. 455–60.

54. Dutchess County Land Records, Liber 95, p. 219, County Clerk's Office, Poughkeepsie, N.Y.; Brown Diary, 29 August 1851, 1 September 1851, 6 September 1851, 14 November 1851, 21 October 1851. Besides Brown, the Union Burying Ground's trustees were Edward Bush, Christian Reynolds, Samuel Gomer, and Samuel Sampson. The 1850 U.S. Census records a "John H. Ross" living in Fishkill in 1850; he is white and only thirty years old but does not reappear ten years later in the census. This Ross was a laborer, thus leading to the speculation that the Colored Burial Ground willingly accepted the dead coming from poor families regardless of race. On the "Negro" cemetery in Fishkill, see "Facts and Figures from J. W. Poucher's *Old Gravestones of Dutchess County*," 1924, http://freepages.genealogy.rootsweb.ancestry.com/~dutchesscemetery/fishkill.htm , accessed 9 October 2009.

55. Charles H. Brooks, *The Official History and Manual of the Grand United Order of Odd Fellows* (Philadelphia: Odd Fellows' Journal Print, 1902), pp. 12–13, 218, 221, 225–26; D. W. Bristol, *The Morals of Odd Fellowship: A Discourse* (Auburn, N.Y.: William J. Moses, 1854), p. 75.

56. In the 1850 U.S. Census, Thomas Hoffman is listed as Aurelia's husband and a seaman. Hoffman, moreover, served as Grand Director of the GUOOF Philomathean Lodge in Manhattan in 1845 and 1846, according to Brooks, *The Official History and Manual*, pp. 28, 31. The Brown Diary, 1 October 1845, strongly suggests that David Thompson was an

Odd Fellow. See also Brown Diary, 19 August 1847, 28 July 1848, 29 July 1848, 2 June 1849, 7 March 1851; Wilder, *In the Company of Black Men*, pp. 75, 117. Regarding other sailor friends of Brown, he mentioned Thomas Bowser, "steward of the steam packet Sarah Sands of Liverpool" (Brown Diary, 26 January 1848) and James Patterson, who worked "on board of the packet ship Ashburton" (Brown Diary, 3 March 1848). In addition, a younger brother or other male relative of Hester Purnell Thompson—George Purnell— was a sailor. James wrote him and David Thompson at the same time, according to the diary, on 2 February 1846, and Purnell is listed as a twenty-three-year-old sailor in the 1850 U.S. Census.

57. Bristol, *The Morals of Odd Fellowship*, p. 75. See Brown Diary, 24 November 1847, for one instance of James's attentions to a dying African American friend, George Washington; Washington did not die until 24 September 1849, according to the diary; in the interim, James wrote letters for him (see Brown Diary, 3 March 1848). Using Cypress Hills Cemetery in Brooklyn as a model for Greenwood Cemetery's fees, James would have paid $6.00 for Hester's burial plot, (52 square feet), a hearse, the opening and closing of the grave, and a sexton to tend to the site, according to the *Brooklyn Daily Eagle*, 3 April 1850, p. 4. He may have purchased the gravesite for Hester from an IOOF burial plot (see the *Brooklyn Daily Eagle*, 9 November 1844, p. 2). James and Julia were extraordinarily attentive to widow Julia Landrick. The Landricks were friends of the Browns, living in Poughkeepsie. Following the husband's death in April 1847, they helped her move her family to Washington, D.C., that September, planted a tree at Edward Landrick's gravesite in Dutchess County that October, and, two years later, assisted her with personal business (see Brown Diary, 3 April 1847, 21 April 1847, 17 June 1847, 14 September 1847, 8 August 1849).

58. Wilder, *In the Company of Black Men*, pp. 103–10.

CONCLUSION

1. Brown Diary, 7 October 1830, 8 December 1839, 31 January 1840, 15 February 1840, 12 September 1841, 7 June 1842, 10 June 1842, 6 August 1842, 26 December 1842, 30 December 1842, 20 December 1843, 9 December 1844, 18 January 1845, 4 December 1846, 24 January 1847, 1 June 1847, 4 June 1847, 7 June 1847, 10 July 1847, 5 December 1847, 24 January 1848, 19 March 1849, 20 March 1849, 2 July 1849, 27 September 1850, 15 January 1851, 6 July 1851, 3 March 1853, 26 February 1854, 8 October 1854, 30 July 1857, 11 August 1857, 13 July 1858, 17 April 1859.

2. Jason Illari, "Unlocking the Past: A History of Poplar Hill Mansion 1795–2005," Masters Thesis, Salisbury University, 2004, pp. 47–50; Linda Duyer, *'Round the Pond: Georgetown of Salisbury, Maryland* (Salisbury, Md.: Linda Duyer, 2007), pp. 33–34; *New York Herald*, 31 October 1844, p. 2; *Boston Daily Atlas*, 1 November 1844, p. 2.

3. John Switala, *The Underground Railroad in Delaware, Maryland, and West Virginia* (Mechanicsburg, Pa.: Stackpole Books, 2004) pp. 61–86; Association for the Benefit of Colored Orphans, "Admissions (With some Indentures and Short Histories, 1837–1866)," Volume 23, p. 408, New-York Historical Society; Worcester County Land Records, AS, p. 446 (7 April 1827), Maryland State Archives (MSA); Worcester County Land Records, AM, p. 150 (9 April 1821), MSA; Worcester County Land Records, AP, p. 685 (18 May 1824), MSA; Worcester County Land Records, AS251 (7 December 1826), MSA; Worces-

ter County Land Records, AQ, p. 210 (23 August 1824), MSA; Worcester County Land Records, AX, pp. 104–5 (9 May 1831), MSA; Worcester County Land Records, AS, p. 84 (14 June 1826), MSA; Worcester County Land Records, AT, p. 509 (5 January 1828), MSA; Somerset County Land Records, GH, Liber 3, p. 228 (17 June 1826), MSA.

4. Somerset County Land Records, JD, Liber 6, p. 112 (14 October 1820), MSA; Somerset County Land Records, GH, Liber 5, p. 165, MSA (14 October 1829), MSA; Somerset County Land Records, GH, Liber 9, p. 504 (22 October 1838), MSA; Somerset County Land Records, WP, Liber 1, p. 466 (31 October 1846), MSA; Somerset County Land Records, LW, Liber 5, p. 168 (30 March 1857), MSA. Dr. Thomas E. Davidson, "Free Black Landowners on the Lower Eastern Shore of Maryland 1783–1861," pp. 3–4, 709, Unpublished paper, Salisbury State College, Edward H. Nabb Research Center for Delmarva History and Culture, Salisbury, Md.

5. Anderson, "Free Black Landowners," pp. 8–9; Somerset County Land Records, WP, Liber 1, p. 465 (31 October 1846), MSA; Somerset County Land Records, WP, Liber 2, p. 407 (18 December 1847), MSA; 1, p. 465 (31 October 1846), MSA; Somerset County Land Records, WP, Liber 2, p. 407 (18 December 1847), MSA; Somerset County Land Records, LW, Liber 4, p. 341 (13 October 1855), MSA; Somerset County Land Records, LW, Liber 5, p. 391 (3 November 1857), MSA.

6. 1820 U.S. Census; 1840 U.S. Census; 1850 U.S. Census; 1860 U.S. Census; Somerset County Land Records, WP, Liber 1, p. 465 (31 October 1846), MSA; Somerset County Land Records, WP, Liber 2, p. 407 (18 December 1847), MSA; Somerset County Land Records, LW, Liber 4, p. 341 (13 October 1855), MSA; Somerset County Land Records, LW, Liber 5, p. 391 (3 November 1857), MSA.

7. 1820 U.S. Census; 1850 U.S. Census.

8. Worcester County Land Records, AT, p. 321 (7 January 1828), MSA; Worcester County Land Records, AT, p. 509 (5 January 1828), MSA; Worcester County Land Records, JAP, Liber 1, p. 161, (20 November 1852), MSA; Worcester County Land Records, JAP, Liber 1, p. 162 (8 March 1848), MSA.

9. *Poughkeepsie Daily Eagle*, 25 April 1861, p. 3; *Poughkeepsie Daily Eagle*, 24 April 1861, p. 2; James H. Smith, *History of Dutchess County, 1683–1882* (Syracuse, N.Y.: D. Mason & Co., 182), pp. 511–12; Frederick Phisterer, *New York in the War of the Rebellion, 1861 to 1865*, 2nd edition (Albany, N.Y.: Weed, Parsons and Company, 1890), pp. 32, 51–52, 60, 136, 468, 502–3; Ruttenber and Tice, *A History of the Town of Newburgh*, p. 189.

10. Steven Mintz and Susan Kellogg, *Domestic Revolutions: A Social History of American Family Life* (New York: The Free Press, 1988), p. 73; Brown Diary, 11 October 1858, 6 May 1860, 14 June 1860, 31 July 1861.

11. Brown Diary, 21 October 1852, 17 March 1860, 25 March 1860, 24 March 1860, 26 March 1860, 22 April 1860, 24 April 1860, 1 June 1860, 4 January 1861, 8 February 1861, 28 July 1861, 29 July 1861, 17 November 1861; 1840 U.S. Census; 1850 U.S. Census; 1860 U.S. Census; 1870 U.S. Census; 1880 U.S. Census; VerPlanck, *History of Abraham Isaacse Ver-Planck*, pp. 206–9; Smith, *History of Dutchess County*, p. 522; *Fishkill Standard*, 4 May 1895.

12. Joseph Alfred Scoville, *The Old Merchants of New York City* (New York: Thomas R. Knox & Co., 1885), p. 157; VerPlanck, *History of Abraham Isaacse VerPlanck*, p. 307; Brown Diary, 3 November 1861; Jim Heron, *Denning's Point: A Hudson River History* (Hensonville, N.Y.: Black Dome Press, 2006); Brown Diary, 24 February 1861; 1860 U.S. Census; Harold Donaldson Eberlein and Cortlandt Van Dyke Hubbard, *Historic Houses of the Hudson Val-*

ley (Toronto: General Publishing, Ltd., 1990), p. 54; *Fishkill Standard*, 4 May 1895; Brown Diary, 7 March 1862, 9 October 1862.

13. Brown Diary, 11 April 1862, 22 February 1863.

14. Lois E. Horton, "From Class to Race in Early America: Northern Post-Emancipation Racial Reconstruction," in Michael A. Morrison and James Brewer Stewart, *Race and the Early Republic: Racial Consciousness and Nation-Building in the Early Republic* (New York: Rowman and Littlefield, 1999), pp. 55, 62–73; David R. Roediger, "The Pursuit of Whiteness: Property, Terror, and Expansion, 1790–1860," in Morrison and Stewart, *Race and the Early Republic*, pp. 5–26; Melish, "The 'Condition' Debate," pp. 85–90; Audrey Smedley, *Race in North America: Origin and Evolution of a Worldview* (Boulder, Colo.: Westview Press, 1999), pp. 169–272.

15. Timothy Shortell, "The Rhetoric of Black Abolitionism: An Exploratory Analysis of Antislavery Newspapers in New York State, *Social Science History*, Volume 28, Number 1 (Spring 2004), pp. 75–109.

16. *Poughkeepsie Eagle*, 8 August 1857, p. 2.

17. Gayle McKeen, "Whose Rights? Whose Responsibility? Self-Help in African-American Thought," *Polity*, Volume 34, Number 4 (Summer 2002), p. 412.

18. Brown Diary, 26 March 1866.

Index

About the Author

MYRA B. YOUNG ARMSTEAD is a professor of history at Bard College. Her books include *"Lord, Please Don't Take Me in August": African Americans in Newport and Saratoga Springs, 1870–1930* and *Mighty Change, Tall Within: Black Identity in the Hudson Valley.*